Nature *and* Nurture

The Complex Interplay of Genetic
and Environmental Influences
on Human Behavior and Development

Nature *and* Nurture

The Complex Interplay of Genetic
and Environmental Influences
on Human Behavior and Development

Edited by

Cynthia García Coll, PhD
Elaine L. Bearer, MD
Brown University

Richard M. Lerner, PhD
Tufts University

LAWRENCE ERLBAUM ASSOCIATES, PUBLISHERS
2004   Mahwah, New Jersey   London

Lawrence Erlbaum Associates, Inc., Publishers
10 Industrial Avenue
Mahwah, NJ 07430

Cover design by Sean Trane Sciarrone

Library of Congress Cataloging-in-Publication Data

Nature and nurture : the complex interplay of genetic and en-
vironmental influences on human behavior and develop-
ment / edited by Cynthia García Coll, Elaine L. Bearer and
Richard M. Lerner.
      p. cm.
Includes bibliographical references and index.
ISBN 0-8058-4387-6 (h : alk. paper)
    1. Nature and nurture. 2. Behavior genetics. 4. Human be-
havior   I. García Coll, Cynthia T.   II. Bearer, Elaine L.
III. Lerner, Richard M.

QH438.5.N38 2003
155.2'34—dc21   2003040816
                                                         CIP

Books published by Lawrence Erlbaum Associates are
printed on acid-free paper, and their bindings are chosen for
strength and durability.

Printed in the United States of America
10   9   8   7   6   5   4   3   2   1

Contents

Foreword
Behavioral Genetics
in the Post-Genomic Era

Steven E. Hyman

As is well documented in this volume, studies of the genetic contributions to behavior have had a highly contentious and at times dark history. At its most extreme, the eugenics movement, which included behavioral geneticists, led to sterilizations in many countries, including the United States, and contributed to mass murder in Nazi Germany. More recently in the United States, controversy about behavioral genetics was rekindled, *inter alia*, by attempts to explain differences in IQ test scores among racial and ethnic groups by the finding from twin studies that demonstrated that genes substantially influence IQ. Despite the fact that little has been known until very recently about human genetic diversity as it relates to peoples with different geographic origins, and even less about the nature of the genetic contributions to behavioral phenotypes, several writers attempted to influence public policy on such matters as education. The history of behavioral genetics in the public sphere has proved problematic for its healthy development within its proper sphere, the laboratory, in several countries, most notably Germany. This history has also posed challenges to the atmosphere of objectivity and neutrality that is critical for any scientific inquiry. Ultimately the scientific community must play a role in managing the results of its inquiries, but in the long term, scientific inquiry cannot and should not be stopped even if we are worried about what we will find. In particular, contributions from behavioral genetics are much in need if we are to give ourselves the best possible chance to understand the panoply of serious illnesses that affect behavior and to devise better treatments for them.

When areas of science appear to have potential public policy relevance, open discussion is critical. While some scientists will approach even their early findings with great enthusiasm for rapid application, a sober discussion of what we really know, what we don't know, and what is speculation is a healthy part of any public discussion. Recognizing that scientists are human and function within a social context, we must still strive for a science that is objective and politically neutral. The scientific community has an obligation to address contentious issues, such as genetic privacy, in the public forum, and difficult as it might be, we must avoid applying emerging scientific notions prematurely or inappropriately to public policy. It is one thing to rush a new cancer drug through its approvals; it is quite another to make global decisions about educational or employment opportunities based on relatively early mixtures of data and surmise.

In the post-genomic era, the ultimate goal of behavioral genetics is not to parse fractional causality to genes or environment, but rather to contribute to the understanding of neural mechanisms that underlie behavior. While this effort will have important implications for human self-understanding, the most pressing need is for advances against disabling illnesses such as autism, schizophrenia, and bipolar disorder. There is no excuse for remaining mired in arguments over the significance of heritabilities, calculated from twin studies, when there is important work to be done. That work is identifying the genetic and nongenetic factors that interact to build our brains, modify them over a lifetime, and, for a large number of our species, lead to serious mental disorders, learning disabilities, and other disabling problems of brain function.

How will genetics help in the study of mental disorders? Because the brain is so complex, information at the genetic level is absolutely required to understand brain development and function. In part because we lack information about the genetic variants (alleles) that influence the risk of autism or schizophrenia, we have limited understanding of what goes wrong in the brain to produce these two terrible illnesses, and indeed we even have difficulty with case definitions. Genetic information can help psychiatry and psychology better define such diseases, a critical step in improving our understanding of them. This is not the only field in which genetic or genomic information will alter our definitions of diseases. For example, many cancers were until recently classified based on how they looked to a pathologist after applying stains. With the advent of functional genomics—the ability to study patterns of gene expression using DNA microarrays—it has become clear that some cancers previously thought to be a single disease actually represent multiple diseases, with different likelihoods of metastasis and different responses to therapy. The hope is that discovering the genomic loci that contribute risk for mental illnesses will also lead to a more rational classification of disorders, and more importantly give us clues for the study of pathophysiology. An improved understanding of pathophysiology is critical because our treatment armamentarium for mental illness is still so limited: the ability to identify more homogeneous populations for study, to have better insight about brain pathways that lead to symptoms, and to identify gene products that might be candidate targets for the development of therapies are all much in need.

Human genetics is not an experimental science for reasons both ethical and practical. For example, one obviously cannot, and ethically must not rigidly control environments for human subjects. Prior to the advent of molecular genetics and the more recent tools provided by the Human Genome Project, human behavioral genetics was limited to a great degree to quantitative analyses of twin studies, adoption studies, and multigenerational family designs that attempted to discriminate genetic from nongenetic influences on behavioral phenotypes and to determine the modes of inheritance. Historically, the most common designs were the comparison of monozygotic twins versus dizygotic twins raised together. On the assumption of a shared environment, one could then examine the role of genes based on the fact that monozygotic twins share 100% of their DNA whereas dizygotic twins share on average 50% of their DNA. Studies of individuals who had been adopted away from their biological families early in life better separated heredity and environment, and studies of twins separated at birth have proven even more useful in terms of their explanatory power. But adoption studies are difficult to perform, since they depend on societies making both records and people available for examination and interview. Multigenerational family designs permit the analysis of modes of inheritance across generations, and even in the pre-molecular era, occasionally facilitated linkage studies, albeit with the very limited number of polymorphic protein markers that were available.

Based on the assumption of environmental equivalence, the analysis of twin studies led to the partitioning of sources of phenotypic variation into (a) a genetic component, (b) a component attributable to the shared family environmental, and (c) a component attributed to idiosyncratic (unshared) environmental factors, plus chance and error. Results were quantified in measures such as heritabilities, the significance of which became a matter of contention. To be sure, the methodology of twin studies has the weakness that the 100% shared-DNA condition (monozygotic twins) cannot truly be balanced by a 100% shared-environment condition in humans—this is difficult enough to achieve in laboratory rats.

Measures frequently used in thinking about disease phenotypes, which can be derived from both twin and family studies, are recurrence risk ratios, which quantify the likelihood of sharing a phenotype with another person as a function of relatedness and therefore as a function of the percentage of DNA shared. Recurrence risk ratios are used to prioritize disease phenotypes for molecular genetic investigation based on the notion that the greater the contribution of genes to a phenotype, the higher the likelihood of identifying the genetic loci that contribute risk. Both heritabilities and recurrence risk ratios attempt to describe the aggregate genetic contribution to a phenotype no matter how complex the genetic contribution, thus a high recurrence risk ration is not a guarantee of success in identifying actual loci contributing to a phenotype.

In the post-genomic era, quantitative genetics will not lose its utility, but rather has become a means to an end. The utility of quantitative analyses will lie in better defining phenotypes deserving molecular genetic analysis, and setting priorities. Twin studies will also prove useful in directing the search for environmental factors that might contribute to phenotypes. One may be guided by such information on the aggregate influence of genes on a phenotype to prioritize molecular investigations toward diseases with high recurrence-risk ratios, such as autism, schizophrenia, and bipolar disorder, and away from syndromes where it is difficult to demonstrate any involvement of genes, such as generalized anxiety disorder. Indeed, this is exactly what we did while I was director of the National Institute of Mental Health from 1996 to 2001, recognizing that such measures, while useful, left important aspects of the feasibility unknown.

At the dawn of the 21st century, the main challenges confronting the genetic study of mental illnesses or for that matter any behavioral phenotype, are twofold: the difficulty of defining phenotypes and the apparently large number of genetic and nongenetic risk factors involved and the complexity (nonlinearity) of their interaction. Complexity is a challenge to our science, but it also has implications for human self-understanding. Complexity does not explain away the aggregate effect of genes. But it also means neither genotype alone nor environmental influences alone are determinative of phenotype.

Ultimately, of course, it is our brains and not our genes that are proximate to the control of behavior. We recognize that although genes are critically important, they do not by themselves cause the brain to be built and therefore do not, except in the case of rare, highly penetrant Mendelian disorders, provide us with a causal description of what has happened to any individual. At the same time, given the complexity of the brain, it is hard to imagine that we will understand it well without important contributions from genetics.

Extensive twin and family studies, along with the occasional adoption studies concerned with mental illness phenotypes, have established beyond question that genes play an important role in risk. The recurrence-risk ratios that have been obtained for many of the serious mental disorders are among the highest in medicine. Genes clearly play a very important role in autism, schizophrenia, and bipolar disorder, and in major depression and other more common disorders, they play a role that is roughly the same magnitude as in type 2 diabetes mellitus. Increasingly, studies comparing monozygotic and dizygotic twins, studies of segregation of phenotypes across generations in extended pedigrees, and frustrating attempts at linkage analysis, suggest that a relatively large number of genes interact with nongenetic factors to produce mental illness. Nongenetic factors might include specific environmental and contextual factors as well as stochastic and chaotic factors (think of the chaotic factors that might influence the wiring up of one hundred trillion synapses in the brain). It is quite possible that so many factors of similar magnitude interact in such complex ways that we will be limited in our capacity to build adequate models. On the other hand, progress with a variety of genetically complex disorders argues that as technology advances and behavioral phenotypes are refined, we can succeed.

While I have focused the foregoing on mental disorders—a far less controversial area for investigation than non-illness related behavioral variation—it must be recognized that behavioral genetics cannot cordon off only disease phenotypes as safe for investigation. Indeed, it is highly likely that many mental disorders, including depression, attention deficit hyperactivity disorder, and even autism, are not discontinuous phenotypes, but rather quantitative traits in which illness represents the left tail of a bell curve. Thus, even research focused on illness will also have powerful implications for "the normal."

There are rare and often severe disease phenotypes, such as Rett syndrome, in which a behavioral syndrome is caused deterministically by a single deleterious mutation in a single gene. Twin and family studies of a very large number of behavioral phenotypes have demonstrated that situations in which a single gene, acting in Mendelian dominant or recessive fashion, causes a phenotype are very rare indeed. Of course there may be rare Mendelian forms of common mental disorders as have been discovered for Alzheimer's disease and Parkinson's disease. If there are, we have not found them yet, but the examples of Mendelian dominant Alzheimer's disease and both dominant and recessive forms of Parkinson's disease suggests that should such families exist, they could be of enormous value to understanding pathogenesis.

Twin studies have also revealed that there are no common behavioral phenotypes for which monozygotic twins have 100% concordance. From this follows something of an irony. Quantitative genetic studies of behavior have not established genetic determinism, as some critics have feared, but rather, have shown that both genetic and nongenetic factors contribute significantly to essentially all common phenotypes—illness phenotypes and normal variant phenotypes alike. The analysis of the nongenetic contribution to behavioral phenotypes has also produced something of a surprise. Given the intellectual prejudices of mid-20th century behavioral science, ranging from behaviorism to psychoanalysis, a surprising finding from a very on large number of twin studies investigating many phenotypes is that nongenetic effects, while quite significant, are only in very small part attributable to shared family environment. Instead, it is the unshared or idiosyncratic aspects of environment, together with the oft-neglected stochastic and chaotic factors involved in brain development, that appear to play the critical roles in influencing phenotypes. In sum, for a large number of behavioral phenotypes and for all common mental disorders, classical quantitative genetics has established that genes play an important role but do not act deterministically; instead, they interact in extremely complex ways with nongenetic factors. Of course, environmental influences can be construed to act as deterministically as genes, so the fact that genes and environment interact, does not, without additional analysis and argument establish free will.

An additional issue is that genetic and nongenetic factors are not simply additive. It has long been recognized that genes and nongenetic factors act hierarchically during early brain development, although an understanding of epistasis has not always informed model building in behavioral genetics. In addition, behavioral geneticists have long pointed out the existence of gene-environment covariation throughout life. Genes affect a child's experience of the environment both by influencing the perceived salience of diverse stimuli and by influencing the environments to which a person may approach or avoid. Genes may even alter the environment itself; for example, a child's temperament, which is partly genetically influenced, may elicit widely divergent behavior on the part of parents, teachers, and peers. In turn, the environment (e.g., lived experience, drugs, illness) influences gene expression throughout life and therefore helps shape the synapses and circuits that ultimately control behavior. In the end, the brain is the great integrator, shaping neural circuits and their responsiveness and remodeling them over time based on genetic factors, a wide diversity of environmental influences, and stochastic and chaotic factors that play at least some role in gene expression within neurons, and the synaptic connections between neurons.

Based on considerations of the sort that I have reviewed, few modern scientists would disagree with the proposition that nature and nurture are inextricably intertwined as they influence brain and behavior. Indeed the nature–nurture debate is often declared to be at an end. Unfortunately, it is not entirely clear that the "resolution" of the nature–nurture dichotamy has fully penetrated general thought, even that of many educated citizens including educators, clinicians, policy makers, and even some social scientists. I fear that in many guises the opposition of nature and nurture continues to exert influence. In many settings, the nature–nurture dichotomy is that seen through the additional distorting lens of Cartesianism which dichotomizes mind from brain (and body). The resulting misguided train of thought is that if a behavioral disorder or undesirable tendency is genetically influenced (in fact this would be the case with most behavioral phenotypes), then amelioration must be accomplished through biological means such as pharmacology, while interventions based on learning or changes in context will have weak impact at best. A pessimistic variant on this idea is that if a behavior is strongly genetically influenced, it is, basically fixed (perhaps pending the development of gene therapy). Of course there are limits set by our genes—we cannot learn to fly—on the other hand, many genetically influenced traits are in fact susceptible to significant change.

The most famous counterexample against fixity is the complete prevention of phenylketonuria by removing phenylalanine from the diet of individuals affected by this Mendelian inborn error of metabolism. There are more germane examples, however, such as secular trends showing increases in height (a highly genetically influenced trait) and in IQ across many human groups throughout the 20th century. The point is that if one thinks about the possibility of environmental influences on brain development, ranging from social context to nutrition, to pharmacologic intervention, there is much that can be done to intervene in genetically influenced traits. Unfortunately, not all genetically influenced traits show trends toward betterment across human history. There are waxing and waning trends in crime and violence. In the clinical domain, eating disorders such as anorexia nervosa and bulimia, which are genetically influenced, have increased in the developed world and are making their debuts in the developing world, perhaps as a result of social context that influences body image, and as a result of peer interactions that produce "contagion" mediated through cognition.

Despite the controversies and despite the contentious history, behavioral genetics is a critical part of our scientific future and is likely to be one of the cornerstones in improving life for people with mental illness. If the goals of early behavioral genetics were to apportion the degree of heritability of a particular behavioral variant, the goals are now very different. Ultimately, the information from behavioral genetics will provide a critical set of tools to understand the brain and the neural underpinnings of behavior. I would argue that the main thrust of behavioral genetics in the near term must be toward an understanding of illness—patterns of behavior that produce distress, disability, and even death. However, the quest for self-understanding and for improving our ability to function will also drive investigation of mechanisms underlying normal behavior. By moving beyond the notion of heritability to mechanisms by which gene-environment interactions shape the brain, we are less likely to succumb to simple deterministic models. While I have warned against premature attempts to influence social policy, we must be attentive to real and immediate social issues. Even though genetic complexity means that information based on genotypes is probabilistic rather than deterministic, it could still be misused in ways that would limit educational or employment opportunities or health insurance. Genetic privacy is an issue that should be addressed now. Moreover, as we redirect the goals of behavioral genetics from the quantitative models to brain mechanisms, we must continue to recognize the risks of harming or stigmatizing individuals even while trying to help them. Overall, we must face the ethical challenges that will certainly arise as we learn more about what makes us tick as human beings. The history of this important science amply demonstrates the danger of failing to do so.

Preface

This book grew out of an interdisciplinary conference held at Brown University, April 5–6, 2001 on the topic "Genetic Influences on Human Behavior and Development." The conference was held under the auspices of the Center for the Study of Human Development and funded by the Mittlemann Family Directorship at the center, the Francis Wayland Collegium for Liberal Learning at Brown University, and the John D. and Catherine T. MacArthur Foundation Research Network on Successful Pathways through Middle Childhood. It brought together scholars from a variety of disciplines—biologists, psychologists, psychiatrists, and economists—for two days to discuss the implications of existing knowledge of genetic-environment transactions for an understanding of human behavior and development. The book represents many, but not all, of the main views presented at the conference.

In addition to those who contributed chapters, the following scholars were part of the conference and of the many discussions and ideas that gave origin to this book: Susan Oyama (City University of New York), Dan Brock (now at the National Institute of Health), Felton Earls (Harvard University), David Reiss (George Washington University), Michael McKeown (Brown University), Hillary Worthen (Harvard Medical School), John Modell (Brown University), Ron Seifer (Brown University), and Kristi Wharton (Brown University). The dynamic and sometimes quite heated discussions at the conference gave impetus for the present collection.

The three coeditors equally shared the editorial work of the book with the assistance of Patricia Balsofiore, executive assistant at the Center for the Study of Human Development. Pat, with great dedication and a good sense of humor, organized all the details of the original conference and coordinated the coeditors' work and the final production of the entire manuscript. We are indebted to her for the careful management of the many details that occur "behind the scene" in a project of this nature.

In addition, we are grateful for the editorial guidance of Karyn Lu, managing editor of the Publications Office of the Applied Developmental Science Institute in the Eliot-Pearson Department of Child Development, Tufts University. Her advice and efforts facilitated and integrated the numerous interactions between authors and editors that undergird the development of a final manuscript. Finally, we would like to acknowledge the contributions of Bill Webber, our editor at Lawrence Erlbaum Associates, the publishers of the book. Bill's enthusiasm for, wisdom about, and support of the project were vital ingredients in the development and completion of this book.

C. G. C.
E. L. B.
R. M. L.

Introduction

Nature and Nurture in Human Behavior and Development: A View of the Issues

Cynthia García Coll
Elaine L. Bearer
Brown University

Richard M. Lerner
Tufts University

In June 2000, a breakthrough announcement was made about the completion of the mapping of the human genome (International Human Genome Sequencing Consortium, 2001; Venter et al., 2001). Heralded as a major scientific accomplishment on its own, the implications of such knowledge for the creation of genetically based interventions for the amelioration and eradication of disease were immediately postulated.

Although it is quite possible that this scientific breakthrough can have a major influence on treatment of diseases such as diabetes, cancer, heart disease, and other physical ailments that run in families, the effect of identifying particular genes or set of genes implicated in human behavior and development is less clear (Rutter, 2002). What does it mean to find a gene or set of genes that are associated with ADHD, schizophrenia, or autism? Does everybody who has that gene manifest the disease: Why or why not? Could it be easier to alter the environment that triggers the behavioral problem given the presence of that gene? Could we eradicate such diseases from our species through gene therapy? If multiple genes are involved in the manifestation of psychopathology, and if single genes are involved in the manifestations of many behaviors, could gene therapy have many unintended behavioral manifestations?

Perhaps more complicated are the implications of identifying genes that are associated with normal variation resulting in individual differences in, for example, temperament, aggression, shyness, intelligence, or activity level. Could we—and should we—eradicate from our genome, as individuals or as a species, genetic material that predisposes us to be too aggressive or too shy or less intelligent, or not active enough? Who has the political power and/or the moral authority to make those decisions? Who will have access to those interventions?

The premise of this book is that the complexity of the transactions between nature and nurture—between genes and the environment from the cellular to the cultural level—make these questions incredibly complex. Oversimplification of rules of how biology and environment operate in human behavior and development can lead to radically different understanding and implications for public policy.

From such simplistic views arise questions such as: "Is this particular behavioral trait biologically determined and, therefore, not amenable to environmental interventions?" or "How much does "genes versus environment" explain individual differences in a particular behavioral trait or developmental process?" (Anastasi, 1958; Gottlieb, 1997; Hirsch, 1997). Such questions risk splitting nature from nurture (Overton, 1998), a split that seems illogical when one considers the data on environmental effects that influence human behavior and development. Such splitting can also lead to the misconception that genes are destiny or that of genetic programming is unresponsive to the environment.

In addition, as shown repeatedly by history, the danger of such oversimplificationis its potential impact on public policy and its ethical implications (e.g., Gould, 1981; Hirsch, 1970; Kamin, 1974; Lerner, 1992; Lewontin, Rose, & Kamin, 1984). For example, such simplistic notions of how human beings' behavior and development operate led in the past to eugenic laws that were designed to eradicate particular developmental deviations such as mental retardation or low IQ through selective breeding (Gould, 1981; Proctor, 1988). Thus, public policy interventions promoting genetic manipulations in certain populations identified as having a particular gene for an undesirable trait, or the lack of a public willingness to intervene if a genetic predisposition rather than environmental etiology has been identified, are two of the possible scenarios derived from this misunderstanding of the complex interplay between genes and the environment.

Fortunately, our current knowledge of biology, developmental systems, and the fused, or synthetic, interplay of environmental and biological influences on behavior and development can illuminate and guide our understanding of such processes and influence the design of appropriate and useful public policies that are appropriate to derive from them (Gottlieb, 1997; Lerner, 2002). Even at the cellular level, genetic codes are expressed within particular environmental circumstances, and alterations on those environments can lead to radically different phenotypic expressions from similar genetic material. Indeed, as explained in several chapters in this volume (e.g., by Gottlieb, Hirsch, and Lerner), developmental systems theories and the research conducted within this framework suggest that genes and environments work together integratively in a complex and closely intertwined fashion. Consequently, theories of human behavior based entirely on either nature or nurture alone are likely to be counterfactual, and research predicated on such dichotomies will produce incomplete and possibly useless data.

However, though state-of-the-art knowledge is available, recent highly visible works (i.e., Herrnstein and Murray, *The Bell Curve*, 1994; Harris, *The Nurture Assumption*, 1998; Rowe, *The Limits of Family Influence*, 1994; and Rushton, *Race, Evolution and Behavior*, 1999/2000) portray pretty simple ideas about the role of genetics in human behavior and development. Such a series of perspectives can have dangerous implications for our understanding of developmental mechanisms and result in public policies and practices that negatively impact society (Rutter, 2002).

Together, the contributors to this book present scholarship that enables research and application to transcend the traditional question of how much significance to attribute to genetics versus environment in the development of a particular behavioral trait. This volume replaces such a dichotomy with the language of dynamic, developmental systems. That is, with an understanding of the character of the plasticity of human development and the flexibility of genetic expression that derives from the interplay of genes with environments from the genetic to the cellular to the macroinstitutional level. This conceptual framework of dynamic interactions between the expression of the genetic program and the influence of the environment has implications for a new set of public policy and social program options for people across the life span. In short, this volume provides a timely contribution to a highly visible and controversial area with profound policy implications for human development and well being.

ORGANIZATION OF THE BOOK

The chapters in this book present a variety of views on the current status of knowledge about the ways in which dynamic, developmental, mutually interactive systems in the genetic and environmental domains operate. As a necessity, the information in this volume is derived from multiple disciplines and from multiple perspectives within these disciplines. The contributors to this volume are distinguished scholars from developmental, comparative, and clinical psychology; biology; and economics. They use their own and others' current and past research to argue for an inclusive and highly dynamic view of the interplay between nature and nurture.

The book is organized around chapters derived from papers presented at a conference held at Brown University in April 2001. Perhaps distinct from other conference-based volumes, conference papers were prepared as initial drafts of chapters for this volume and not as end products per se. Conference participants were given copies of all manuscripts prior to the meeting, and as a consequence, the presentation of each paper was followed by an informed and rich interdisciplinary discussion of its contents, in the form of both prepared commentaries by conference participants and as well by an open discussion among conference members after the commentaries. The volume includes as chapters papers finalized by the authors after attending the conference and formal versions of several of the commentaries delivered by discussants.

Each chapter in the volume represents a contribution from different and perhaps even contradictory perspectives. Participants do not represent a whole, unified view. They all, however, address the complexities of understanding gene-human development relations with their own unique synthesis and alternative interpretation. No other volume that we know of presents the breadth of cutting-edge perspectives that are included in this book.

In the first chapter, Lerner contrasts hereditarian versus developmental system views of human development from their knowledge of human functioning to their implications for policy and programs. He argues that a developmental systems approach provides a richer and more accurate view of human development that is theoretically and empirically useful for grounding policies and programs to promote positive human development.

In the second chapter, Suomi provides empirical evidence to support the dynamic interplay of genes and environment from his programmatic work on primates reared in laboratory settings. His findings suggest that both heritable and early experiential factors together influence the development of excessive physical aggression and these influences depend on abnormal serotonin metabolism in rhesus monkeys. He concludes that gene-environment interactions are ubiquitous, diverse in nature, and detectable within the first month of life, whereas genetic effects independent of environmental influences represent the exception rather than the rule.

Spencer and Harpalani start the third chapter by elucidating misunderstandings of basic concepts such as behavioral genetics, heritability, and gene-environment interactions. Subsequently, they propose their own theoretical framework, a phenomenological variant of bio-ecological and ecological systems theory, as an alternative view of how the genotype changes its expression as a function of context and developmental history. Within this model, particular alleles can be treated as risk or protective factors, acting as sources of vulnerability or resilience for individuals within particular contexts.

A commentary on the three previous chapters, by biologist Anne Fausto Sterling, uses her research on gender to illustrate the shortcomings of dualistic, cultural determinist views and of various psychological views, which purport to integrate biological or genetic functioning with behavior. She indicates that splitting nature and nurture is an impoverished concept, and goes on to explain why the developmental systems approach enriches our understanding of the processes by which genes and behavior interface. She challenges proponents of developmental systems theories to aim their scholarship at understanding the development of gender, sexuality, and sexual expression.

In the fourth chapter, Gottlieb argues that genes require environmental and behavioral inputs to function appropriately during the normal course of individual development. He criticizes an unidirectional view, where the activity of genes and the maturational process are pictured as relatively insulated, and proposes a bidirectional view—a probabilistic-epigenetic view—where function, activity and experience affect genetic activity and maturation. The environment in his conceptualization is seen not only as the agent of natural selection in promoting evolution but also as a crucial feature influencing the outcome of genetic expression and determining the individual's development.

Rende, in the fifth chapter, elucidates the strengths and weaknesses and the present and likely future developments of behavioral genetic techniques and their core concept, heritability. He proposes that behavioral genetics is a useful "way to uncover the developmental dance between biological process and social context." Reviewing the literature for the development of various psychiatric disorders (i.e., autism, schizophrenia, depression, etc.), he suggests that there are multiple genes implicated in many of these disorders, that such genes merely confer risk for the disease but that interaction between these genes and environmental factors determines whether the risk produces the disease. The same studies support a polygenic view, where any single gene is not a necessary or sufficient condition for the expression of the disease. This represents a clear contrast to the earlier, and perhaps still prevalent view, of a single-locus etiology.

In contrast, Hirsch tackles the task of explaining theoretically and/or computationally the concepts of uniqueness, diversity, similarity, repeatability, and heritability in terms of calculating and estimating the number of possible genotypes for specie and genetic influences on populations and individuals. He argues that traditional conceptualizations have undermined the complexity of genetic processes.

In her commentary, biologist Lundy Braun decries the crude genetic or environmental determinism that derives from dualistic, nature versus nurture conceptions. Agreeing with Hirsch that simplistic, split conceptions of genetic activity can obscure understanding, she emphasizes that behaviorial genetics, even as revised in Rende's proposals, fails to grasp the ways in which biological systems function. Braun endorses, therefore, integrative, developmental systems ideas, as represented for instance in the theory and research of Gottlieb. She believes that only through research based on such dynamic models will understanding of human development and disease be advanced.

In the next chapter, Dickens and Cohen contend that there are many misconceptions and false assumptions about behavioral genetics and evolutionary psychology, both of which are useful fields for understanding decision-making processes in humans. They begin by arguing that for a behavior to be genetically influenced, it does not mean that the behavior is either ethical or unchangeable. Then they proceed to posit that within an economist model of rational choice, genetic influences can be hypothesized to occur (a) on tastes which influence preferences, (b) on constraints on the range of behaviors from which one may choose, or (c) on the decision-making process itself. They conclude that the field of evolutionary psychology has much to inform the work of behavioral economics, with clear social implications of such analyses.

Bearer, in the next chapter, elucidates first how the social and physical environment influences the genetic program through a multistep system of complex, flexible, biochemical reactions. She then presents evidence from the Cichlid fish of how behavior can drive genetic change over time and posits discrimination as a source of bias underlying kin selection, which can thereby influence the gene pool over evolutionary time. She ends with a cautionary note that misuse of this fundamental ability to distinguish between those people who are similar ("us") and those who are different ("them") may be at the root of existing inequities in health care access around the world. Such inequities could further promote a genetic bottleneck, thus reducing the variety of the human gene pool over only a few generations.

In the final chapter, Overton uses the notion of embodiment as a fundamental way of understanding human development, moving away from the Cartesian split approach of explaining behavior as if it were the product of two distinct processes: nurture or nature. Within this framework, biology and culture are seen as dialectical, relational complementaries, not as fundamental dichotomies. Using a person-center focus, Overton argues for the use of theory that defines humans as embodied persons functioning as a self-organizing dynamic system of cognitive, emotional, and motivational meanings.

Finally, in the closing commentary, the book editors indicate that one key conclusion derives from the scholarship presented across the volume—that human development occurs through a fused process of dynamic relations involving variables from biological through sociocultural and historical levels of organization. Influences from all levels—genes, individual behavior, parental rearing practices, or social policies, for instance—contribute integratively, and only integratively, to the structure and function of human behavior and development.

Accordingly, the scholarship in this volume provides scientific legitimization for innovative, relational approaches to the study of nature and nurture and its applications to policy and social programs. For those concerned with using the best of science to inform the policies and programs affecting the quality of human development within and across the nations of our world, developmental systems approaches and other relational theories can serve as templates through which scholars may develop or extend their knowledge about the systemic bases of human development. Only then, we will be in the position of creating the necessary multidisciplinary and scientist-practitioner-community collaborations needed to enhance human development.

REFERENCES

Anastasi, A. (1958). Heredity, environment, and the question "how?" *Psychological Review, 65,* 197–208.

Gottlieb, G. (1997). *Synthesizing nature–nurture: Prenatal roots of instinctive behavior.* Mahwah, NJ: Lawrence Erlbaum Associates.

Gould, S. J. (1981). *The mismeasure of man.* New York: Norton.

Hirsch, J. (1970). Behavior-genetic analysis and its biosocial consequences. *Seminars in Psychiatry, 2,* 89–105.

Hirsch, J. (1997). Some history of heredity-vs-environment, genetic inferiority at Harvard (?), and The (incredible) Bell Curve. *Genetica, 99,* 207–224.

International Human Genome Sequencing Consortium. (2001). Initial sequencing and analysis of the human genome. *Nature, 409,* 860–921.

Kamin, L. J. (1974). *The science and politics of IQ.* Potomac, MD: Wiley.

Lerner, R. M. (1992). *Final solutions: Biology, prejudice, and genocide.* University Park: Pennsylvania State University Press.

Lerner, R. M. (2002). *Concepts and theories of human development* (3rd ed.). Mahwah, NJ: Lawrence Erlbaum Associates.

Lewontin, R. C., Rose, S., & Kamin, L. J. (1984). *Not in our genes: Biology, ideology, and human nature.* New York: Pantheon.

Overton, W. F. (1998). Developmental psychology: Philosophy, concepts, and methodology. In W. Damon (Series Ed.) & R. M. Lerner (Ed.), *Handbook of child psychology: Vol. 1. Theoretical models of human development* (5th ed., pp. 107–187). New York: Wiley.

Proctor, R. N. (1988). *Racial hygiene: Medicine under the Nazis.* Cambridge, MA: Harvard University Press.

Rutter, M. (2002). Nature, nurture, and development: From evangelism through science toward policy and practice. *Child Development, 73,* 1–21.

Venter, J. C., Adams, M. D., Myers, E. W., Li, P. W., Mural, R. J. [plus 270 others]. (2001). The sequence of the human genome. *Science, 291,* 1304–1351.

1

Genes and the Promotion of Positive Human Development: Hereditarian Versus Developmental Systems Perspectives

Richard M. Lerner
Tufts University

Many experimental biologists outside of the biomedical-industrial complex are just now coming (back) to grips with the facts of epigenesis; with the profound mystery that developmental biology is, with the poverty of gene programs as an explanatory device; and with a crisis defined by the realization that an increasingly deficient theory of developmental genetics is the *only* theory currently available. The question remains: if biologists are starting to learn this lesson, will the psychologists be far behind?

—Richard C. Strohman (1993a, p. 101)

Genes are part of the developmental system in the same sense as other components (cell, tissue, organism), so genes must be susceptible to influence from other levels during the process of individual development.

—Gilbert Gottlieb (1992, p. 167).

Contemporary theories of human development are predicated on dynamic, relational, and systems perspectives (Lerner, 1998a, 1998b). The complexity of these theories can be daunting to scholars, both in regard to the conceptual difficulties involved in integratively understanding the multiple levels of organization fused within the developmental system and in respect to the methodological challenges involved in using such theories as a frame for research.

If challenging to scholars, such theories are often seen as virtually impossible to grasp by nonspecialists, for instance, by the "Person in the Street" (to use the term suggested by Horowitz, 2000, p. 8), by media representatives, or by policy makers who influence the allocation of funds to programs aimed at promoting health and human development. These groups may gravitate to "single-variable stories" (Horowitz, 2000, p. 3) about human development—such as "genes cause behavior" (e.g., see Rushton, 1999)—to understand, communicate about, or support policies and programs to improve people's lives, respectively.

Such a simplistic—indeed a distortingly simplistic—alternative to developmental systems theories of human development is embodied in hereditarian views of behavioral development; that is, views that "split" nature from it relation to nurture (Overton, 1998) and that reduce the complexity of the human developmental system to mechanistically acting genetic determinants (e.g., Plomin, 1986, 2000; Rowe, 1994; Rushton, 1999, 2000). Fields such as human sociobiology and behavior genetics are examples of such hereditarian positions. However, because it is often the case that sociobiologists (e.g., Rushton, 1999, 2000; Wilson, 1980) claim that data derived from behavior genetics research pertinent to the concept of heritability provide key evidence in support of the validity of their ideas, behavior genetics constitutes an important sample case for the evaluation of hereditarian thinking. Accordingly, we may note the observations of Horowitz (2000) in regard to the behavior genetics approach to theory and research about human development. Horowitz (2000, p. 3) indicated:

> Against the media popularity of single-variable stories, the science itself is moving inexorably toward greater and greater data-driven, integrative theoretical complexity. An exception to this is behavioral genetics. In contrast to the dynamic nonlinear interactive models full of reciprocity between and among levels and variables, behavioral genetics presents a relatively non-dynamic linear additive model that tries to assign percentages of variance in behavior and development that can be attributed to genes. The enterprise rests on the assumption that genetic influence can be expressed as a value accounting for a portion of the variance in a nondynamic linear equation for predicting behavioral functioning and furthermore, that the individual experiences of shared and nonshared environments can be assessed inferentially by the degree of biological relatedness of individuals without empirical observations of experience (Hoffman, 1991; Horowitz 1993, p. 3).

> Behavioral genetics involves a relatively simplistic approach when compared with the kinds of dynamic systems theories currently being elaborated. Perhaps that is why, in the mode of wanting simple answers to simple questions, behavior genetic reports are so media attracting.

What then is the view of human development presented by behavior genetics? Why is this view not a viable, nature alternative to dynamic and integrative developmental systems conceptions of human development? What is the frame offered by behavior genetics for application to public policies and social programs aimed at reducing or preventing the problems of young people or promoting their positive development? And, if behavior genetics fails as a useful model for understanding human development, what potential harm is done to the children, adolescents, and families of our nation if this instance of hereditarian thinking influences policies and programs? Can potential harm be counteracted by forwarding a developmental systems perspective as a frame for applications to policies and programs? To address these questions, it is useful to define the field of behavior genetics.

DEFINITION OF THE FIELD OF BEHAVIOR GENETICS

According to Robert Plomin (2000), a prolific contributor to the behavior genetics literature, "Behavioural genetics is the genetic study of behaviour, which includes quantitative genetics (twin and adoption studies) as well as molecular genetics (DNA studies) of human and animal behaviour broadly defined to include responses of the organism from responses measured in the brain such as functional neuroimaging to self-report questionnaires" (p. 30). Plomin, DeFries, and McClearn (1980) indicate that "behavioral genetics lies at the interface between genetics and the behavioral sciences" (p. 12), and Plomin (1986) notes that "behavioral geneticists explore the etiology of individuality, differences among individuals in a population (p. 5). He further explains that "the three basic methods used in human behavioral genetics are family, twin, and adoption studies" (p. 11).

Across all these methods, the goal of behavior genetic analysis is to separate (partition) the variation in a distribution of scores (e.g., for a personality trait, temperamental characteristic, or intelligence) into the proportion due to genes and the proportion due to the environment. Although behavior geneticists admit that genes and environments may be correlated and/or may interact, they most typically seek to compute a score (termed a "heritability coefficient") that in its most frequently used form denotes the independent contribution of genetic variance to the overall differences in the distribution of scores for a given individual characteristic.

For such heritability scores to be meaningful, the methodologies of behavior genetics rest on a model of gene function that sees as possible genetic contributions that are independent of (not correlated or interactive with) the context within which genes exist. Genes, however, do not work in the way that behavior geneticists imagine.

Fatal Flaws in the Behavior Genetics Model of Gene Function

As illustrated in the epigraphs by Strohman (1993a) and Gottlieb (1992), as well as in the writings of other molecular geneticists (e.g., Elman, et al., 1998; Ho, 1984; Müller-Hill, 1988; Venter, et al., 2001) and cell biologists (McEwen, 1997, 1998, 1999; Meaney, Aitken, Berkel, Bhatnager, & Sapolsky, 1988) more generally, molecular biologists do not place credence in the model of genetic function involved in behavioral genetics. In fact, Venter and his colleagues (2001), the group that successfully mapped the sequence of the human genome, emphasize that there are two conceptual errors that should not be made in the face of the advances they and other scientists are making in understanding the structure and functional consequences of the human genome. They stressed:

> There are two fallacies to be avoided: determinism, the idea that all characteristics of the person are "hard-wired" by the genome; and reductionism, the view that with complete knowledge of the human genome sequence, it is only a matter of time before our understanding of gene functions and interactions will provide a complete causal description of human variability. (p. 1348)

Contemporary thought in molecular genetics thus rejects the idea that genes are structures that act on supragenetic levels; instead, these scientists adopt the dynamic, developmental systems view noted in the epigraph by Gottlieb (1992; see also Ford & Lerner, 1992; Lerner, 1998b; Lewis, 1997; Magnusson, 1990, 1995, 1996, 1999a, 1999b; Magnusson & Stattin, 1998; Smith & Thelen, 1993; Thelen & Smith, 1994, 1998). This view emphasizes the integration—or fusion—of genes with the other levels of organization that comprise the person and his or her context. In such dynamic systems, the specific features of the interactions of the processes associated with these multiple levels create both the individuality of behavior at any point in time and the integrated character of human functioning that gives behavior its generality and cross-time predictability (Lerner, 1978; Smith & Thelen, 1993; Thelen & Smith, 1998).

In essence, then, we have in the field of behavior genetics (e.g., Plomin, 1986, 2000; Rowe, 1994) the use of a model of genetic structure and function that is specifically rejected by those scientists who study the action of genes directly. This rejection occurs because the field of behavioral genetics not only employs a counterfactual and scientifically atavistic conception of the role of genes in human development (Elman, et al., 1998; Ho, 1984; Strohman, 1993a, 1993b; Venter, et al., 2001) but also because behavior genetics is a viewpoint with a conceptually flawed and empirically deficient view of developmental process and, as well, involves the conflation of description and explanation.

For instance, in regard to process, the structural account of genetic action behavior genetics offer suffers from the flaws of all structural accounts of development; that is, as explained by Thelen and Smith (1994, 1998; Smith & Thelen, 1993), such conceptions are inherently incomplete. These views do not explain individual behavioral performance (actions), other than to express empirically unsubstantiated confidence that in some way genetic structures translate—through the levels of cells, tissues, organs, the individual, and his or her actual context—into real-time actions.

For example, without any specification of the pathways of influence from genes to behaviors, Rowe (1994) asserted:

Genes can produce dispositions, tendencies, and inclinations, because people with subtly different nervous systems are differently motivated ... [and] given enough environmental opportunities [for selection of environments], the ones chosen are those most reinforcing for a particular nervous system created by a particular genotype ... the direction of the growth curve of development, and the limit ultimately attained, is set in the genes. (p. 91)

However, because behavior geneticists believe that genetic structure transcends and is independent of real-time actions, an adequate, empirically verifiable account of actual individual-in-context behavior is beyond theoretical range (Smith & Thelen, 1993). Moreover, because of the inability to explain individual performance of actual individual-in-context behavior, behavior genetics, like other structural theories (Smith & Thelen, 1993), cannot explain the global order of behavior or developmental change itself.

In turn, in regard to the conflation of description and explanation, behavior genetics describes variability in trait distributions in a specific sample and then explains the distribution it has observed by reference to a label it has applied to one (or the other) of the sources of the variability—genes or environment. Not only is this reification an instance of the nominal fallacy, but—to paraphrase the parody of structural explanations presented by Smith and Thelen (1993, p. 159)—the cause of the distribution of interindividual differences in a trait distribution is merely an abstract description of the trait distribution itself: Behavior genetics describes the variability in a distribution, labels it with a fancy source term (i.e., heritability), and then imputes that there is a gene, or set of genes, that explains the distribution.

To illustrate, Rowe (1994) notes that "understanding the growth and development of a single individual has been confused with understanding the origin of different traits in a population" (p. 3). However, this confusion about the distinction between interindividual differences and intraindividual change, as well as the problem of the conflation of description and explanation, exists in behavior genetics. On the basis of heritability data, writers such as Rowe seamlessly slide from talking about descriptive sources of variation within a trait distribution into talking about the genetic basis of individual development, that is, about the "causal influence on such child outcomes as intelligence, personality, and psychopathology" (p. 1).

One key basis of the lack of an adequate treatment in behavior genetics of performance, of developmental sequence and process, as well as of the distinction between description and explanation, is that these conceptual problems are coupled in behavior genetics with a lack of an adequate theoretical understanding both of supragenetic intraorganism processes (Gottlieb, 1991a, 1991b, 1992, 1997; Gottlieb, Wahlsten, & Lickliter, 1998) and of extraorganism contextual or ecological processes (Bronfenbrenner & Ceci, 1994; Horowitz, 2000; Lewis, 1997; Magnusson, 1999a, 1999b; Sameroff, 1983; Thelen & Smith, 1998). Accordingly, behavior genetics fails to adequately measure the environment, or ecology (Hoffman, 1991) of human development. In short, to paraphrase Goldberger (1980), in his discussion of Hearnshaw's (1979) account of the scientific fraud behavior geneticist Cyril Burt perpetrated regarding the study of the heritability of intelligence, behavior geneticists have methods that give them a lot of numbers but very little sensible or useful data about human development.

BEHAVIOR GENETICS AS THE EMPEROR'S NEW CLOTHES

That these egregious conceptual and methodological problems exist is not news, not even in psychology. Hirsch (e.g., 1970, 1976a, 1976b, 1990a, 1990b, 1997a, 1997b) has written repeatedly about these problems for about a quarter of a century, and Schneirla (1956, 1957), Kuo (1967, 1970, 1976), Lehrman (1953, 1970), Tobach (1981; Tobach & Greenberg, 1984; Tobach & Schneirla, 1968), Gottlieb (1970, 1983, 1992), Bronfenbrenner (1979, 1989; Bronfenbrenner & Ceci, 1994), Collins, Maccoby, Steinberg, Hetherington, & Bornstein (2000), Ford and Lerner (1992), Horowitz, (1993, 2000), Lerner (1978, 1984, 1986, 1991), Lewis (1997); Magnusson (1999a, 1999b; Magnusson & Stattin, 1998), Overton (1998), and Thelen and Smith (1994, 1998; Smith & Thelen, 1993) have contributed consonant commentaries both prior to and during the period of Hirsch's still ongoing work.

Yet, despite this criticism by their colleagues in the field of psychology, as well as by the lack of credence given to behavior genetics by molecular geneticists—as well as by eminent population geneticists (e.g., Feldman & Lewontin, 1975) and evolutionary biologists (e.g., Gould, 1981, 1996)—many psychologists continue to act as if behavioral genetics provides evidence for the inheritance of behaviors as varied as intelligence (Jensen, 1969, 1998), parenting (Scarr, 1992), morality (Wilson, 1975), temperament (Buss & Plomin, 1984), television viewing (Plomin, Corley, DeFries, & Faulker, 1990), and even the role in human development of the environment (Harris, 1998; Plomin, 1986, 2000; Plomin & Daniels, 1987; Rowe, 1994)! It should be noted that "environment" is the too general, and now outmoded, term used by behavior geneticists to refer to the integrated, multilevel context, or the ecology, involved in the dynamic system of person-context relations that characterizes human development (e.g., Bronfenbrenner, 1979, Bronfenbrenner & Ceci, 1994; Bronfenbrenner & Morris, 1998; Thelen & Smith, 1998).

The breadth and depth of these continuing criticisms of behavior genetics have been somewhat invisible or, at least, ignored by Plomin (2000), who claimed that "The controversy that swirled around behavioural genetics research during the 1970s has largely faded. During the 1980s and especially during the 1990s, the behavioural sciences became much more accepting of genetic influence" (p. 30).

This view is wrong in at least two ways. First, the controversy regarding the legitimacy of behavioral genetics—both as a conceptual frame for understanding the role of genes in behavioral development and as a methodology for studying the role of genes in behavioral development—has not diminished at all. One need only note the controversy associated with the publication of *The Bell Curve* (Herrnstein & Murray, 1994; e.g., see Goldberger & Manski, 1995; Hirsch, 1997a) or the criticisms leveled at the hereditarian views of J. Philippe Rushton (1996, 1997a, 1997b, 1999; e.g., see Lerner, 1992a, 2002), which rely heavily on information derived from behavior genetics, to recognize that Plomin's (2000) "declaration of victory" is an inadequate attempt to either ignore or deny the persisting flaws of behavior genetics theory and method identified by scientists from numerous disciplines (e.g., see the critiques published throughout the 1990s and into the twenty-first century by Collins, Maccoby, Steinberg, Hetherington, & Bornstein, 2000; Gottlieb, 1997; Hirsch, 1997a, 1997b; Horowitz, 1993, 2000; Lerner & von Eye, 1992; Lewontin, 2000; Peters, 1995; Strohman, 1993a, 1993b; Winston, 1996, 1997a, 1997b).

To illustrate, in a critique of the explanatory model and method associated with behavior genetic analyses of parent behaviors and of the effects of parenting on child and adolescent development, Collins, et al. (2000) noted:

Large-scale societal factors, such as ethnicity or poverty, can influence group means in parenting behavior—and in the effects of parenting behaviors—in ways that are not revealed by studies of within group variability. In addition, highly heritable traits also can be highly malleable. Like traditional correlational research on parenting, therefore, commonly used behavior-genetic methods have provided an incomplete analysis of differences among individuals. (p. 220)

Accordingly, Collins, et al. (2000) concluded:

Whereas researchers using behavior-genetic paradigms imply determinism by heredity and correspondingly little parental influence (e.g., Rowe, 1994), contemporary evidence confirms that the expression of heritable traits depends, often strongly, on experience, including specific parental behaviors, as well as pre-dispositions and age-related factors in the child. (p. 228)

Second, Plomin rewrites history by stating that it was not until the 1990s that behavioral science accepted the role of genes in behavioral development. For well more than a half century (e.g., Anastasi, 1958; Maier & Schneirla, 1935; Novikoff, 1945a, 1945b; Schneirla, 1956, 1957), genes have been accepted as part of the developmental system that propels human life across time. The issue is not the one that Plomin points to, then, that of accepting that genes are involved in development. Instead, the issue is how do genes contribute to development. Plomin's (2000) approach and that of other behavior geneticists (e.g., Rowe, 1994) involves a split, nature-reductionist treatment of this issue (Overton, 1998). Most contemporary developmental scientists take an integrated, relational developmental systems approach to the issue (Lerner, 1998a, 1998b; Overton, 1998).

In fact, Plomin (2000) conceptually approaches the vacuity of the behavior genetics approach, at least as it has been pursued through the twentieth century. Although he maintains that "twin and adoption research and genetic research using nonhuman animal models will continue to thrive" in the twenty-first century (p. 30), Plomin perhaps admits to the serious flaws in this approach to understanding the role of genes in behavioral development when he acknowledges that "the greatest need is for quantitative genetic research that goes beyond heritability, that is, beyond asking whether and how much genetic factors are important in behavioral development (p. 31). Moreover, he then goes on to ask a series of important questions about the role of genes in behavioral development: "How do genetic effects unfold developmentally? What are the biological pathways between genes and behaviour? How do nature and nurture interact and correlate?" (p. 31). Unfortunately, he seeks answers to these questions through the flawed model and methods of behavior genetics and never explores the potential usefulness of developmental systems approaches. Nevertheless, such exploration would be very useful because Plomin admits that it would be a major mistake:

> To think that genes determine outcomes in a hard-wired, there's-nothing-we-can-do-about-it way. For thousands of rare single-gene disorders, such as the gene on chromosome 4 that causes Huntington's disease, genes do determine outcomes in this hard-wired way. However, behavioral disorders and dimensions are complex traits influenced by many genes as well as many environmental factors. For complex traits, genetic factors operate in a probabilistic fashion like risk factors rather than predetermined programming. (p. 33)

Thus, ultimately, Plomin (2000) admits that a probabilistic, nature-nurture relation is involved in accounting for the role of genes in behavioral development. Still, his views about single-gene disorders reflect an ahistorical conception of such problems of human development. That is, in respect to other such single-gene disorders, for example, as involved with phenylketonuria (PKU), genetic research has found means to counteract the problems produced by the genetic inheritance and has thus shown that a hard-wired genetic influence is not that hard-wired after all (Scriver & Clow, 1980a, 1980b). As such, Plomin maintains a narrow view of the probabilistic developmental system; it apparently does not include the ingenuity of scholars who capitalize on the plasticity within the developmental system to demonstrate that what might seem to be hard-wired is in reality amenable to change as a consequence of the embeddedness of genes within a dynamic system. Nevertheless, in admitting to the importance of a probabilistic system in behavioral development, Plomin (2000) is in actuality defeating his own split approach to the nature and nurture of behavioral development.

Moreover, other scholars are not as convinced as is Plomin (2000) that the various methodologies he associates with behavior genetics will generate useful data. For example, Collins, et al. (2000) noted:

> One criticism is that the assumptions, methods, and truncated samples used in behavior-genetic studies maximize the effects of heredity and features of the environment that are different for different children and minimize the effects of shared family environments ... A second criticism is that estimates of the relative contributions of environment and heredity vary greatly depending on the source of data ... heritability estimates vary considerably depending on the measures used to assess similarity between children or between parents and children ... The sizable variability in estimates of genetic and environmental contributions depending on the

paradigms and measures used means that no firm conclusions can be drawn about the relative strength of these influences on development. (pp. 220–221)

Similarly, and again counter to Plomin's (2000) assertion that the controversy surrounding behavior genetics faded by the 1990s, Horowitz, in 2000, noted:

One sees increasing skepticism about what is to be learned from assigning variance percentages to genes ... The skepticism is informed by approaches that see genes, the central nervous system and other biological functions and variables as contributors to reciprocal, dynamic processes which can only be fully understood in relation to sociocultural environmental contexts. It is a perspective that is influenced by the impressive recent methodological and substantive advances in the neurosciences. (p. 3)

The cutting-edge study of the neurosciences within the developmental systems perspective noted by Horowitz (2000) is exemplified by the work of Suomi (1997, 2000; Bennett, et al., in press) who sought to identify how genes and context fuse within the developmental system. Because of the close genetic similarity of rhesus moneys to humans, he studied such organisms as a means to provide a model for the investigation of this system. In one recent instance of this long-term research program, Suomi (2000; Bennett, et al., in press) found that young rhesus monkeys show individual differences in their emotional reactivity (or "temperament"). Some young monkeys are highly reactive; for example, they become quite excited and agitated when they experience environmental stress, for instance, separation from their mothers; other monkeys show low reactivity in such situations, for instance, they behave calmly in the face of such separation. Suomi (2000; Bennett, et al., in press) discovered that these individual differences in behavior are associated with different genetic inheritances related to the functioning of serotonin, a brain chemical involved in neurotransmission and linked to individual differences in such conditions as anxiety, depression, and impulsive violence.

Accordingly, to study the interrelation of serotonergic system genes and environmental influences on behavioral development, Suomi (2000; Bennett, et al., in press) placed high or low reactivity rhesus young with foster rhesus monkeys that were also either high or low in emotional reactivity. When young monkeys with the genetic inheritance marking high reactivity were reared for the first six months of life with a low reactivity mother, they developed normally and, despite their genes, did not show high reactivity even when removed from their foster mothers and placed in a group of peers and unknown adults. In fact, these monkeys showed a high level of social skill; for example, they took leadership positions in their group. However, when young monkeys with this same genetic marker for high reactivity were raised by high reactivity foster mothers, they did not fare well under stressful conditions and proved socially inept when placed in a new social group.

Moreover, Suomi (2000; Bennett, et al., in press) found that the interaction between the serotonin transporter genotype and early experience not only influences rhesus monkey behavior but, as well, brain chemistry regarding the use of serotonin. Despite have a high reactivity genotype, the monkeys whose early life experiences were with the low reactivity foster mothers had brain chemistry that corresponded to monkeys with a low reactivity genotype. Accordingly, Suomi (2000, p. 31) concluded:

> The recent findings that specific polymorphisms in the serotonin transporter gene are associated with different behavioral and biological outcomes for rhesus monkeys as a function of their early social rearing histories suggest that more complex gene-environment interactions actually are responsible for the phenomenon. It is hard to imagine that the situation would be any less complex for humans.

Behavior Genetics Constitutes the Maintenance of a Scientific Fiction

Clearly, many human developmentalists do not believe the causal story line of behavior genetics. Nevertheless, research in behavior genetics—studies that, in effect, involve obtaining samples of people with differing degrees of biological relatedness and applying, typically, state-of-the-art measures of traits and inadequate measures of the ecology of human development (Bronfenbrenner & Ceci, 1994; Hoffman, 1991)—is well-funded and widely disseminated, both through articles in the best scientific journals and in books produced through excellent publication houses.

But, behavior genetics is really like the story of the emperor's new clothes. Despite the positive regard some researchers hold for this area, there is actually nothing there. The naked truth is that conceptual errors and misapplied models—no matter how often repeated or published—do not by dint of their numbers make for an adequate contribution to science. The conceptual problems of the split, nature-mechanistic model of human development of behavior genetics and the several limitations of the scientific methods it uses to try to support this model, for example, in regard to the computation and interpretation of heritability estimates, are well known (e.g., see Lerner, 2002, for a recent review) and will be discussed in other chapters in this book. Together, these sources indicate the technical (statistical) problems associated with heritability research and underscore the myriad conceptual and methodological shortcomings of behavior genetics and why any purported evidence it presents for the split, hereditarian view of behavior development is more apparent than real. Nevertheless, despite scientific limitations that should reduce a field to scholarly irrelevancy, behavior geneticists continue to pursue their "research," to obtain government and foundation funding for it, and to promulgate their ideas about the import of their work for public policies and social programs pertinent to young people and their families (e.g., Rowe, 1994; Rushton, 1999, 2000).

Such extensions of flawed ideas to the arena of public policy and social programs can be dangerous to human welfare, social justice, and civil society (Lerner, 1992a, 1992b, 2002). To illustrate, in the mid 1960s, T. C. Schneirla wrote about the social policy implications of Konrad Lorenz's hereditarian ideas about the existence of a human instinct for aggression. In a review of Lorenz's *On Aggression* (1966), Schneirla (1966) wrote:

> It is as heavy a responsibility to inform man about aggressive tendencies assumed to be present on an inborn basis as it is to inform him about "original sin," which Lorenz admits in effect. A corollary risk is advising societies to base their programs of social training on attempts to inhibit hypothetical innate aggressions, instead of continuing positive measures for constructive behavior. (p. 16)

Despite such risks, hereditarians adopting a behavior genetics approach to human behavior advise society about the social import of their counterfactual views of genetic contributions to development. It is important to illustrate and evaluate such applications.

THE CONCEPTUAL FRAMES PROVIDED BY BEHAVIOR GENETICS AND DEVELOPMENTAL SYSTEMS FOR HUMAN DEVELOPMENT APPLICATIONS

The purported uses for applications to policies and programs pertinent to human development of behavior genetics rest on the secondary (or even epiphenomenal) role assigned within this perspective to the ecology of human development in contributing to the causal bases of individual functioning. If context is not of primary significance in the determination of behavior and development, then any policies or programs aimed at enhancing the context of human development (e.g., prevention programs pertinent to youth risk behaviors or policies aimed at changing the family, school, or community experiences of poor children to promote their positive life chances) would be at best of only secondary importance. If context is, however, not at all causal—or if purported contextual influences on human development are seen as only illusory or epiphenomenal influences that can be reduced completely to genetic influences (e.g., Rowe, 1994; Rushton, 1999, 2000)—then attempts to change the context to enhance human development are irrelevant, misguided, and wasteful exercises. They could be construed, in fact, as inhumane exercises that falsely elevated the hopes of people whose problematic plights were due not to their social circumstances (e.g., social injustice or the absence of opportunity, equity, or democracy) but rather to their fixed and immutable genetic inheritances.

Such a view of the impotence of the ecology of human development as a source of plasticity in behavior would result then in applications directed to the only causal source of variance in human development, that is, genetic ones. If the genes that caused the problems afflicting the human condition could not be changed through antenatal repair, then the only policies and programs that would make scientific and societal sense would be ones aimed at, in the short term, diminishing the chances of possessors of the problematic genes from reproducing and thus passing their affliction onto another generation (e.g., see Lorenz, 1940a,

1940b, 1943a, 1943b; cf. Gould, 1981, 1996; Lerner, 1992a; Proctor, 1988). The long-term, or final, policy or program solution would be the elimination of the genes from the human genetic pool. The view of context associated with hereditarian conceptions (e.g., see Rowe, 1994; Rushton, 1999, 2000) contrast significantly with the fused conception of person and context variables found in developmental systems perspectives about the bases of human development (Lerner, 2002).

The Dynamic, Developmental Systems "Alternative" to Behavior Genetics

The developmental process envisioned in the dynamic developmental systems perspective stands in marked contrast to the hereditarian view of developmental process found in behavior genetics. As Gottlieb (1992) explained, in a developmental systems view of process, the key "conception is one of a totally interrelated, fully coactional system in which the activity of genes themselves can be affected through the cytoplasm of the cell by events originating at any other level in the system, including the external environment" (pp. 144–145). As such, Gottlieb (1992, 1997) and other developmental systems theorists (e.g., Thelen & Smith, 1998) emphasized that neither genes nor context by themselves cause development. The fusion among levels within the integrated developmental system means that relations among variables—not splits between nature and nurture—constitute the core of the developmental process.

Accordingly, although hereditarians argue that biological contributions are isomorphic with genetic influences (e.g., Rushton, 1999), this equivalence is not seen as veridical with reality from the perspective of developmental systems theory. For instance, although some hereditarians see constitutional variables (e.g., relating to brain volume, head size, size of reproductive organs, and stature) as all based on heredity (Rushton, 1999), within developmental systems:

> "Constitutional" is not equivalent to "genetic," and purposely so. Constitutional includes the expressed functions of genes—which, in themselves require some environmental input—but constitutional includes the operations of the central nervous system and all the biological and environmental experiences that impact organismic functioning and that make constitutional variables part of the dynamic change across the life span as they affect the development of and the decline of behavior. (Horowitz, 2000, p. 8)

In short, developmental science and developmental scientists should stop engaging in the pursuit of theoretically anachronistic and counterfactual conceptions of gene function. Indeed, significant advances in the science of human development will rest upon embedding the study of genes within the multiple, integrated levels of organization comprising the dynamic developmental system of person-context relations.

As Thelen and Smith (1994, 1998; Smith & Thelen, 1993) noted, pursuing this dynamic interactionist, developmental systems perspective will surely be an arduous path, one likely filled with conceptual and empirical difficulties, mistakes, and uncertainties. Nevertheless, there is more than sufficient reason to continue to pursue this approach to behavioral development.

First, the nature-mechanistic approach of behavior genetics fails completely as an adequate theoretical or empirical approach to understanding human development. Second, and to paraphrase the epigraph by Strohman (1993a, p. 101) that opened this paper, we have no better option available than to pursue a dynamic developmental systems approach. And third, great progress is being made. To appraise this progress it is useful to return again to the ideas of Horowitz (2000).

The Contributions of Horowitz to Understanding the Importance of Developmental Systems Theories

Summarizing the status at the beginning of the twenty-first century of theory and research pertinent to developmental systems perspectives, Horowitz (2000) noted that there exists:

> extremely important information about structural plasticity in neuro-psychological function. Most critically, this structural and functional plasticity across developmental time is being tied directly to the amplifications and constraints of the social/cultural contexts that determine the opportunities that children and adults have to experience and to learn. (p. 3)

To help frame these data, Horowitz (2000) introduced a model of the dynamic developmental system that she notes corresponds to those of other developmental systems theorists (e.g., Gottlieb, et al., 1998; Lerner, 1998a, 1998b, in press). As such, Horowitz indicated:

> In this model, as in some of the others, the assumption is made (supported by data) that from the moment of conception development is influenced by constitutional, social, economic and cultural factors and that these factors, furthermore, continue in linear and nonlinear relationships, to affect development across the life span, with development broadly defined to accommodate both the increase and decrease in ability and function. (p. 4)

Moreover, in the context of presenting her model of the human developmental system, Horowitz (2000) compared the approach to developmental analysis represented by hereditarian approaches to behavior development, such as behavior genetics, with the approach pursued in the sorts of theories represented in her model. While recognizing the attractiveness to the "average person" and the media of the simplistic answers provided by nature-oriented theorists, Horowitz (2000) observed:

> The conundrum for many is to explain the regularities of the postnatal emergence of the normal universal species-typical behaviors in each individual child despite the

seeming variations in the gross nature of environments. The nativists answer is recourse to instincts, to predetermined, architecturally and genetically driven explanations both for the species as a whole and for the individuals in particular (Chomsky, 1965; Pinker, 1994; Spelke, Breinlinger, Macomber, & Jacobson, 1992; Spelke & Newport, 1998). To the Person in the Street these explanations seem to provide the simple answers to simple questions though the nativist position is by no means simplistic and the position is often supported by very interesting data.

The alternative view and, I believe, the more compelling view is to consider that within all the gross environmental variations there is present the essential minimal experience necessary for the acquisition—the learning—of the basic universal behaviors of our species. There is a growing agreement that universal behaviors and physical structures are not built into the organism but that humans are, at the very least, evolutionary primed to take advantage of the transactional opportunities provided by what Brandtstädter (1998) sees as the universal physical and social ecologies available to all normal human organisms—the kinds of transactional opportunities so beautifully analyzed by Thelen and her colleagues with respect to early motor development (Thelen & Ulrich, 1991). As a result of these transactional experiences, the forms and function of the universal developmental domains are constructed, whether as described in Thelen's dynamic systems approach to motor development (Thelen & Smith, 1994; Thelen & Ulrich, 1991), or in Katherine Nelson's (1996) powerful analysis and synthesis of the role of language in cognitive development, or in Kurt Fischer's notion of the "constructive web" and his attempts to document the linear and nonlinear mechanisms involved in the construction and development of the hierarchies of skills (Fischer, 1980; Fischer & Bidell, 1998). (p. 5)

In short, given the myriad theoretical and methodological problems associated with behavior genetics, little can be gained either for advancing the science of human development or for adequately informing or serving Horowitz's (2000) "Person in the Street" by continuing to invest resources in the behavior genetics approach. There seem to be compelling reasons to make human and financial investments elsewhere given, on one hand, the counterfactual view of genetic activity inherent in behavior genetics and the several insurmountable conceptual and computational problems involved in the derivation of heritability estimates and, on the other hand, the availability of the theoretically rich and empirically productive developmental systems alternative to hereditarian approaches such as behavior genetics.

I believe, then, that both science and society may be well served by embarking on the scholarly path envisioned by Horowitz (2000). To both enhance understanding of human development, and to best promote its healthy progression across ontogeny, we should begin to devote our theoretical and research efforts to the exploration of the dynamic developmental system depicted by her and others (e.g., Collins, et al., 2000; Ford & Lerner, 1992; Lerner, 1991, 1996, 1998, 1998a, 1998b, 2002; Levine & Fitzgerald, 1992; Lewis, 1997; Sameroff, 1983; Smith & Thelen, 1993; Thelen & Smith, 1994, 1998). Such an initiative would be important because the hereditarian and the developmental systems viewpoints have quite different implications for policies and programs pertinent to the promotion of positive human development.

Contrasts Between Hereditarian and Developmental Systems Perspectives About Human Development Policies and Programs

Table 1.1 presents one view of the different implications of hereditarian and developmental systems ideas for promoting positive human development through policy and program initiatives. The table displays a 2x2 contingency table that contrasts (A) beliefs about whether the hereditarian, split conception is believed to be either (1) true or (2) false; and (B) public policy and social program implications that would be associated with the hereditarian split position were it in fact (1) true or (2) false under either of the two belief conditions involved in "A."

The format for this table was suggested by Jensen (1973) in a discussion of what he saw as the social and educational policy dangers that might arise from viewing his genetic differences hypothesis (Jensen, 1969) about the source of racial and socioeconomic status variation in IQ scores as false when it might in fact be true. The dangers Jensen (1973) saw are among those presented in cell A2, B2 of Table 1.1 (the cell that would be followed in the developmental systems perspective were believed to be true).

Table 1.1 displays as well the severe implications for the treatment of some people that would derive from policies and programs if the hereditarian position were accepted as true. These implications would occur whether it was in fact the case that the hereditarian position was veridical with reality. In turn, the table presents (in cell A2, B2) the implications for positive human development that would derive from policies and programs if the hereditarian viewpoint was generally accepted to be what it in fact is, that is, false, and if the developmental systems alternative was used instead as a frame for human development policies and programs.

Though I have argued that the hereditarian position is counterfactual, I have also acknowledged that beliefs about its falsity are not unanimous. Given the quite negative human development policy and program implications of the belief in the truth of a hereditarian position, it is important to do more that just (a) appreciate the contrasts between hereditarian and developmental systems perspectives in their respective visions for the sources of influence that may be engaged to improve human development, or (b) note that behavior genetics merges a counterfactual view of gene action with a naive and impoverished understanding of the ecology of human development. In addition, as Lewontin (1992) has cautioned, it is crucial for human welfare that scholars remain vigilant about the presentation of hereditarian ideas potentially pertinent to human development policies and programs and, as well, about the actual use of these ideas in policy statements and program recommendations. A key example of this need for vigilance occurs in regard to the book by David Rowe (1994), *The Limits of Family Influence: Genes, Experience, and Behavior.*

ROWE'S HEREDITARIAN IDEAS ABOUT THE IRRELEVANCE OF CONTEXTUAL INFLUENCES ON HUMAN DEVELOPMENT

Rowe's (1994) central idea is that "broad differences in family environments, except those that are neglectful, abusive, or without opportunity—may exert little in-

TABLE 1.1

Policy and Program Implications if Hereditarian "Split" Conception of Genes (A) Believed True or False; (B) In Fact True or False

		B. Hereditarian "split" conception in fact:	
		1. True	2. False
A. Hereditarian "split" conception believed:	1. True	* Repair inferior genotypes, making them equal to superior genotypes * Miscegenation laws * Restrictions of personal liberties of carriers of inferior genotypes (separation, discrimination, distinct social tracts) * Sterilization * Elimination of inferior genotypes from genetic pool	* Same as A1, B1
	2. False	* Wasteful and futile humanitarian policies * Wasteful and futile programs of equal opportunity, affirmative action, equity, and social justice * Policies and programs to quell social unrest because of unrequited aspirations of genetically constrained people * Deterioration of culture and destruction of civil society	* Equity, social justice, equal opportunity, affirmative action * Celebration of diversity * Universal participation in civic life * Democracy * Systems assessment and engagement * Civil society

fluence on personality development over the life course" (p. 1). However, he also claims that his "book's thesis [is] shared family environments have little effect on developmental outcomes" (p. 4).

Thus, to Rowe (1994), it does not matter (except in extreme circumstances) whether family environments are, across children, different or common (i.e., shared): It is his thesis that in neither case does environment influence developmental outcomes (see also Scarr, 1992). There are several problems with this stance, ones prototypic of the behavior genetics approach to the environment.

A key problem is that Rowe (1994) fails to recognize that family influences can strongly influence individual development, perhaps especially when there is no variation in them, that is, when they are shared equally across children. Elder's (1974) classic work on the effects of family economic hardship on children developing during the Great Depression is one excellent case in point. Another is provided by the recent work of Conger, Elder, and their colleagues (e.g., Conger et al., 1991; Conger et al., 1992; Ge et al., 1992) linking family economic hardship to adolescent distress, adjustment, and problems of substance use. Yet, because such invariant ecological influences contribute nothing to the variance across children or adolescents, their effects may be underestimated—especially when the ANOVA analytic techniques used in behavior genetics are ill-advisedly employed to estimate environmental contributions—a point that Hebb (1970) and Feldman and Lewontin (1975) made.

Another example of the problematic view of the context of human development Rowe (1994) used occurs when he explains what he means by the term "socialization science." Here, Rowe appears to be referring to an area of social and behavioral science that is predicated on the view that characteristics of the ecology of human development, such as culture, socioeconomic status, family milieu, and nonnormative life events, may have some causal influence on human development. He claimed that socialization science "may miss entirely which experiences are influential for personality development, and in many cases these may be experiences we cannot grasp to change our children's lives" (p. 5).

Of course, causal influences may not be identified in a given study. But, such omission would seem to be especially likely when—as is typically the case in behavior genetics—the context of human development is represented by, or better reduced to, a single score on a personality or intelligence test. For instance, consider behavior genetic studies using adoption designs. Here, assessments of the relative contributions to child outcomes of (a) the conception through point-of-adoption family context provided by a biological parent versus (b) the family context of an adopting parent to child outcomes, are indexed by differences in the relations (e.g., by differences between correlations) in trait scores for the biological parent and child compared to the adopting parent and child (cf. Hoffman, 1991). To illustrate, in discussing how the influence of selective placement in adoptions can be understood, Rowe (1994, p. 39) noted that "its quantitative strength is the correlation between the trait as measured in the biological parent (usually the unwed mother of the adoptee) and as measured in the adoptive parent." All contextual influences associated with families are reduced, therefore, to a single score, for example, to an IQ score.

Such adoption studies underestimate the possible contribution to the variance of context and of dynamic person-context relations, and, at the same time, overestimate the contribution of genetic variance because:

1. Variance due to intrauterine contextual influences (and typically also to post-birth, preadoption contextual influences) is not measured and is attributed instead to genetic variance; in fact, Rowe (1994) admits that "all the accidents of embryological development are unshared; they can affect siblings differently, because each child has a different birth history" (p. 34);

2. Data sets of trait correlations involving different degrees of biological family resemblance represent findings-to-be-explained; the presence of correlations does not prove anything about the role of genes or of genetic differences in causing the correlations; and

3. The multiple levels of organization comprising the ecology of human development (Bronfenbrenner, 1979, 1989; Bronfenbrenner & Ceci, 1994) cannot even begin to be measured by a score for a single trait measure, or even by a multivariate array of scores from several trait measures. To the contrary, and as again illustrated by the work of Elder (1974) and Conger (e.g., Conger, et al., 1991, 1992; Ge, et al., 1992), multilevel-multivariate representations of the context are needed to adequately represent the ecology of human development.

The reason Rowe (1994) omitted these theoretical and empirical contributions to the study of the context of human development is that behavior genetics is theoretically anachronistic. In splitting genes from environment, in divorcing the genes from the developmental system in which they are fused (Gottlieb, 1997; Horowitz, 2000; Overton, 1998; Thelen & Smith, 1998), Rowe focused on the environment of human development though a lens that reduces the scope of his vision and has him looking at past theories instead of contemporary ones (Lerner, 1998a). That is, to Rowe (1994), the theories that are seen as relevant to the context, or ecology, of human development or, in his terms, that represent the breadth of "socialization science" are Freudian theory (pp. 9–10), early behaviorism (pp. 10–12), and social learning theory (pp. 12–13), as represented by two references to the work of Bandura (1965, 1971). Bandura's (1986) later work—which is dynamically interactional and developmental—is not mentioned.

Indeed, nowhere in Rowe's (1994) book, or in the more recent hereditarian books published by Rushton (1999, 2000), is there an appreciation of this complex ecology of human development or, even more surprising, of the major theoretical contributions that have occurred over about the last 30 years in the understanding of context in human development and of the dynamic systems linking the individual to his or her multilevel context (e.g., Baltes, Lindenberger, & Staudinger, 1998; Baltes, Staudinger, & Lindenberger, 1999; Brim & Kagan,

1980; Bronfenbrenner, 1979, 1989; Bronfenbrenner & Morris, 1998; Elder, 1980, 1998; Elder, Modell, & Parke, 1993; Ford & Lerner, 1992; Gottlieb, 1983, 1991a, 1991b, 1992, 1997; Horowitz, 2000; Lerner, 1978, 1986, 1991, 1996, 2002; Levine & Fitzgerald, 1992; Lewis, 1997; Magnusson, 1995, 1996, 1999a, 1999b; Sameroff, 1975, 1983; Thelen & Smith, 1998; Wapner & Demick, 1998).

Moreover, the absence of reference to dynamic developmental systems theory is a particularly striking omission, given Rowe's (1994) biological orientation and the fact that it was in biology (von Bertalanffy, 1933) and later in comparative psychology (e.g., Gottlieb, 1976, 1991, 1992; Kuo, 1976; Schneirla, 1957; Tobach, 1971, 1981) where such perspectives had much of their genesis and (and continue to have) influence. The errors of scientific omission and commission in hereditarian positions, such as the one Rowe (1994) presented, have important implications for the ways in which such positions are applied to human development policies and programs. As I have suggested, these implications and their developmental systems alternatives are important to consider from the standpoints of both science and human welfare.

Hereditarian Versus Developmental Systems "Pathways" From Science to Social Policy and Social Action

I have argued that the conceptualization of genes and, superordinately, of nature as separable from nurture, found within behavior genetics is known—at least among molecular geneticists and some developmental and/or comparative scientists—to be counterfactual. Yet, I have noted that the field associated with this conceptual mistake continues to flourish. Indeed, despite a continuing failure by hereditarians to demonstrate the scientific validity of their nature-mechanistic ideas, new versions of the same flawed ideas continue to arise and attract research funding and, as described by Horowitz (2000), public, political, and media attention (e.g., Herrnstein, 1971; Herrnstein & Murray, 1994; Jensen, 1969, 1998; Lorenz, 1943a, 1943b, 1965; Rushton, 1987, 1996, 1999, 2000; Wilson, 1975).

Scholars in the field of human development must, therefore, confront several questions as a consequence of this curious situation: How did the biological, social, and behavioral sciences that attempt to contribute to the understanding and enhancement of human behavior and development arrive at this point? Why do we not just declare that the "emperor has no clothes?" Why, instead, why do we award grants and journal space to work having this fatal conceptual flaw?

Most important, why do we allow such mistaken reductionistic and mechanistic thinking to influence both science policy and social policy? In turn, why do we not more generally embrace policies informed by the scientifically valid alternative, developmental systems models of the role of biology-context relations?

In response to these questions, I believe that we can acknowledge, on one hand, that behavior genetics *has* helped social and behavioral science recall that both biology and context must be considered in any adequate theory of human development. On the other hand, however, I believe it is appropriate at this point in the history of the field of human development to reject the oversimplified and incorrect view of context and of biology, respectively, found in behavior genetics. We are at a point in the science of human development where we must move on to the more arduous task of understanding the integration of biological and contextual influences in terms of the developmental system of which they are a dynamic part. This change in scientific attention is important for reasons of both the production of adequate developmental scholarship and the generation of useful social policy.

To illustrate, I may note that for Rowe (1994), as for other behavior geneticists as well (e.g., Plomin, 1986, 2000), as long as variance can be partitioned, there is a belief that genes can be shown to give rise to any aspect of human functioning—even the environment in which the individuals—the "lumbering robots" (Dawkins, 1976)—housing the genes are embedded. For instance, Rowe (1994) asserted that "the measures we label as environmental (including such central ones as social class) may hide genetic variation" (p. 5). And how do genes create the environment? To Rowe, "the answer is that the genes may construct a nervous system—and that hormones and neurotransmitters may then motivate behaviors resulting in the dramatic redesign of an environment. The way a beaver will restructure its environment is as genetically shaped as its flat tail and keen hearing" (p. 90). Thus, Rowe's (1994) answer, which is his description of a process termed "niche picking," illustrates not only the mechanism and reductionism of behavior genetics but, as well, the acontextual, asystemic, superficial, and even magical, thinking about developmental process that exists within the field of behavior genetics.

Moreover, it is in the incautious dissemination of work based on such thinking wherein pernicious implications for social policy can arise (Lerner, 1992a, 1992b). Rowe (1994) argued: "My thesis here is that social class may capture not variation in rearing and environmental social background, but instead variation in genes. This idea returns genes to socialization science by a back door—*by the very variable (social class) thought to have liberated social science from hereditarian thinking!*" (p. 135).

Rowe's (1994) idea is redolent of the late-nineteenth- and early-twentieth-century social Darwinists in America and Europe (Proctor, 1988; Tobach, Gianutsos, Topoff, & Gross, 1974). In particular, his idea is consistent with the thinking involved in the German racial hygiene movement during this period (Proctor, 1988). Here, writers such as Alfred Ploetz, Wilhelm Schallmayer, Karl Binding, and Alfred Hoche maintained that members of low socioeconomic status groups—among other weaker members of society (e.g., the chronically sick or the lame)—were in their respective societal niches because of the inheritance of particular (i.e., inferior) genes (Lerner, 1992a; Proctor, 1988).

At this point, however, similarity to the thinking of Rowe (1994) disappears. This is because these racial hygienists went on to recommend—in a manner consistent with Cells A1, B1 and A1, B2 of Table 1.1—that, if the overall health of society were to be improved, then policies must be instituted to rid society of these inferior genes. For instance, social programs and health care could be denied to the people possessing these genes and, as a result, they would have neither the economic, social, nor medical resources to long survive on their own (Proctor, 1988). As a consequence, it was thought that these policies would—in perhaps only a generation or two—eliminate poverty as well as weak, medically fragile, or handicapped persons. Simply, then, it was argued that the overall health of the German people would be enhanced because the carriers of the inferior genes would not be present to reproduce.

While again underscoring my belief that Rowe (1994) would find such policy recommendations reprehensible, my point is that the assertion that social class differences are due to genetic differences has been used in the past to justify horrible, and indeed criminal, social policies and political actions (Lifton, 1986; Müller-Hill, 1988; Proctor, 1988). Moreover, ideas about genetic differences may influence social policy today. For example, former NIMH Director Frederick K. Goodwin drew a link between violent behavior among nonhuman primates and the presence of violence among urban males and asserted that these youth have lost the social controls humans have had imposed by civilization over thousands of years of evolution (Psychological Science Agenda, 1992).

Goodwin's thinking is not very distant from that of Rushton (1999, 2000), who proposed that the bases for what he believes are reproductive rate and associated behavioral differences among racial groups lies in the different reproductive strategies characterizing them. Rushton (1999, 2000) describes a continuum of reproductive strategies wherein "at one end of this scale are r-strategies that rely on high reproductive rates. At the other end are K-strategies that rely on high levels of parental care" (p. 24).

The different strategies depicted across this continuum are useful in biology to depict the reproductive rates of separate species (that are trying to survive and reproduce in diverse ecological niches; Johanson & Edey, 1981). For instance, a sponge, living and reproducing on the ocean floor, will produce literally thousands of offspring during a given reproductive cycle, and this rate will increase the probability of a few offspring withstanding the harsh currents and otherwise dangerous ecology of the ocean bottom for a period sufficient for their survival and eventual perpetuation of the species. In turn, given elephants' enormous nutritional needs during their lengthy prenatal gestation period and postnatal years, the probability of offspring survival is enhanced when a small number, most typically one, offspring, is produced during a reproductive cycle.

Thus, the r-K distinction is useful for describing differences between species in how their rate of reproduction fits the ecological niche within which they live. However, there is no validity for applying this concept to differences within a species in the reproductive rates of different individuals or groups. Yet, this is an error that Rushton (1999) makes, and in fact admits that he does! He noted that the r-K "scale is generally used to compare the life histories of different species of animals. I have used it to explain the small but real differences between the human races" (p. 24).

Hence, Rushton (1999) misapplies the r-K distinction in two ways. First, he takes a concept that describes differences between species and applies it to differences within a species without any biological evidence of the validity of such an application. Nevertheless, without any documentation, Rushton (1999) asserts that, in response to the question of whether his r-K concept applies only to differences between species and not to within-species differences, "it applies to both" (p. 103).

Second, Rushton (1999) used a descriptive concept to explain differences within a species—and his explanation is that, basically, the group he called "Blacks" represent an evolutionarily less advanced form of organism, in that their reproductive strategy is more closely aligned with more primitive, r-like organisms. Indeed, Rushton used his r-K explanation to account for purported differences between "Orientals" and "Whites," who he claims are more "K-selected" and "Blacks," who he contends are more "r-selected," in their investment in their children.

He indicated that "highly K-selected men invest time and energy in their children rather than the pursuit of sexual thrills. They are "dads" rather than "cads" (Rushton, 1999, p. 24). Moreover, Rushton (1999) asserted—without any citation whatsoever to bolster his statements—that "in Africa, the female-headed family is part of an overall social pattern. It consists of early sexual union and the procreation of children with many partners. It includes fostering children away from home, even for several years, so mothers remain sexually active …. In Black Africa and the Black Caribbean, as in the American underclass ghetto, groups of pre-teens and teenagers are left quite free of adult supervision" (pp. 35–36).

Amazingly, Rushton (1999) showed no awareness (e.g., through discussion or even mere citation) of the rich literature pertinent to the African American family (e.g., Demo, Allen, & Fine, 2000; McAdoo, 1977, 1991, 1993a, 1993b, 1995, 1998, 1999; McCubbin, Thompson, Thompson, & Futrell, 1998). This literature presents data providing a point-for-point contradiction of Rushton's undocumented assertions. Accordingly, when Rushton (1999) asserted that "scientists have a special duty to examine the facts and tell the truth" (p. 105) one may wonder if he included himself within the group held to this standard.

In any case, it seems clear, from the evaluations that have been made of the quality of the "data" Rushton forwarded regarding his ideas, that the "truth" is not being told by either the data he presented or the interpretations he made of his data (see Lerner, 2002, for a review). For example, Cernovsky (1997) noted that Rushton's studies of racial differences (e.g., Rushton, 1988a, 1988b, 1990a, 1990b, 1991a, 1991b, 1995) as well as those of other researchers working to support his findings (e.g., Lynn, 1993)

are noteworthy for their excessive reliance on very low correlation coefficients from obsolete data sets to postulate causal relationships. When a given method produces findings inconsistent with their … views, they conveniently switch to a different method. An independent statistical re-examination of the same source of data by others may produce dramatically different results. (p. 1)

To illustrate, Cernovsky and Litman (1993) reanalyzed the data that Rushton (1990) used to demonstrate that there were significant race differences (involving what Rushton termed "Mongoloid," "Caucasoid," and "Negroid" groups) across nations in crime rates (e.g., involving homicide, rape, and serious assault). The data, Rushton (1990a, 1990b) claimed, indicated that the Negroid group had higher rates of crime than did either of the other two groups. However, Cernovsky and Litman (1993) found that the race differences Rushton (1990a, 1990b) reported were not strong and, in fact, were largely weak and inconsistent. Not only does Rushton (1990a, 1990b) not present any evidence why these small differences among races should be considered genetic in origin, but in addition, Cernovsky and Litman (1993) found that in Rushton's own data reliance on race to predict an individual's likelihood of committing a crime "would result in an absurdly high rate (99.9%) of false positives" (p. 31).

Given the numerous dimensions of critical scientific problems associated with Rushton's work, we may agree with Cernovsky's (1995) view:

> Although Rushton's writings and public speeches instill the vision of Blacks as small-brained, oversexed criminals who multiply at a fast rate and are afflicted with mental disease, his views are neither based on a bona fide scientific review of literature nor on contemporary scientific methodology. His dogma of bioevolutionary inferiority of Negroids is not supported by empirical evidence. (p. 677)

In sum, given the weak science that is associated with hereditarian position and the fact that, despite its limitations, this counterfactual view of human diversity and development finds its ways into the thinking of not only the "Person in the Street" but also media representatives and policy makers (and even science policy makers), it becomes necessary for scholars with understandings of human development distinct from hereditarian ones to integrate their roles as scientists and citizens. Indeed, and to note a point of agreement with Rowe (1994), scientists, as citizens, might serve both their science and society best by working with other sectors of their community "to try to understand how things really work and what levers for change may exist in them" (p. 224).

CONCLUSIONS

To understand how things really work will require knowledge far beyond that which could be gained from partitioning variance into genetic and environmental components. We will need knowledge about all the levels of organization that comprise the ecology of human development and, as well, and perhaps most critical, about the dynamic system of developmental relations that comprise this ecology.

To obtain such knowledge, we must go beyond the limits of any one area of scholarship. Indeed, we will have to go beyond the limits of academe. How things really work in the real world involves people from all walks of life. In the end, then, each of our perspectives is limited. To effect important and sustained social changes through our actions, communities of scholars in concert with communities of citizens will have to coalesce to learn how desired individual, family, and societal changes can be created.

In such efforts, we would do well to heed the advice of Horowitz (2000) in regard to how, in the face of the simplistically seductive ideas of hereditarianism, we must find the will to act in a manner supportive of social justice. She noted:

> If we accept as a challenge the need to act with social responsibility then we must make sure that we do not use single-variable words like genes or the notion of innate in such a determinative manner as to give the impression that they constitute the simple answers to the simple questions asked by the Person in the Street lest we contribute to belief systems that will inform social policies that seek to limit experience and opportunity and, ultimately, development, especially when compounded by racism and poorly advantaged circumstances. Or, as Elman and Bates and their colleagues said in the concluding section of their book *Rethinking Innateness* (Elman et al., 1998), "If our careless, under-specified choice of words inadvertently does damage to future generations of children, we cannot turn with innocent outrage to the judge and say 'But your Honor, I didn't realize the word was loaded.'" (p. 8)

The challenge Horowitz articulated is one that is quite real for human development scientists who have been involved with trying to provide ideas and evidence countering the behavior genetics approach to human development. As I have emphasized already, I believe that we must pay heed to Lewontin's (1992) caution that the price society must pay for the continued presence of hereditarian conceptions is the need to remain vigilant about their appearance. We must be prepared to discuss the poor science they reflect and the inadequate bases they provide for public policy and applications pertinent to improving human life (see also Schneirla, 1966; Tobach, 1994). We must be ready to suggest alternatives, such as developmental systems ones, to hereditarian views of research about and applications for human development.

Given the enormous, indeed historically unprecedented, challenges facing the families of America and the world, perhaps especially as they strive to raise healthy and successful children capable of leading civil society productively, responsibly, and morally across the twenty-first century (Benson, 1997; Damon, 1997; Lerner, 1995; Lerner, et al., 2000a, 2000b), there is no time to lose in the development of such a commitment by the scholarly community.

Colleagues involved in the developmental systems approach to understanding the role of genes in human development have an opportunity through their work to serve both scholarship and the communities, families, and people of our nation and world. By informing policies and programs sensitive to the diversity and richness of the dynamic relations between individuals and the ecology of human development, we demonstrate that nothing is of greater value to civil society than a science devoted to using its scholarship to improve the life chances of all people.

REFERENCES

Anastasi, A. (1958). Heredity, environment, and the question "how?" *Psychological Review, 65,* 197–208.

Baltes, P. B., Lindenberger, U., & Staudinger, U. M. (1998). Life-span theory in developmental psychology. In W. Damon (Series Ed.) & R. M. Lerner (Vol. Ed.), *Handbook of child psychology: Vol. 1 Theoretical models of human development* (5th ed., pp. 1029–1144). New York: Wiley.

Baltes, P. B., Staudinger, U. M., & Lindenberger, U. (1999). Lifespan psychology: Theory and application to intellectual functioning. In J. T. Spence, J. M. Darley, & D. J. Foss (Eds.), *Annual Review of Psychology* (Vol. 50, 471–507). Palo Alto, CA: Annual Reviews.

Bandura, A. (1965). Influence of models' reinforcement of contingencies on the acquisition of imitative responses. *Journal of Personality and Social Psychology, 1,* 589–595.

Bandura, A. (1971). *Social learning theory.* Morristown, NJ: General Learning Press.

Bandura, A. (1986). *Social foundations of thought and action: A social cognitive theory.* Englewood Cliffs, NJ: Prentice-Hall.

Bennett, A. J., Lesch, K. P., Heils, A., Long, J., Lorenz, J., Shoaf, S. E., Champoux, M., Suomi, S. J., Linnoila, M., & Higley, J. D. (in press). Serotonin transporter genotype and early experience interact to influence nonhuman primate CNS serotonin turnover. *Molecular Psychiatry.*

Benson, P. (1997). *All kids are our kids: What communities must do to raise caring and responsible children and adolescents.* San Francisco: Jossey-Bass.

Brandtstädter, J. (1998). Action perspectives on human development. In W. Damon (Series Ed.) & R. M. Lerner (Vol. Ed.), *Handbook of child psychology: Vol. 1. Theoretical models of human development* (5th ed., pp. 807–863). New York: Wiley

Brim, O. G., Jr., & Kagan, J. (Eds.). (1980). *Constancy and change in human development.* Cambridge, MA: Harvard University Press.

Bronfenbrenner, U. (1979). *The ecology of human development: Experiments by nature and design.* Cambridge, MA: Harvard University Press.

Bronfenbrenner, U. (1989). Ecological systems theory. In R. Vasta (Ed.), *Six theories of child development: Revised formulations and current issues* (pp. 185–246). Greenwich, CT: JAI Press.

Bronfenbrenner, U., & Ceci, S. J. (1994). Nature-nurture reconceptualized in developmental perspective: A bioecological model. *Psychological Review, 101,* 568–586.

Bronfenbrenner, U., & Morris, P. A. (1998). The ecology of developmental process. In W. Damon (Series Ed.) & R. M. Lerner (Vol. Ed.), *Handbook of child psychology: Vol. 1. Theoretical models of human development* (5th ed., pp. 993—1028). New York: Wiley.

Buss, A. H., & Plomin, R. (1984). *Temperament: Early developing personality traits.* Hillsdale, NJ: Lawrence Erlbaum Associates.

Cernovsky, Z. Z. (1995). On the similarities of American blacks and whites. *Journal of Black Studies, 25,* 672–679.

Cernovsky, Z. Z. (1997). *Statistical methods and behavioral similarities of blacks and whites.* Paper presented at the 58th Annual Convention of the Canadian Psychological Association, Toronto, Canada, June 12-14.

Cernovsky, Z. Z., & Litman, L. C. (1993). Re-analyses of J. P. Rushton's crime data. *Canadian Journal of Criminology, 35,* 31–36.

Chomsky, N. (1965). *Aspects of a theory of syntax.* Cambridge, MA: MIT Press.

Collins, W. A., Maccoby, E. E., Steinberg, L., Hetherington, E. M., & Bornstein, M. H. (2000). Contemporary research on parenting: The case of nature and nurture. *American Psychologist, 55,* 218–232.

Conger, R. D., Conger, K. J., Elder, G. H., Jr., Lorenz, F. O., Simons, R. L., & Whitbeck, L. B. (1992). A family process model of economic hardship and adjustment of early adolescent boys. *Child Development, 63,* 526–541.

Conger, R. D., Lorenz, F. O., Elder, G. H., Jr., Melby, J. N., Simons, R. L., & Conger, K. J. (1991). A process model of family economic pressure and early adolescent alcohol use. *Journal of Early Adolescence, 11,* 430–449.

Damon, W. (1997). *The youth charter: How communities can work together to raise standards for all our children.* New York: The Free Press.

Dawkins, R. (1976). *The selfish gene.* New York: Oxford University.

Demo, D. H., Allen, K. R., & Fine, M. A. (2000). *Handbook of family diversity.* New York: Oxford University Press.

Elder, G. H., Jr. (1974). *Children of the Great Depression.* Chicago: University of Chicago Press.

Elder, G. H., Jr. (1980). Adolescence in historical perspective. In J. Adelson (Ed.), *Handbooks of adolescent psychology* (pp. 3–46). New York: Wiley.

Elder, G. H., Jr. (1998). The life course and human development. In W. Damon (Series Ed.) & R. M. Lerner (Vol. Ed.), *Handbook of child psychology: Vol. 1. Theoretical models of human development* (5th ed., pp. 939–991). New York: Wiley.

Elder, G. H., Jr., Modell, J., & Parke, R. D. (Eds.). (1993). *Children in time and place: Developmental and historical insights.* New York: Cambridge University Press.

Elman, J. L., Bates, E. A., Johnson, M. H., Karmiloff-Smith, A., Parisi, D., & Plunkett, K. (1998). *Rethinking innateness: A connectionist perspective on development (neural network modeling and connectionism).* Cambridge, MA: MIT Press.

Feldman, M. W., & Lewontin, R. C. (1975). The heritability hang-up. *Science, 190,* 1163–1168.

Fischer, K. W. (1980). A theory of cognitive development: The control and construction of hierarchies of skills. *Psychological Review, 87,* 477–531.

Fischer, K. W., & Bidell, T. (1998). Dynamic development of psychological structures in action and thought. In W. Damon (Series Ed.) & R. M. Lerner (Vol. Ed.), *Handbook of child psychology: Vol. 1. Theoretical models of human development* (5th ed., pp. 467–561). New York: Wiley.

Ford, D. L., & Lerner, R. M. (1992). *Developmental systems theory: An integrative approach.* Newbury Park, CA: Sage.

Ge, X., Conger, R. D., Lorenz, F. O., Elder, G. H., Montague, R. B., & Simons, R. L. (1992). Linking family economic hardship to adolescent distress. *Journal of Research on Adolescence, 2,* 351–378.

Goldberger, A. S. (1980). Review of "Cyril Burt, Psychologist." *Challenge: The Magazine of Economic Affairs, 23,* 61–62.

Goldberger, A. S., & Manski, C. F. (1995). [Review of the book *The Bell Curve*]. *Journal of Economic Literature, 33,* 762–776.

Gottlieb, G. (1970). Conceptions of prenatal behavior. In L. R. Aronson, E. Tobach, D. S. Lehrman, & J. S. Rosenblatt (Eds.), *Development and evolution of behavior: Essays in memory of T. C. Schneirla* (pp. 111–137). San Francisco: Freeman.

Gottlieb, G. (1976). Conceptions of prenatal development: Behavioral embryology. *Psychological Review, 83,* 215–234.

Gottlieb, G. (1983). The psychobiological approach to developmental issues. In M. M. Haith & J. Campos (Eds.), *Handbook of child psychology: Infancy and biological bases* (Vol. 2, pp. 1–26). New York: Wiley.

Gottlieb, G. (1991a). Experiential canalization of behavioral development: Theory. *Developmental Psychology, 27,* 4–13.

Gottlieb, G. (1991b). Experiential canalization of behavioral development: Results. *Developmental Psychology, 27,* 39–42.

Gottlieb, G. (1992). *Individual development and evolution: The genesis of novel behavior.* New York: Oxford University Press.

Gottlieb, G. (1997). *Synthesizing nature-nurture: Prenatal roots of instinctive behavior.* Mahwah, NJ: Lawrence Erlbaum Associates.

Gottlieb, G., Wahlsten, D., & Lickliter, R. (1998). The significance of biology for human development: A developmental psychobiological systems view. In W. Damon (Series Ed.) & R. M. Lerner (Vol. Ed.), *Handbook of child psychology: Vol. 1. Theoretical models of human development* (5th ed., pp. 233–273). New York: Wiley.

Gould, S. J. (1981/1996). *The mismeasure of man.* New York: Norton.

Harris, J. R. (1998). *The nurture assumption: Why children turn out the way they do.* New York: Free Press.

Hearnshaw, L. S. (1979). *Cyril Burt, psychologist.* New York: Cornell University Press.

Hebb, D. O. (1970). A return to Jensen and his social critics. *American Psychologist, 25,* 568.

Herrnstein, R. J., & Murray, C. (1994). *The bell curve: Intelligence and class structure in American life.* New York: Free Press.

Herrnstein, R. J. (1971). IQ. *Atlantic Monthly, September,* 43–64.

Hirsch, J. (1970). Behavior-genetic analysis and its biosocial consequences. *Seminars in Psychiatry, 2,* 89–105.

Hirsch, J. (1976a). Jensenism: The bankruptcy of "science" without scholarship. *United States Congressional Record, Vol. 122*: no. 73, E2671-2; no. 74, E2693-5; no. 75, E2703-5, E2716-8, E2721-2.

Hirsch, J. (1976b). Review of "Sociobiology," by E.O. Wilson. *Animal Behavior, 24,* 707–709.

Hirsch, J. (1990a). Correlation, causation, and careerism. *European Bulletin of Cognitive Psychology, 10,* 647–652.

Hirsch, J. (1990b). A nemesis for heritability estimation. *Behavioral and Brain Sciences, 13,* 137–138.

Hirsch, J. (1997a). Some history of heredity-vs.-environment, genetic inferiority at Harvard (?), and The (incredible) Bell Curve. *Genetica, 99,* 207–224.

Hirsch, J. (1997b). The triumph of wishful thinking over genetic irrelevance. *Current Psychology of Cognition, 16,* 711–720.

Ho, M. W. (1984). Environment and heredity in development and evolution. In M.-W. Ho & P. T. Saunders (Eds.), *Beyond neo-Darwinism: An introduction to the new evolutionary paradigm* (pp. 267–289). London: Academic Press.

Hoffman, L. W. (1991). The influence of family environment on personality: Accounting for sibling differences. *Psychological Bulletin, 110,* 187–203.

Horowitz, F. D. (1993). Bridging the gap between nature and nurture. A conceptually flawed issue and the need for a comprehensive and new environmentalism. In R. Plomin & G. E. McClearn (Eds.), *Nature, nurture and psychology* (pp. 341–354). Washington, D.C.: APA Books.

Horowitz, F. D. (2000). Child development and the PITS: Simple questions, complex answers, and developmental theory. *Child Development, 71,* 1–10.

Jensen, A. R. (1969). How much can we boost IQ and scholastic achievement? *Harvard Educational Review, 39,* 1–123.

Jensen, A. R. (1973). *Educability and group differences.* New York: Harper & Row.

Jensen, A. R. (1998). Jensen on "Jensenism." *Intelligence, 26,* 181–208.

Johanson, D. C., & Edey, M. A. (1981). *Lucy: The beginnings of humankind.* New York: Simon & Schuster.

Kuo, Z.-Y. (1967). *The dynamics of behavior development.* New York: Random House.

Kuo, Z.-Y. (1970). The need for coordinated efforts in developmental studies. In A. Aronson, E. Tobach, D. S. Lehrman, & J. S. Rosenblatt (Eds.), *Development and evolution of behavior: Essays in memory of T. C. Schneirla* (pp. 181–193). San Francisco: W. H. Freeman.

Kuo, Z.-Y. (1976). *The dynamics of behavior development: An epigenetic view.* New York: Plenum.

Lehrman, D. S. (1953). A critique of Konrad Lorenz's theory of instinctive behavior. *Quarterly Review of Biology 28,* 337–363.

Lehrman, D. S. (1970). Semantic and conceptual issues in the nature–nurture problem. In L. R. Aronson, E. Tobach, D. S. Lehrman, & J. S. Rosenblatt (Eds.), *Development and evolution of behavior: Essays in memory of T. C. Schneirla* (pp. 17–52). San Francisco: Freeman.

Lerner, R. M. (1978). Nature, nurture, and dynamic interactionism. *Human Development, 21,* 1–20.

Lerner, R. M. (1984). *On the nature of human plasticity.* New York: Cambridge University Press.

Lerner, R. M. (1986). *Concepts and theories of human development* (2nd ed.). New York: Random House.

Lerner, R. M. (1991). Changing organism-context relations as the basic process of development: A developmental contextual perspective. *Developmental Psychology, 27,* 27–32.

Lerner, R. M. (1992a). *Final solutions: Biology, prejudice, and genocide.* University Park: Pennsylvania State University Press.

Lerner, R. M. (1992b). Nature, nurture and mass murder. *Readings: A Journal of Reviews and Commentary on Mental Health, 7,* 8–15.

Lerner, R. M. (1995). *America's youth in crisis: Challenges and options for programs and policies.* Thousand Oaks, CA: Sage.

Lerner, R. M. (1996). Relative plasticity, integration, temporality, and diversity in human development: A developmental contextual perspective about theory, process, and method. *Developmental Psychology, 32,* 781–786.

Lerner, R. M. (Ed.). (1998a). *Handbook of child psychology: Vol. 1. Theoretical models of human development* (5th ed.). Damon. New York: Wiley.

Lerner, R. M. (1998b). Theories of human development: Contemporary perspectives. In R. M. Lerner (Ed.), *Handbook of child psychology: Vol. 1. Theoretical models of human development* (5th ed., pp. 1–24). New York: Wiley.

Lerner, R. M. (2002). *Concepts and theories of human development* (3rd ed.). Mahwah, NJ: Lawrence Erlbaum Associates.

Lerner, R. M., Fisher, C. B., & Weinberg, R. A. (2000a). Toward a science for and of the people: Promoting civil society through the application of developmental science. *Child Development, 71,* 11–20.

Lerner, R. M., Fisher, C. B., & Weinberg, R. A. (2000b). Applying developmental science in the twenty-first century: International scholarship for our times. *International Journal of Behavioral Development, 24,* 24–29.

Lerner, R. M., & von Eye, A. (1992). Sociobiology and human development: Arguments and evidence. *Human Development, 35,* 12–33.

Levine, R. L., & Fitzgerald, H. E. (Eds.). (1992). *Analysis of dynamic psychological systems* (Vol. 1 & 2). New York: Plenum.

Lewis, M. (1997). *Altering fate.* New York: Guilford Press.

Lewontin, R. C. (1992). Foreword. In R. M. Lerner (Ed.), *Final solutions: Biology, prejudice, and genocide* (pp. vii–viii). University Park: Pennsylvania State University Press.

Lewontin, R. C. (2000). *The triple helix.* Cambridge, MA: Harvard University Press.

Lifton, R. J. (1986). *The Nazi doctors: Medical killing and the psychology of genocide.* New York: Basic Books.

Lorenz, K. (1940a). Durch Domestikation verursachte St<@2146>rungen arteigenen Verhaltens. *Zeitschrift für angewandte Psychologie und Charakterkunde, 59,* 2–81.

Lorenz, K. (1940b). Systematik und Entwicklungsgedanke im Unterricht. *Der Biologe 9,* 24–36.

Lorenz, K. (1943a). Die angeborenen Formen möglicher Erfahrung. *Zeitschrift für Tierpsychologie, 5,* 235–409.

Lorenz, K. (1943b). Psychologie and stammesgeschichte. In G. Heberer (Ed.), *Die evolution der organismen* (pp. 105–127). Jena, Germany: G. Fischer.

Lorenz, K. (1965). *Evolution and modification of behavior.* Chicago: University of Chicago Press.

Lorenz, K. (1966). *On aggression.* New York: Harcourt Brace.

Lynn, R. (1993). Further evidence for the existence of race and sex differences in cranial capacity. *Social Behavior and Personality, 21,* 89–92.

Magnusson, D. (1990). Personality development from an interactional perspective. In L. Pervin (Ed.), *Handbook of personality* (pp. 193–222). New York: Guilford Press.

Magnusson, D. (1995). Individual development: A holistic integrated model. In P. Moen, G. H. Elder, & K. Lusher (Eds.), *Linking lives and contexts: Perspectives on the ecology of human development* (pp. 19–60). Washington, DC: APA Books.

Magnusson, D. (1996). *The life-span development of individuals: Behavioral, neurobiological, and psychosocial perspectives. A synthesis.* Cambridge, UK: Cambridge University Press.

Magnusson, D. (1999a). Holistic interactionism: A perspective for research on personality development. In L. A. Pervin & O. P. John (Eds.), *Handbook of personality: Theory and research* (2nd ed., pp. 219–247). New York: The Guilford Press.

Magnusson, D. (1999b). On the individual: A person-oriented approach to developmental research. *European Psychologist, 4,* 205–218.

Magnusson, D., & Stattin, H. (1998). Person-context interaction theories. In W. Damon (Series Ed.) & R. M. Lerner (Vol. Ed.), *Handbook of child psychology: Vol. 1 Theoretical models of human development* (5th ed., pp. 685–759). New York: Wiley.

Maier, N. R. F., & Schneirla, T. C. (1935). *Principles of animal behavior.* New York: McGraw-Hill.

McAdoo, H. P. (1977). A review of the literature related to family therapy in the Black community. *Journal of Contemporary Psychotherapy, 9,* 15–19.

McAdoo, H. P. (1991). Family values and outcomes for children. *Journal of Negro Education, 60,* 361–365.

McAdoo, H. P. (1993a). Family equality and ethnic diversity. In K. Altergott (Ed.), *One world, many families* (pp. 52–55). Minneapolis, MN: National Council on Family Relations.

McAdoo, H. P. (1993b). The social cultural contexts of ecological developmental family models. In P. Boss, W. Doherty, & W. Schyumm (Eds.), *Sourcebook of family theories and methods: A contextual approach* (pp. 298–301). New York: Plenum.

McAdoo, H. P. (1995). Stress levels, family help patterns, and religiosity in middle- and working-class African American single mothers. *Journal of Black Psychology, 21,* 424–449.

McAdoo, H. P. (1998). African American families: Strength and realities. In H. I. McCubbin, E. A. Thompson, A. I. Thompson, & J. E. Fromer, (Eds.), *Resiliency in ethnic minority families: African American families* (pp. 17–30). Thousand Oaks, CA: Sage.

McAdoo, H. P. (1999). Diverse children of color. In H. E. Fitzgerald, B. M. Lester, & B. S. Zuckerman (Eds.), *Children of color: Research, health, and policy issues* (pp. 205–218). New York: Garland Publishing.

McCubbin, H. I., Thompson, E. A., Thompson, A. I., & Futrell, J. A. (Eds.). (1998). *Resiliency in ethnic minority families: African-American families.* Thousand Oaks, CA: Sage.

McEwen, B. S. (1997). Possible mechanisms for atrophy of the human hippocampus. *Molecular Psychiatry, 2,* 255–262.

McEwen, B. S. (1998). Protective and Damaging Effects of Stress Mediators, *New England Journal of Medicine, 338,* 171–179.

McEwen, B. S. (1999). Stress and hippocampal plasticity. *Annual Review of Neuroscience, 22,* 105–122.

Meaney, M., Aitken, D., Berkel, H., Bhatnager, S., & Sapolsky, R. (1988). Effect of neonatal handling of age-related impairments associated with the hippocampus. *Science, 239,* 766–768.

Müller-Hill, B. (1988). Murderous science: Elimination by scientific selection of Jews, Gypsies, and others. Germany, 1933–1945 (G. R. Fraser, Trans.). New York: Oxford University.

Nelson, K. (1996). *Language in cognitive development: Emergence of the mediated mind.* New York: Cambridge University Press.

Novikoff, A. B. (1945a). The concept of integrative levels and biology. *Science 101,* 209–215.

Novikoff, A. B. (1945b). Continuity and discontinuity in evolution. *Science 101,* 405–406.

Overton, W. F. (1998). Developmental psychology: Philosophy, concepts, and methodology. In W. Damon (Series Ed.) & R. M. Lerner (Ed.), *Handbook of child psychology: Vol. 1 Theoretical models of human development* (5th ed., pp. 107–187). New York: Wiley.

Peters, M. (1995). Does brain size matter? A reply to Rushton and Ankney. *Canadian Journal of Experimental Psychology, 47,* 751–756.

Pinker, S. (1994). *The language instinct.* New York: William Morrow.

Plomin, R. (1986). *Development, genetics, and psychology.* Hillsdale, NJ: Lawrence Erlbaum Associates.

Plomin, R. (2000). Behavioural genetics in the 21st century. *International Journal of Behavioral Development, 24,* 30–34.

Plomin, R., Corley, R., DeFries, J. C., & Faulker, D. W. (1990). Individual differences in television viewing in early childhood: Nature as well as nurture. *Psychological Science, 1,* 371–377.

Plomin, R., & Daniels, D. (1987). Why are children in the same family so different from each other? *Behavioral and Brain Sciences, 10,* 1–16.

Plomin, R., DeFries, J. C., & McClearn, G. E. (1980). *Behavioral genetics: A primer.* San Francisco: Freeman.

Proctor, R. N. (1988). *Racial hygiene: Medicine under the Nazis.* Cambridge, MA: Harvard University.

Psychological Science Agenda (1992, May/June). APA, mental health community react to Goodwin's resignation (pp. 1,8). American Psychological Association.

Rowe, D. (1994). *The limits of family influence: Genes, experience, and behavior.* New York: Guilford Press.

Rushton, J. P. (1987). An evolutionary theory of health, longevity, and personality: Sociobiology, and r/K reproductive strategies. *Psychological Reports, 60,* 539–549.

Rushton, J. P. (1988a). Do r/K reproductive strategies apply to human differences? *Social Biology, 35,* 337–340.

Rushton, J. P. (1988b). Race differences in behavior: A review and evolutionary analysis. *Personality and Individual Differences, 9,* 1009–1024.

Rushton, J. P. (1990a). Sex, ethnicity, and hormones. *Behavioral & Brain Sciences, 13,* 194, 197–198.

Rushton, J. P. (1990b). Why we should study race differences. *Psychologische Beitraege, 32,* 128–142.

Rushton, J. P. (1991a). Do r-K strategies underlie human race differences? A reply to Weizmann et al. *Canadian Psychology, 32,* 29–42.

Rushton, J. P. (1991b). Race, brain size, and intelligence: Another reply to Cernovsky. *Psychological Reports, 66,* 659–666.

Rushton, J. P. (1995). *Race, evolution, and behavior.* New Brunswick, NJ: Transaction.

Rushton, J. P. (1996). Political correctness and the study of racial differences. *Journal of Social Distress & the Homeless, 5,* 213–229.

Rushton, J. P. (1997a). Cranial size and IQ in Asian Americans from birth to age seven. *Intelligence, 25,* 7–20.

Rushton, J. P. (1997b). More on political correctness and race differences. *Journal of Social Distress and the Homeless, 6,* 195–198.

Rushton, J. P. (1999/2000). *Race, evolution, and behavior* (Special Abridged Ed.). New Brunswick, NJ: Transaction Publishers.

Sameroff, A. (1975). Transactional models in early social relations. *Human Development, 18,* 65–79.

Sameroff, A. J. (1983). Developmental systems: Contexts and evolution. In W. Kessen (Ed.), *Handbook of child psychology: Vol. 1, History, theory, and methods* (pp. 237–294). New York: Wiley.

Scarr, S. (1992). Developmental theories for the 1990s: Development and individual differences. *Child Development, 63,* 1–19.

Schneirla, R. C. (1956). Interrelationships of the innate and the acquired in instinctive behavior. In P. P. Grassé (Ed.), *L'instinct dans le comportement des animaux et de l'homme.* Paris: Mason et Cie.

Schneirla, T. C. (1957). The concept of development in comparative psychology. In D. B. Harris (Ed.), *The concept of development: An issue in the study of human behavior* (pp. 78–108). Minneapolis: University of Minnesota Press.

Schneirla, T. C. (1966). Instinct and aggression: Reviews of Konrad Lorenz, *Evolution and modification of behavior* (Chicago: University of Chicago Press, 1965), and *On aggression* (New York: Harcourt Brace, 1966). *Natural History, 75,* 16.

Scriver, C. R., & Clow, C. L. (1980a). Phenylketonuria: Epitome of human biochemical genetics (first of two parts). *New England Journal of Medicine, 303,* 1336–1342.

Scriver, C. R., & Clow, C. L. (1980b). Phenylketonuria: Epitome of human biochemical genetics (second of two parts). *New England Journal of Medicine, 303,* 1394–1400.

Smith, L. B., & Thelen, E. (Eds.). (1993). *A dynamic systems approach to development: Applications.* Cambridge, MA: MIT Press.

Spelke, E. S., Breinlinger, K., Macomber, J., & Jacobson, K. (1992). Origin of knowledge. *Psychological Review, 99,* 605–632.

Spelke, E. S., & Newport, E. L. (1998). Nativism, empiricism, and the development of knowledge. In W. Damon (Series Ed.) & R. M. Lerner (Vol. Ed.), *Handbook of child psychology: Vol. 1. Theoretical models of human development* (5th ed., 275–340). New York: Wiley.

Strohman, R. C. (1993a). Organism and experience. [Review of the book *Final Solutions*]. *Journal of Applied Developmental Psychology, 14,* 147–151.

Strohman, R. C. (1993b). Book Reviews: *Final Solutions,* Richard M. Lerner, Pennsylvania State University Press, 1992, and *Individual Development and Evolution: The genesis of novel behavior,* Gilbert Gottlieb, Oxford University Press, 1992. *Integrative Physiological and Behavioral Science, 28,* 99–104.

Suomi, S. J. (1997). Early determinants of behavior: Evidence from primate studies. *British Medical Bulletin, 53,* 170–184.

Suomi, S. J. (2000). A behavioral perspective on developmental psychopathology: Excessive aggression and serotonergic dysfunction in monkeys. In A. J. Sameroff, M. Lewis, & S. Miller (Eds.), *Handbook of developmental psychopathology* (2nd ed., pp. 237–256). New York: Plenum Press.

Thelen, E., & Smith, L. B. (1994). *A dynamic systems approach to the development of cognition and action.* Cambridge, MA: MIT Press.

Thelen, E., & Smith, L. B. (1998). Dynamic systems theories. In W. Damon (Series Editor) & R.M. Lerner (Vol. Ed.), *Handbook of child psychology: Vol. I Theoretical models of human development* (5th ed., pp. 563–633). New York: Wiley.

Thelen, E., & Ulrich, B.D. (1991). Hidden skills: A dynamical systems analysis of treadmill stepping during the first year. *Monographs of the Society for Research in Child Development, 56* (1), 104.

Tobach, E. (1978). The methodology of sociobiology from the viewpoint of a comparative psychologist. In A. L. Caplan (Ed.), *The sociobiology debate* (pp. 411–423). New York: Harper & Row.

Tobach, E. (1971). Some evolutionary aspects of human gender. *Journal of Orthopsvchiatrv, 41,* 710–715.

Tobach, E. (1981). Evolutionary aspects of the activity of the organism and its development. In R. M. Lerner & N. A. Busch-Rossnagel (Eds.), *Individuals as producers of their development: A life-span perspective* (pp. 37–68). New York: Academic Press.

Tobach, E. (1994). … Personal is political is personal is political …. *Journal of Social Issues, 50,* 221–224.

Tobach, E., Gianutsos, J., Topoff, H. R., & Gross, C. G. (1974). *The four horses: Racism, sexism, militarism, and social Darwinism.* New York: Behavioral publications.

Tobach, E., & Greenberg, G. (1984). The significance of T. C. Schneirla's contribution to the concept of levels of integration. In G. Greenberg & E. Tobach (Eds.), *Behavioral evolution and integrative levels* (pp. 1–7). Hillsdale, NJ: Lawrence Erlbaum Associates.

Tobach, E., & Schneirla, T. C. (1968). The biopsychology of social behavior of animals. In R. E. Cooke & S. Levin (Eds.), *Biologic basis of pediatric practice* (pp. 68–82). New York: McGraw-Hill.

Venter, J. C., Adams, M. D., Myers, E. W., Li, P. W., Mural, R. J., et al. (2001). The sequence of the human genome. *Science, 291,* 1304–1351.

von Bertalanffy, L. (1933). *Modern theories of development.* London: Oxford University Press.

Wapner, S., & Demick, J. (1998). Developmental analysis: A holistic, developmental, systems-oriented perspective. In W. Damon (Series Ed.) and R. M. Lerner (Vol. Ed.), *Handbook of child psychology: Vol. 1. Theoretical models of human development* (5th ed., pp. 761–805). New York: Wiley.

Wilson, E. O. (1975). *Sociobiology: The new synthesis.* Cambridge, MA: Harvard University Press.

Wilson, E. O. (1980). A consideration of the genetic foundation of human social behavior. In G. W. Barlow & J. Silverberg (Eds.), *Sociobiology: Beyond nature/nurture* (pp. 295–305). Boulder, CO: Westview.

Winston, A. S. (1996). The context of correctness: A comment on Rushton. *Journal of Social Distress and the Homeless, 5,* 231–250.

Winston, A. S. (1997a). Genocide as a scientific project. *American Psychologist, 52,* 182–183.

Winston, A. S. (1997b). Rushton and racial differences: Further reasons for caution. *Journal of Social Distress and the Homeless, 6,* 199–202.

2 How Gene-Environment Interactions Influence Emotional Development in Rhesus Monkeys

Stephen J. Suomi
National Institutes of Health

INTRODUCTION

The question of whether the characteristics that make us unique as individuals are largely determined by our heritage or shaped by our personal experiences has been debated since at least the time of Aristotle. Those who grew plants or raised animals practiced selective breeding long before anything was known about specific genes, and educators and philosophers alike asserted that "the child is the father of the man" centuries before any formulation of explicit theories of reinforcement by twentieth-century behaviorists. In recent years, we have heard claims by some behavioral geneticists that going shopping or getting a divorce is highly heritable, as well as arguments not about whether personality is determined by experience but whether the experience that really counts is with one's parents or with one's peers (e.g., Harris, 1998). Clearly, the nature–nurture debate is not new.

What has been relatively new among those who study development is an emerging realization that the basic questions underlying the nature–nurture debate over the years may have been largely misguided. Instead of arguing whether behavioral and biological characteristics that appear during development are genetic in origin or the product of specific experiences, these individuals acknowledge that both genetic and environmental factors can play crucial roles in shaping individual developmental trajectories. Behavioral geneticists, among others, have tried to determine the relative contributions of specific genetic and environmental factors

35

to a variety of physical, physiological, cognitive, emotional, and behavioral features that different humans and animals exhibit. Other investigators have been more interested in determining to what extent developmental phenomena result from interactions between genetic and environmental factors (Collins, Maccoby, Steinberg, Hetherington, & Bornstein, 2000; Rutter, 2001).

This chapter summarizes recent research examining the development of emotional regulation in rhesus monkeys, with a major focus on identifying certain genetic and environmental factors—and their multiple interactions—that consistently predispose some monkeys to be unusually fearful in novel or mildly challenging circumstances and others to be excessively and inappropriately aggressive. In both cases, difficulties in the regulation of these two emotions not only are evident early in life but also appear to be linked to a variety of behavioral and physiological problems that emerge later in development and typically persist thereafter.

By way of background, it is now generally accepted that humans do not have a monopoly on emotionality. Over a century ago, Darwin (1872) argued that some mammals are clearly capable of expressing emotions, and an impressive body of recent research has demonstrated that many mammals possess the same basic neural circuitry and exhibit the same general patterns of neurochemical change that have been implicated in human emotional expression (e.g., Panksepp, 1998). Monkeys and apes, in particular, display characteristic patterns of emotional expression that seem strikingly similar to, if not homologous with, those routinely exhibited by infants and young children in virtually every human culture studied to date. To be sure, some complex emotions such as shame are most likely exclusively human, but those apparently require cognitive capabilities well beyond those of human infants and nonhuman primates of any age (cf. Lewis, 1992). Most other emotions are clearly expressed soon after birth by human and nonhuman primate infants alike, and they appear to serve as highly visible and salient social signals to those around them (cf. Suomi, 1997b). Among the most obvious are expressions of fear and those of anger and rage associated with aggression.

Ethologists have long argued that these basic patterns of emotional expression each serve important adaptive functions, having been largely conserved over mammalian evolutionary history. Consider the case of fear: In a world filled with predators and competitors who have the potential to maim or even kill, an individual fully without fear is unlikely to survive long. On the other hand, excessive or inappropriate fear can essentially paralyze any individual, in effect limiting those very interactions with the environment needed for physical and social survival. Thus, while every human and nonhuman primate is born with the capacity to be fearful, each must learn which particular stimuli merit fearful responses, as well as how to inhibit the expression of fear in nonthreatening situations that present little risk to life or limb (Suomi & Harlow, 1976).

Similarly, the capability to engage in aggressive attack and defense in the service of protecting self, family, and friends from predators and competitors is seemingly crucial for the survival of the individual and the maintenance of any social group across successive generations. Excessive and/or inappropriate aggression by any individual, however, has the potential of destroying the very social fabric that binds the group together. The expression of aggression must, therefore, be regulated; that is, individual group members must come to know which social stimuli merit an aggressive response and which do not, and for those that do, to what degree, and for how long, if the group is to maintain its social cohesion over time. Learning how and when to avoid an aggressive encounter and when and how to end it once begun may be at least as important as learning how and when to start or respond to an aggressive act (Suomi, 2000a).

The development of proficiency in regulating fear and aggression appears to be especially important for those advanced primate species whose members live in large social groups that are well defined in terms of both kinship relationships and social dominance hierarchies. Among the most complex are those of rhesus monkeys (*Macaca mulatta*), a highly successful species of macaque monkey that lives throughout most of the Indian subcontinent and beyond. In their natural habitats, rhesus monkeys typically reside in large, distinctive social groups (termed "troops") composed of several female-headed families, each spanning three or more generations of kin, plus numerous immigrant adult males. This form of social group organization derives from the fact that all rhesus monkey females spend their entire life in the troop into which they were born, whereas virtually all males emigrate from their natal troop around the time of puberty and eventually join other troops. Rhesus monkey troops are also characterized by multiple social dominance relationships, including distinctive hierarchies both between and within families, as well as a hierarchy among the immigrant adult males (Lindburg, 1971).

The complex familial and dominance relationships seen in rhesus monkey troops seemingly require that any well-functioning troop member not only be able to regulate its expressions of fear and aggression but also to become familiar with the specific kinship and dominance status of other monkeys toward whom those emotions might be expressed. An impressive body of both laboratory and field data strongly suggests that the acquisition of such knowledge represents an emergent property of the species-normative pattern of socialization that rhesus monkey infants experience as they are growing up (Sameroff & Suomi, 1996).

NORMATIVE DEVELOPMENT OF EMOTIONAL REGULATION IN RHESUS MONKEYS

Rhesus monkey infants are born with the capacity to express multiple emotions, including both fear and anger. These infants begin life highly dependent upon their biological mother for essentially all their initial biological and psychological needs, and they spend virtually all their first month in almost continuous physical contact with their mother. During this time, a strong and enduring social bond between mother and infant naturally emerges (Harlow, 1958). This bond, largely homologous with Bowlby's (1969) characterization of human mother–infant attachment, is unique in terms of its exclusivity, constituent behavioral features, and long-term duration—it is like no other relationship a monkey will experience again in its lifetime, except (in reciprocal form) for females when they become mothers themselves (Suomi, 1999).

Once an infant has developed an attachment relationship with its mother, it can use her as a secure base from which to begin exploring its immediate social and nonsocial environment. Most infant monkeys soon learn that if they become frightened or otherwise threatened, they can always run back to their mother for immediate safety and comfort via mutual ventral contact. Numerous studies have documented that initiation of ventral contact with the mother promotes rapid decreases in hypothalamic-pituitary-adrenal (HPA) activity, as indexed by a drop in plasma cortisol concentrations (e.g., Gunnar, Gonzalez, Goodlin, & Levine, 1981; Mendoza, Smotherman, Miner, Kaplan, & Levine, 1978), and in sympathetic nervous system arousal, as indexed by reductions in heart rate (e.g., Reite, Short, Selier, & Pauley, 1981), along with other physiological changes commonly associated with soothing. Secure attachment relationships thus help infants learn to manage the fears they will inevitably experience in the course of exploring their ever-expanding world. On the other hand, if a rhesus monkey infant develops an insecure attachment relationship with its mother, both its ability to regulate fear and its willingness to explore may be compromised, consistent with Bowlby's (1988) observations regarding human attachment relationships (Suomi, 1999).

During their second and third months of life, rhesus infants begin interacting with monkeys other than their mother, and they soon develop distinctive social relationships with specific individuals outside of their immediate family, especially with peers—other infants of like age and comparable physical, cognitive, and social capabilities. Following weaning (usually in the fourth and fifth months), play with peers emerges as a predominant social activity for young monkeys and essentially remains so until puberty (Ruppenthal, Harlow, Eisele, Harlow, & Suomi, 1974). During this developmental period, play interactions become more and more behaviorally and socially complex, increasingly involving interaction patterns that appear to simulate most aspects of adult social behavior. By the time they reach puberty, most rhesus monkey juveniles have had ample opportunities to develop, practice, and perfect behavioral routines that will be crucial for normal adult functioning, especially with respect to dominance interactions and aggressive exchanges.

Aggression typically emerges in a young monkey's behavioral repertoire prior to 6 months of age, and it initially appears in the context of rough-and-tumble play (Symonds, 1978). Sham-biting, hair-pulling, wrestling, and other forms of physical contact are basic components of rough-and-tumble play directed toward peers, occurring with increasing frequency among males in the second half of their first year of life and, in fact, becoming their predominate form of play behavior throughout the juvenile years. Although some form of virtually all basic physical components of adult aggressive exchanges can be seen in these rough-and-tumble play bouts, the intensity of such interactions is usually quite controlled and seldom escalates to the point of actual physical injury—if it does, the play bout is almost always terminated immediately, either by adult interven- tion or by one or more of the participants backing away themselves. The impor- tance of these play bouts with peers for the socialization of aggression becomes apparent when one considers that rhesus monkey infants reared in laboratory en- vironments that deny them regular access to peers during their initial months in- evitably exhibit excessive and socially inappropriate aggression later in life (cf. Suomi & Harlow, 1975).

The onset of puberty is associated with major life transitions for both males and females, involving major hormonal alterations, pronounced growth spurts, and other obvious physical changes and also major social changes for both sexes. Males experience the most dramatic social disruptions: When they leave home, they sever all social contact not only with their mother and other kin but also with all others in their natal social troop. Virtually all these adolescent males soon join all-male "gangs," and after several months to a year, most of them then attempt to join a different troop, usually composed entirely of individuals largely unfamiliar to the immigrant males (Berard, 1989). The process of natal troop emigration is ex- ceedingly dangerous for adolescent males—the mortality rate from the time they leave their natal troop until they become successfully integrated into another troop can approach 50%, depending on local circumstances (e.g., Dittus, 1979). Recent field studies have identified and characterized striking variability in both the tim- ing of emigration and the basic strategies followed by these males in their attempts to join other established social groups.

Adolescent females, by contrast, never leave their natal troop. Puberty for them is instead associated with increases in social activities directed toward maternal kin, especially when they begin to have offspring of their own. Indeed, the birth of a new infant (especially to a new mother) often has the effect of brings extended family members closer both physically and socially and, in the process, provides a buffer for the new mother and her infant from external threats and stressors. These females' ties to both family and troop are facilitated throughout adulthood by ap- propriate regulation of fear and aggression; conversely, these ties can be compro- mised whenever such emotional regulation goes awry (Suomi, 1998).

INDIVIDUAL DIFFERENCES IN THE REGULATION OF FEAR

While the basic developmental sequence outlined above is typical for most rhesus monkeys growing up both in the wild and in captive social groups, there are never- theless substantial differences among individuals in the precise timing and relative ease with which they make major developmental transitions, as well as how they manage the day-to-day challenges and stresses that are an inevitable part of com- plex social group life. In particular, recent research has identified a subgroup of in- dividuals, comprising approximately 15 to 20% of both wild and captive populations, who seem excessively fearful. These monkeys consistently respond to novel and/or mildly challenging situations with extreme behavioral disruption and pronounced physiological arousal, including significant and often prolonged activation of the HPA axis, sympathetic nervous system arousal, and increased noradrenergic turnover (Suomi, 1986).

These excessively fearful or "uptight" monkeys can usually be identified during their first few weeks of life. Most begin leaving their mothers later chronologically and exploring their physical and social environment less than other infants in their birth cohort. Highly fearful youngsters also tend to be shy and withdrawn in their initial encounters with peers—laboratory studies have shown that they exhibit significantly higher and more stable heart rates and greater secretion of cortisol in such interactions than do their less reactive age-mates. However, when these monkeys are in familiar and stable social settings, they become virtually indistinguishable, both behaviorally and physiologically, from others in their peer group. In contrast, when fearful monkeys encounter extreme and/or prolonged stress, their behavioral and physiological differences from others in their social group usually become exaggerated (Suomi, 1991a).

For example, young rhesus monkeys growing up in the wild typically experience functional maternal separations during the 2-month-long annual breeding season when their mothers repeatedly leave the troop for brief periods to consort with selected males (Berman, Rasmussen, & Suomi, 1994). The sudden loss of access to its mother is a major social stressor for any young monkey, and not surprising, virtually all youngsters initially react to their mother's departure with short-term behavioral agitation and physiological arousal, much as Bowlby (1960, 1973) described for human infants experiencing involuntary maternal separation. Whereas most youngsters soon begin to adapt to the separation and readily seek out the company of others in their social group until their mother returns, highly fearful individuals typically lapse into a behavioral depression characterized by increasing lethargy, lack of apparent interest in social stimuli, eating and sleeping difficulties, and a characteristic hunched-over, fetal-like posture (Suomi, 1991b). Laboratory studies simulating those naturally occurring maternal separations have shown that relative to their like-reared peers, highly fearful monkeys not only are more likely to exhibit depressive-like behavioral reactions to short-term social separation but also to show greater and more prolonged HPA activation, more dramatic sympathetic arousal, more rapid central noradrenergic turnover, and greater immunosuppression (Suomi, 1991a). These differential patterns of biobehavioral response to separation tend to remain remarkably stable throughout prepubertal development and may be maintained through adolescence and even into adulthood (Suomi, 1995). There is compelling evidence of significant heritability for at least some components of these differential patterns of separation response (e.g., Higley et al., 1993).

In naturalistic settings, fearful rhesus juveniles have greater adrenocortical activity, higher parasite loads, and lower antibody titers following tetanus vaccination than do others in their birth cohort (Laudenslager, Rasmussen, Berman, Broussard, & Suomi, 1993; Laudenslager et al., 1999). When they reach adolescence, fearful males tend to emigrate from their natal troop at significantly older ages than the rest of their male cohort and, when they do finally leave, they typically employ much more conservative strategies for entering a new troop than do their less-reactive peers. Such strategies actually appear to enhance the prospects of surviving the emigration process for these fearful males (Rasmussen, Fellows, & Suomi, 1990). Thus, although excessive fearfulness apparently puts an individual male at increased risk for adverse biobehavioral reactions to stress throughout development, in some circumstances, this characteristic may actually be adaptive (Suomi, 2000b).

A parallel situation exists for females: Highly fearful young mothers in the wild tend to reject and punish their infants at higher rates around the time of weaning than do other mothers in their troop (Rasmussen, Timme, & Suomi, 1997), and in the absence of social support they appear to be at increased risk for infant neglect and/or abuse (Suomi & Ripp, 1983). Yet, under stable social circumstances these fearful females may not only turn out to be highly competent mothers but also often achieve relatively high positions of social dominance (Rasmussen, Timme, & Suomi, 1997; Suomi, 1999). In sum, excessive fearfulness in infancy appears to be associated with increased risk for developing anxious- and depressive-like symptoms and potential problems in parenting in response to stressful circumstances later in life; however, such long-term outcomes are far from inevitable.

Recent research has demonstrated that individual differences in biobehavioral measures of fearfulness obtained during infancy are also predictive of differential responses to other situations experienced later in life. One of the most striking of these involves differences in the propensity to consume alcohol in a "happy hour" situation. Over the past decade, J. D. Higley and his colleagues have developed an experimental paradigm in which group-living rhesus monkeys are given the opportunity to consume an aspartame-flavored 7% ethanol beverage, a nonalcoholic aspartame-flavored beverage, and/or plain tap water for daily 1-hour periods within their familiar social group (e.g., Higley, Hasert, Suomi, & Linnoila, 1991). Falke et al. (2000) found that monkey infants who exhibited high levels of plasma cortisol following brief separations at 6 months of age subsequently consumed significantly more alcohol in this happy hour situation when they were 5 years of age than did monkeys whose 6-month cortisol responses were more moderate, independent of gender or rearing background. These monkeys appeared to be self-medicating in that particular situation.

INDIVIDUAL DIFFERENCES IN THE REGULATION OF AGGRESSION

A second subgroup of rhesus monkey exhibit problems in regulating their aggressive behavior. These monkeys, comprising approximately 5 to 10% of the population, seem unusually impulsive, insensitive, and overly aggressive in their interactions with other troop members. Impulsive young monkeys, especially males, often are unable to moderate their behavioral responses to rough-and-tumble play initiations from peers, frequently escalating initially benign play bouts into full-blown, tissue-damaging aggressive exchanges (Higley, Suomi, & Linnoila, 1996). Not surprisingly, peers tend to avoid most

of these males during play bouts, and as a result they become increasingly isolated socially. In addition, they appear unwilling (or unable) to follow the rules
inherent in rhesus monkey social dominance hierarchies. For example, they
may directly challenge a dominant adult male, a foolhardy act that can result in
serious injury, especially when the juvenile refuses to back away or exhibit sub-
missive behavior once defeat becomes obvious. Impulsive juvenile males also
show a propensity for making dangerous leaps from treetop to treetop in outdoor settings (Mehlman et al., 1994).

Overly impulsive monkeys, male and female alike, consistently exhibit chronic
deficits in central serotonin metabolism, as reflected by unusually low
cerebrospinal fluid (CSF) concentrations of the primary central serotonin metabolite 5-hydroxyindoleacetic acid (5-HIAA). Laboratory studies have shown that
these deficits in serotonin metabolism emerge early in life and tend to persist
throughout development, as was the case for HPA responsiveness among highly
fearful monkeys. Monkeys who exhibit such deficits are also likely to show poor
state control and visual orienting capabilities during early infancy (Champoux,
Suomi, & Schneider, 1994), poor performance on delay-of-gratification tasks during childhood (Bennett et al., 1999), and excessive cerebral glucose metabolism
under mild isoflurine anesthesia as adults (Doudet et al., 1995). In addition, both
laboratory and field studies have reported that individual differences in 5-HIAA
concentrations are highly heritable among monkeys of similar age and comparable
rearing background (e.g., Higley et al., 1993).

Recent field studies have found that the timing of natal troop emigration typically experienced by impulsive males is seemingly the reverse of that shown by
fearful males, with a long-term prognosis that is not particularly promising. Ostra-
cized by their peers and frequently attacked by adults of both sexes, most of these
excessively aggressive young males are physically driven out of their natal troop
prior to the onset of puberty and long before most of their male cohort begins the
normal emigration process (Mehlman et al., 1995). These males tend to be grossly
incompetent socially, and lacking the requisite social skills necessary for successful entrance into another troop or even to join an all-male gang, most of them become solitary and typically perish within a year (Higley et al., 1996b).

Young females who have chronically low CSF levels of 5-HIAA also tend to be
impulsive, aggressive, and generally rather incompetent socially. Unlike the
males, however, they are not expelled from their natal troop but instead remain
with their families throughout their lifetime, although studies of captive rhesus
monkey groups suggest that these females usually remain at the bottom of their respective dominance hierarchies (Higley et al., 1996a). Although most of these females eventually become mothers, recent research indicates that their maternal
behavior often leaves much to be desired (Suomi, 2000a). In sum, rhesus monkeys
who exhibit poor regulation of impulsive and aggressive behavior and low central
serotonin turnover early in life tend to follow developmental trajectories that often
result in premature death for males and chronically low social dominance and poor
parenting for females.

As was the case for excessively fearful monkeys, overly impulsive and aggressive individuals tend to consume excessive amounts of alcohol when placed in the aforementioned happy hour experimental paradigm. Interestingly, their pattern of alcohol consumption during the 1-hour sessions appears to be more like binge-drinking than the self-medication pattern typically exhibited by excessively fearful individuals (Higley, Suomi, & Linnoila, 1996). Recent studies have demonstrated a significant relationship between degree of alcohol intoxication and serotonin transporter availability in these monkeys (Heinz et al., 1998), as well as among alcohol intake, innate tolerance, and serotonin transporter availability (Higley et al., in press).

EFFECTS OF EARLY PEER REARING ON THE REGULATION OF FEAR AND AGGRESSION

Although the findings from both the field and laboratory studies cited previously have consistently shown that differences among rhesus monkeys in their expressions of fearfulness and impulsive aggression tend to be quite stable from infancy to adulthood and are at least in part heritable, this does not mean that they are necessarily fixed at birth or are immune to subsequent environmental influence. To the contrary, an increasing body of evidence from laboratory studies has demonstrated that patterns of emotional expression can be modified substantially by certain early social experiences, especially with respect to early attachment relationships.

Perhaps the most compelling evidence comes from studies of rhesus monkey infants raised with peers instead of their biological mothers. In these studies, infants typically have been permanently separated from their biological mothers at birth; hand-reared in a neonatal nursery for their first month of life; housed with same-aged, like-reared peers for the rest of their first 6 months; and then moved into larger social groups containing both peer-reared and mother-reared age-mates. During their initial months, these infants readily establish strong social bonds with each other, much as mother-reared infants develop attachments to their own mothers (Harlow, 1969). However, because peers are not nearly as effective as typical monkey mothers in reducing fear in the face of novelty or in providing a secure base for exploration, the attachment relationships that these peer-reared infants develop are almost always anxious in nature (Suomi, 1995). As a result, although peer-reared monkeys show completely normal physical and motor development, most appear to be excessively fearful—their early exploratory behavior tends to be somewhat limited, they seem reluctant to approach novel objects, and they tend to be shy in initial encounters with unfamiliar peers (Suomi, 1997a).

Even when peer-reared youngsters interact with their rearing partners in familiar settings, their emerging social play repertoires are usually retarded in both frequency and complexity. One explanation for their relatively poor play performance is that their peer partners have to serve both as attachment figures and playmates, a dual role that neither mothers nor mother-reared peers have to fulfill. Another obstacle peer-reared monkeys face is that all of their early play bouts involve partners who are basically as socially incompetent as themselves. Perhaps as a result of these factors, peer-reared youngsters typically drop to the bottom of their respective dominance hierarchies when they are subsequently housed with mother-reared monkeys their own age (Higley, Suomi, & Linnoila, 1996).

Several prospective longitudinal studies have found that peer-reared monkeys consistently exhibit more extreme behavioral, adrenocortical, and noradrenergic reactions to social separation than do their mother-reared cohorts, even after they have been living in the same social groups for extended periods (e.g., Higley & Suomi, 1989; Higley, Suomi, & Linnoila, 1992). Such differences in reactions to separation persist from infancy to adolescence, if not beyond. Interestingly, the general nature of the separation reactions that peer-reared monkeys exhibit seems to mirror that shown by naturally occurring highly fearful mother-reared subjects. In this regard, peer-rearing early in life appears to have the effect of making rhesus monkeys generally more fearful than they might have been if reared by their biological mothers (Suomi, 1997a).

Early peer-rearing has another long-term developmental consequence for rhesus monkey—they tend to become excessively aggressive, especially if they are males. Like the previously described impulsive monkeys growing up in the wild, peer-reared males initially exhibit overly aggressive tendencies in the context of juvenile play; as they approach puberty, the frequency and severity of their aggressive episodes typically exceed those of their same-age mother-reared counterparts. Peer-reared females tend to groom (and be groomed by) others in their social group less frequently and for shorter durations than mother-reared females, and as noted earlier, they usually stay at the bottom of their respective dominance hierarchies. The differences between peer-reared and mother-reared age-mates in rates of aggression and grooming and in dominance rankings remain relatively robust throughout the prepubertal and adolescent years (Higley, Suomi, & Linnoila, 1996). Peer-reared monkeys also consistently have lower CSF concentrations of 5-HIAA than their mother-reared counterparts. These group differences in 5-HIAA concentrations appear well before 6 months of age, and they remain stable at least throughout adolescence and into early adulthood (Higley & Suomi, 1996). Thus, peer-reared monkeys exhibit the same general tendencies that characterize excessively impulsive wild-living (and mother-reared) rhesus monkeys, not only behaviorally but also in terms of decreased serotonergic functioning.

Given these findings, it should perhaps come as no surprise that peer-reared adolescent monkeys as a group consume larger amounts of alcohol under comparable ad libitum conditions than their mother-reared agemates (Higley, Hasert, Suomi, & Linnoila, 1991). They also rapidly develop a greater tolerance for alcohol, and as previously noted, this tendency appears to be associated with differences in serotonin turnover rates (Higley et al., in press) and with differential serotonin transporter availability (Heinz et al., 1998). In sum, early rearing with peers seems to make rhesus monkey infants both more fearful and more impulsive, and their resulting developmental trajectories resemble those of naturally occurring subgroups of rhesus monkeys growing up in the wild.

GENE-ENVIRONMENT INTERACTIONS

Studies examining the effects of peer-rearing and other variations in early rearing history (e.g., Harlow & Harlow, 1969), along with the previously cited heritability findings, clearly provide compelling evidence that both genetic and early experiential factors can affect a monkey's capacity to regulate expression of fear and aggression. Do these factors operate independently, or do they interact in some fashion in shaping individual developmental trajectories? Ongoing research capitalizing on the discovery of a polymorphism in one specific gene—the serotonin transporter gene—suggests that gene-environment interactions not only occur but also can be expressed in multiple forms.

The serotonin transporter gene (5-HTT), a candidate gene for impaired serotonergic function (Lesch et al., 1996), has length variation in its promoter region that results in allelic variation in 5-HTT expression. A heterozygous "short" allele (LS) confers low transcriptional efficiency to the 5-HTT promoter relative to the homozygous "long" allele (LL), raising the possibility that low 5-HTT expression may result in decreased serotonergic function (Heils et al., 1996), although evidence in support of this hypothesis in humans has been decidedly mixed to date (e.g., Furlong et al., 1998). The 5-HTT polymorphism was first characterized in humans, but it also appears in a largely homologous form in rhesus monkeys but interestingly not in many other species of primates and other mammals (Lesch et al., 1997).

We recently utilized polymerase chain reaction (PCR) techniques to characterize the genotypic status of monkeys in the studies comparing peer-reared monkeys with mother-reared controls described earlier with respect to their 5-HTT polymorphic status. Because extensive observational data and biological samples had been previously collected from these monkeys throughout development, it became possible to examine a wide range of behavioral and physiological measures for potential 5-HTT polymorphism main effects and interactions with early rearing history. Analyses completed to date suggest that such interactions are widespread and diverse.

For example, Bennett et al. (2002) reported that CSF 5-HIAA concentrations did not differ as a function of 5-HTT status for mother-reared subjects, whereas among peer-reared monkeys individuals with the LS allele had significantly lower CSF 5-HIAA concentrations than those with the LL allele. One interpretation of this interaction is that mother-rearing appeared to buffer any potentially deleterious effects of the LS allele on serotonin metabolism. A different form of gene-environment interaction was suggested by the analysis of alcohol consumption data: Whereas peer-reared monkeys with the LS allele consumed more alcohol than peer-reared monkeys with the LL allele, the reverse was true for mother-reared subjects, with individuals possessing the LS allele actually consuming less alcohol than their LL counterparts (Bennett et al., 1998). In other words, the LS allele appeared to represent a risk factor for excessive alcohol consumption among peer-reared monkeys but a protective factor for mother-reared subjects. In another set of analyses, Champoux et al. (2002) examined the relationship between early rearing history and serotonin transporter gene polymorphic status on measures of neonatal neurobehavioral development during the first month of life and found further evidence of maternal buffering. Specifically, infants possessing the LS allele who were reared in the laboratory neonatal nursery showed significant deficits in measures of attention, activity, and motor maturity relative to nursery-reared infants possessing the LL allele, whereas both LS and LL infants who were being reared by competent mothers exhibited normal values for each of these measures.

In sum, the consequences of having the LS allele have been found to differ dramatically for peer-reared and mother-reared monkeys: Whereas peer-reared individuals with the LS allele exhibit deficits in measures of neurobehavioral development during their initial weeks of life and reduced serotonin metabolism and excessive alcohol consumption as adolescents, mother-reared subjects with the very same allele are characterized by normal early neurobehavioral development and serotonin metabolism, as well as reduced risk for excessive alcohol consumption later in life. Indeed, it could be argued on the basis of these findings that having the short allele of the 5-HTT gene may well lead to psychopathology among monkeys with poor early rearing histories but might actually be adaptive for monkeys who develop secure early attachment relationship with their mothers.

IMPLICATIONS FOR UNDERSTANDING THE DEVELOPMENT OF EMOTIONAL REGULATION IN HUMANS

Earlier in this chapter, it was argued that emotional regulation represents a process that is not limited to humans. To what extent can studies of its development and possible biological correlates in rhesus monkeys enhance our understanding of how genetic and environmental factors might influence the development of emotional regulation in children, particularly those who display debilitating fearfulness or excessive aggression as they are growing up? To be sure, rhesus monkeys are clearly not furry little humans with tails but rather members of another (albeit closely related) species, and one should be especially cautious when making comparisons between humans and other primate species with respect to the expression of fearful and aggressive behavior, given that there exist obvious age, gender, and cultural differences in what is considered excessive or abnormal for humans. Nevertheless, some general principles emerge from research with rhesus monkeys that might be relevant for the human case.

First, the results of these studies have clearly demonstrated that both nature and nurture are at play in the development of most, if not all, biobehavioral features of excessive fearfulness and impulsive aggressiveness. On one hand, evidence of significant heritability has been reported for certain neonatal reflex and activity patterns, HPA reactivity, CSF 5-HIAA concentrations, and behavioral expressions of both fear and aggression. On the other hand, many of these studies have also demonstrated significant effects of differential early rearing experiences on the developmental trajectories of virtually all of these very same behavioral and physiological systems, their significant heritabilities notwithstanding. Thus, the manner in which a rhesus monkey has been reared can markedly affect its pattern of neonatal reflex development, its daily distribution of activity states, its propensity to activate its HPA axis and to exhibit fear in the face of novelty, as well as its likelihood of escalating play bouts into aggressive episodes and its chronic CSF concentrations of 5-HIAA, respectively, no matter how many genes might be involved in each instance. Clearly, both nature and nurture can contribute to the development of both excessive fearfulness and impulsive aggressiveness in this species—and most likely in other primate species as well.

Perhaps the more interesting principle concerns the manner and degree to which heritable factors can interact with environmental influences to shape individual developmental trajectories with respect to these two emotions. The recent findings that a specific polymorphism in the serotonin transporter gene is associated with different behavioral and biological outcomes for rhesus monkeys as a function of their early social rearing histories suggest that more complex gene-environment interactions may actually be responsible for the phenomena in question. Whether comparable instances of gene-environment interactions can be demonstrated for other biobehavioral characteristics is currently the focus of ongoing research efforts; preliminary findings to date have been exceedingly encouraging in that respect. Nevertheless, even highly definitive demonstrations of additional gene-environment interactions would scarcely begin to address issues regarding the actual cascades of protein synthesis presumably initiated by expression of the genes in question; the extent and manner in which such expression might be enhanced, blocked, or otherwise modified by specific environmental factors; and the biological pathways and mechanisms through which such expression might be translated into specific physiological and behavioral characteristics exhibited by individual monkeys. Although nature and nurture can obviously interact, exactly how, when, and why has yet to be fully determined—be it for rhesus monkeys or for our fellow humans.

REFERENCES

Bennett, A. J., Lesch, K. P., Heils, A., &. Linnoila, M. (1998). Serotonin transporter gene variation, CSF 5-HIAA concentrations, and alcohol-related aggression in rhesus monkeys (*Macaca mulatta*). *American Journal of Primatology, 45,* 168–169.

Bennett, A. J., Lesch, K. P., Heils, A., Long, J., Lorenz, J., Shoaf, S. E., Champoux, M., Suomi, S. J., Linnoila, M., & Higley, J. D. (2002). Early experience and serotonin transporter gene variation interact to influence primate CNS function. *Molecular Psychiatry, 17,* 118–122.

Bennett, A. J., Tsai, T., Hopkins, W. D., Lindell, S. G., Pierre, P. J., Champoux, M., & Shoaf, S. E. (1999). Early social rearing environment influences acquisition of a computerized joystick task in rhesus monkeys (*Macaca mulatta*). *American Journal of Primatology, 49,* 33–34.

Berard, J. (1989). Male life histories. *Puerto Rican Health Sciences Journal, 8,* 47–58.

Berman, C. M., Rasmussen, K. L. R., & Suomi, S. J. (1994). Responses of free-ranging rhesus monkeys to a natural form of maternal separation: I. Parallels with mother-infant separation in captivity. *Child Development, 65,* 1028–1041.

Bowlby, J. (1960). Separation anxiety. *International Journal of Psycho-Analysis, 51,* 1–25.

Bowlby, J. (1969). *Attachment.* New York: Basic Books.

Bowlby, J. (1973). *Separation.* New York: Basic Books.

Bowlby, J. (1988). *A secure base.* New York: Basic Books.

Champoux, M., Bennett, A. J., Lesch, K. P., Heils, A., Nielson, D. A., Higley, J. D., & Suomi, S. J. (2002). Serotonin transporter gene polymorphism and neurobehavioral development in rhesus monkey neonates. *Molecular Psychiatry, 7,* 1058–1063.

Champoux, M., Suomi, S. J., & Schneider, M. L. (1994). Temperamental differences between captive Indian and Chinese-Indian hybrid rhesus macaque infants. *Laboratory Animal Science, 44,* 351–357.

Collins, W. A., Maccoby, E. E., Steinberg, L., Hetherington, E. M., & Bornstein, M. H. (2000). Contemporary research on parenting: The case for nature *and* nurture. *American Psychologist, 55,* 218–232.

Darwin, C. (1872). *The expression of emotions in man and animals.* New York: D. Appleton.

Dittus, W. P. J. (1979). The evolution of behaviours regulating density and age-specific sex ratios in a primate population. *Behaviour, 69,* 265–302.

Doudet, D., Hommer, D., Higley, J. D., Andreason, P. J., Moneman, R., Suomi, S. J., & Linnoila, M. (1995). Cerebral glucose metabolism, CSF 5-HIAA, and aggressive behavior in rhesus monkeys. *American Journal of Psychiatry, 152,* 1782–1787.

Fahlke, C., Lorenz, J. G., Long, J., Champoux, M., Suomi, S. J., & Higley, J. D. (2000). Rearing experiences and stress-induced plasma cortisol as early risk factors for excessive alcohol consumption in nonhuman primates. *Alcoholism: Clinical and Experimental Research, 24,* 644–650.

Furlong, R. A., Ho, L., Walsh, C., Rubinsztein, J. S., Jain, S., Pazkil, E. S., Eaton, D. F., & Rubinsztein, D. C. (1998). Analysis and meta-analysis of two serotonin transporter gene polymorphisms in bipolar and unipolar affective disorders. *American Journal of Medical Genetics, 81,* 58–63.

Gunnar, M. R., Gonzalez, C. A., Goodlin, B. L., & Levine, S. (1981). Behavioral and pituitary-adrenal responses during a prolonged separation period in rhesus monkeys. *Psychoneuroendocrinology, 6,* 65–75.

Harlow, H. F. (1958). The nature of love. *American Psychologist, 13,* 673–685.

Harlow, H. F. (1969). Age-mate or peer affectional system. In D. S. Lehrman, R. A. Hinde, & E. Shaw (Eds.), *Advances in the study of behavior* (Vol. 2, pp. 333–383). New York: Academic Press.

Harlow, H. F., & Harlow, M. K. (1969). Effects of various mother–infant relationships on rhesus monkey behaviors. In B. M. Foss (Ed.), *Determinants of infant behaviour* (Vol. 4, pp. 15–36). London: Metheun.

Harris, J. R. (1998). *The nurture assumption: Why children turn out the way they do.* New York: Free Press.

Heils, A., Teufel, A., Petri, S., Stober, G., Riederer, P., Bengel, B., & Lesch, K. P. (1996). Allelic variation of human serotonin transporter gene expression. *Journal of Neurochemistry, 6,* 2621–2624.

Heinz, A., Higley, J. D., Gorey, J. G., Saunders, R. C., Jones, D. W., Hommer, D., Zajicek, K., Suomi, S. J., Weinberger, D. R., & Linnoila, M. (1998). *In vivo* association between alcohol intoxication, aggression, and serotonin transporter availability in nonhuman primates. *American Journal of Psychiatry, 155,* 1023–1028.

Higley, J. D., Hasert, M. L., Suomi, S. J., & Linnoila, M. (1991). A new nonhuman primate model of alcohol abuse: Effects of early experience, personality, and stress on alcohol consumption. *Proceedings of the National Academy of Sciences, 88,* 7261–7265.

Higley, J. D., Hommer, D., Lucas, K., Shoaf, S., Suomi, S. J., & Linnoila, M. (in press). CNS serotonin metabolism rate predicts innate tolerance, high alcohol consumption, and aggression during intoxication in rhesus monkeys. *Archives of General Psychiatry.*

Higley, J. D., King, S. T., Hasert, M. F., Champoux, M., Suomi, S. J., & Linnoila, M. (1996a). Stability of individual differences in serotonin function and its relationship to severe aggression and competent social behavior in rhesus macaque females. *Neuropsychopharmacology, 14,* 67–76.

Higley, J. D., Mehlman, P. T., Taub, D. M., Higley, S., Fernald, B., Vickers, J. H., Suomi, S. J., & Linnoila, M. (1996b). Excessive mortality in young free-ranging male nonhuman primates with low CSF 5-HIAA concentrations. *Archives of General Psychiatry, 53,* 537–543.

Higley, J. D., & Suomi, S. J. (1989). Temperamental reactivity in nonhuman primates. In G. A. Kohnstamm, J. E. Bates, & M. K. Rothbard (Eds.), *Handbook of temperament in children* (pp. 153–167). New York: Wiley.

Higley, J. D., & Suomi, S. J. (1996). Reactivity and social competence affect individual differences in reaction to severe stress in children: Investigations using nonhuman primates. In C. R. Pfeffer (Ed.), *Intense stress and mental disturbance in children* (pp. 3–58). Washington, DC: American Psychiatric Press.

Higley, J. D., Suomi, S. J., & Linnoila, M. (1992). A longitudinal assessment of CSF monoamine metabolite and plasma cortisol concentrations in young rhesus monkeys. *Biological Psychiatry, 32,* 127–145.

Higley, J. D., Suomi, S. J., & Linnoila, M. (1996). A nonhuman primate model of Type II alcoholism?: Part 2: Diminished social competence and excessive aggression correlates with low CSF 5-HIAA concentrations. *Alcoholism: Clinical and Experimental Research, 20,* 643–650.

Higley, J. D., Thompson, W. T., Champoux, M., Goldman, D., Hasert, M. F., Kraemer, G. W., Scanlan, J. M., Suomi, S. J., & Linnoila, M. (1993). Paternal and maternal genetic and environmental contributions to CSF monoamine metabolites in rhesus monkeys *(Macaca mulatta). Archives of General Psychiatry, 50,* 615–623.

Laudenslager, M. L., Rasmussen, K. L. R., Berman, C. M., Broussard, C. L., & Suomi, S. J. (1993). Specific antibody levels in free-ranging rhesus monkeys: Relationship to plasma hormones, cardiac parameters, and early behavior. *Development Psychobiology, 26,* 407–420.

Laudenslager, M. L., Rasmussen, K. L. R., Berman, C. J., Lilly, A., Shelton, S. E., Kalin, N. H., & Suomi, S. J. (1999). A preliminary analysis of individual differences in rhesus monkeys following brief capture experiences: Endocrine, immune, and health indicators. *Brain, Behavior, & Immunology, 13,* 124–137.

Lesch, K. P., Bengel, D., Heils, A., Sabol, S. Z., Greenberg, B. D., Petri, S., Benjamin, J., Muller, C. R., Hamer, D. H., & Murphy, D. L. (1996). Association of anxiety-related traits with a polymorphism in the serotonin transporter gene regulatory region. *Science, 274,* 1527–1531.

Lesch, L. P., Meyer, J., Glatz, K., Flugge, G., Hinney, A., Hebebrand, J., Klauck, S. M., Poustka, A., Poustka, F., Bengel, D., Mossner, R., Riederer, P., & Heils, A. (1997). The 5-HT transporter gene-linked polymorphic region (5-HTTLPR) in evolutionary perspective: Alternative biallelic variation in rhesus monkeys. *Journal of Neural Transmission, 104,* 1259–1266.

Lewis, M. (1992). *Shame: The exposed self.* New York: The Free Press.

Lindburg, D.G. (1971). The rhesus monkey in north India: An ecological and behavioral study. In L. A. Rosenblum (Ed.), *Primate behavior: Developments in field and laboratory research* (Vol. 2, pp. 1–106). New York: Academic Press.

Mehlman, P. T., Higley, J. D., Faucher, I., Lilly, A. A., Taub, D. M., Vickers, J. H., Suomi, S. J., & Linnoila, M. (1994). Low cerebrospinal fluid 5 hydroxyindoleacetic acid concentrations are correlated with severe aggression and reduced impulse control in free-ranging primates. *American Journal of Psychiatry, 151,* 1485–1491.

Mehlman, P. T., Higley, J. D., Faucher, I., Lilly, A. A., Taub, D. M., Vickers, J. H., Suomi, S. J., & Linnoila, M. (1995). CSF 5-HIAA concentrations are correlated with sociality and the timing of emigration in free-ranging primates. *American Journal of Psychiatry, 152,* 901–913.

Mendoza, S. P., Smotherman, W. P., Miner, M., Kaplan, J., & Levine, S. (1978). Pituitary-adrenal response to separation in mother and infant squirrel monkeys. *Developmental Psychobiology, 11,* 169–175.

Panksepp, J. (1998). *Affective neuroscience: The foundations of human and animal emotions.* New York: Oxford University Press.

Rasmussen, K. L. R., Fellows, J. R., & Suomi, S. J. (1990). Physiological correlates of emigration behavior and mortality in adolescent male rhesus monkeys on Cayo Santiago. *American Journal of Primatology, 20,* 224–225.

Rasmussen, K. L. R., Timme, A., & Suomi, S. J. (1997). Comparison of physiological measures of Cayo Santiago rhesus monkey females within and between social groups. *Primate Reports, 47,* 49–55.

Reite, M., Short, R., Selier, C., & Pauley, J. D. (1981). Attachment, loss, and depression. *Journal of Child Psychology and Psychiatry, 22,* 141–169.

Ruppenthal, G. C., Harlow, M. K., Eisele, C. D., Harlow, H. F., & Suomi, S. J. (1974). Development of peer interactions of monkeys reared in a nuclear family environment. *Child Development, 45,* 670–682.

Rutter, M. L. (2001). How can we know environment really matters? In F. Parker-Lamb, J. Hagen, & R. Robinson (Eds.), *Developmental and contextual transition of children and families: Implications for research, policy, and practice* (pp. 5–18). New York: Columbia University Press.

Sameroff, A. J., & Suomi, S. J. (1996). Primates and persons: A comparative developmental understanding of social organization. In R. B. Cairns, G. H. Elder, & E. J. Costello (Eds.), *Developmental science* (pp. 97–120). Cambridge, UK: Cambridge University Press.

Suomi, S. J. (1986). Anxiety-like disorders in young primates. In R. Gittelman (Ed.), *Anxiety disorders of childhood* (pp. 1–23). New York: Guilford.

Suomi, S. J. (1991a). Up-tight and laid-back monkeys: Individual differences in the response to social challenges. In S. Brauth, W. Hall, & R. Dooling (Eds.), *Plasticity of development* (pp. 27–56). Cambridge, MA: MIT Press.

Suomi, S. J. (1991b). Primate separation models of affective disorders. In J. Madden (Ed.), *Neurobiology of learning, emotion, and affect* (pp. 195–214). New York: Raven.

Suomi, S. J. (1995). Influence of Bowlby's attachment theory on research on nonhuman primate biobehavioral development. In S. Goldberg, R. Muir, & J. Kerr (Eds.), *Attachment Theory: Social, developmental, and clinical perspectives* (pp. 185–201). Hillsdale, NJ: Analytic Press.

Suomi, S. J. (1997a). Early determinants of behaviour: Evidence from primate studies. *British Medical Bulletin, 53,* 170–184.

Suomi, S. J. (1997b). Nonverbal communication in nohuman primates: Implications for the emergence of culture. In P. Molnar & U. Segerstrale (Eds.), *Where nature meets culture: Nonverbal communication in social interaction* (pp. 131–150). Hillsdale, NJ: Lawrence Erlbaum Associates.

Suomi, S. J. (1998). Conflict and cohesion in rhesus monkey family life. In M. Cox & J. Brooks-Gunn (Eds.), *Conflict and cohesion in families* (pp. 283–296). Mahwah, NJ: Lawrence Erlbaum Associates.

Suomi, S. J. (1999). Attachment in rhesus monkeys. In J. Cassidy & P. R. Shaver (Eds.), *Handbook of attachment: Theory, research, and clinical applications* (pp. 181–197). New York: Guilford.

Suomi, S. J. (2000a). A biobehavioral perspective on developmental psychopathology: Excessive aggression and serotonergic dysfunction in monkeys. In A. J. Sameroff, M. Lewis, & S. Miller (Eds.), *Handbook of developmental psychopathology* (pp. 237–256). New York: Plenum.

Suomi, S. J. (2000b). Behavioral inhibition and impulsive aggressiveness: Insights from studies with rhesus monkeys. In L. Balter & C. Tamis-Lamode (Eds.), *Child psychology: A handbook of contemporary issues* (pp. 510–525). New York: Taylor & Francis.

Suomi, S. J., & Harlow, H. F. (1975). The role and reason of peer friendships. In M. Lewis & L. A. Rosenblum (Eds.) *Friendships and peer relations* (pp. 310–334). New York: Basic Books.

Suomi, S. J., & Harlow, H. F. (1976). The facts and functions of fear. In M. Zuckerman & C. D. Spielberger (Eds.), *Emotions and anxiety: New concepts, methods, and applications* (pp. 3–34). Hillsdale, NJ: Lawrence Erlbaum Associates.

Suomi, S. J., & Ripp, C. (1983). A history of motherless mother monkey mothering at the University of Wisconsin Primate Laboratory. In M. Reite & N. Caine (Eds.), *Child abuse: The nonhuman primate data* (pp. 49–77). New York: Alan R. Liss.

Symonds, D. (1978) *Play and aggression: A study of rhesus monkeys.* New York: Columbia University Press.

3

Nature, Nurture, and the Question of "How?": A Phenomenological Variant of Ecological Systems Theory

Margaret Beale Spencer
Vinay Harpalani
University of Pennsylvania

Few areas of inquiry have captivated the entire realm of social sciences like the nature–nurture question. The study of genetic and environmental influences on human behavior and development has been one of the most significant investigations that social scientists have undertaken. Behavioral genetics is the field most associated with the nature–nurture question. Behavioral genetic research focuses, however, on determining how much variance within populations can be attributed genetic or environmental factors; it does not say much about how nature and nurture interact to produce observable outcomes. For developmental psychologists, "how?" rather than "how much?" is the pertinent question. In this chapter, we discuss the need for a process-oriented approach to the nature–nurture question and present Spencer's Phenomenological Variant of Ecological Systems Theory as a guiding conceptual framework to address the question of "how?" Our analysis attempts to explicate the nature–nurture question and integrate issues of race/ethnicity, gender, socioeconomic status, cultural dissonance, and other contextual factors, as they interact with normative developmental and identity processes that are mediated by gene-environment interaction. We will also pose ideas for application of the PVEST framework in future research on the nature–nurture question.

Few areas of inquiry have captivated the entire realm of social sciences like the nature versus nurture debate. Investigating the impact of genetic and environmental influences on human development, and the processes involved in mediating these influences, poses perhaps the most fundamental question we can ask about human nature. The nature–nurture question continues to garner attention, and with the swift progress of the Human Genome Project, interest in this issue will only grow.

Historically, the intellectual battleground between hereditarians and environmentalists spanned a variety of academic disciplines, including psychology, sociology, and anthropology, along with professional realms such as education and medicine. The primary debate, in the eyes of the public, was whether nature or nurture was responsible for a given outcome. In later years, the focus shifted from contention to cooperation; rather than asking whether genetic or environmental factors determine a given outcome, researchers recognized the importance of both (Plomin, 1996). Although still often misunderstood by the public, the realization that both heredity and environment play a role in practically all human behavior superseded myopic notions such as genetic determinism or strict environmentalism. Thus, through methods such as twin and adoption studies, behavioral geneticists began to study the relative impact of heredity and environment on human behavior (see Plomin, DeFries, McClearn, & McGuffin, 2001).

Social scientists have also recognized, however, that the calculation of heritabilities for traits and the partitioning of variance into genetic and environmental components—the traditional domain of behavioral genetics—is of limited value (Bronfenbrenner & Ceci, 1994; Turkheimer, 1998). While it may be useful to know, the determination of how much variance is accounted for by genetic and environmental factors does not reveal how the two interact to yield developmental outcomes. The ultimate nature–nurture question, as originally posed by Anastasi (1958) and restated by Bronfenbrenner and Ceci (1993), is not, "How much?"— but rather, "How?"

Behavioral genetics does not typically pose answers to this question. Though it is the discipline most typically associated with the nature–nurture question, behavioral genetics focuses on the sources of variation within populations rather than on the developmental processes involved (Gottlieb, 1995). Thus, a process-oriented model of human development is necessary to understand the nature–nurture issue more completely.

In this chapter, we attempt to shed light on the question of how nature and nurture interact to produce developmental outcomes. First, we briefly review the shortcomings of the behavioral genetic approach, focusing on the concept of heritability and the consideration of environment and gene-environment interaction. We examine Bronfenbrenner and Ceci's (1993, 1994) ideas on heritability and the interaction of nature and nurture in human development. Next, we transition this analysis to Bronfenbrenner's (1979, 1989, 1993) Ecological Systems Theory, analyzing it in terms of the nature–nurture question. Bronfenbrenner's work presents an ideal conceptual bridge between our work and more traditional perspectives on the nature–nurture issue. We propose Spencer's (1995, 1999)

Phenomenological Variant of Ecological Systems Theory (PVEST) as a model for analyzing human development, and as an identity-focused, cultural-ecological framework to analyze processes involved in the interaction of nature and nurture. We discuss how PVEST might inform traditional findings and theories in behavioral genetics, and its possible application in research on the nature–nurture question—particularly in light of advances in human genetics and human development research. Our approach to the nature–nurture question considers issues of race/ethnicity, gender, socioeconomic status, cultural dissonance, and other contextual factors as they interact with the normative developmental and identity processes that are mediated by gene-environment interaction. Throughout, our analysis emphasizes the need for, and utility of, a process-oriented approach.

SOME BASIC CRITIQUES OF THE BEHAVIORAL GENETIC PARADIGM

The central shortcoming of behavioral genetics is the lack of a broader, developmentally sensitive framework to integrate and explain how genetic and environmental influences affect human behavior. Ironically, the consequences of this shortcoming are illustrated by the very name of the discipline, *behavioral genetics*. As Plomin (1990) stated, rather than talking about genes for particular behaviors, "we should talk about genetic influences on individual differences in height and on behavior. There are no genes for behavior ... genes do not determine behavior. What we are talking about is a probabilistic connection between genetic factors and behavioral differences among people" (pp. 20–21).

To extend this reasoning further, the term "behavioral genetics" is somewhat misleading, as the immediate objects of behavioral genetic studies are usually traits, not behaviors. Though one can directly study behavior, most behavioral genetic studies focus on traits such as personality measures and IQ tests (see Plomin et al., 2001 for an overview of findings from these studies). Traits are essentially defined as individual differences within a population. As Robert Plomin (1990) noted, genes do not determine behavior; they only influence traits that define the propensity to engage in particular behaviors. Although Plomin and most behavioral geneticists understand this relationship between genes and behavior quite well, the term "behavioral genetics" can easily confuse those who are not as well versed in the pertinent theories and relationships underlying the discipline. A term such as "psychological genetics" or "genetic psychology" would be more accurate and appropriate.

A clarification of terminology is particularly important given that the relationship between heredity and environment in human development has been perhaps the most misrepresented and misunderstood area of inquiry in all of science. While genetic influences on human behavior and development undeniably exist and are significant in many realms, concepts and terminology from behavioral genetics have led many to misconstrue these influences. In fact, the very term, "behavioral genetics," is misleading in the same manner as many terms and concepts within the discipline. As such, our primary objective in this paper is to pose a theoretical framework to mitigate these kinds of misunderstandings and to demonstrate its utility for the analysis of genetic and environmental influences on human development.

Heritability

The primary and perhaps most misunderstood concept in behavioral genetics is that of heritability—the proportion of variance in a given trait, within a particular sample, that can be attributed to genetic influences. Typically, in behavioral genetic studies, quantitative genetic techniques are used to estimate relative genetic and environmental components of traits within a given sample. Variance within a sample is vital in behavioral genetic studies; if a trait does not show much variability within a population, then its examination is not assisted by behavioral genetic methods (Gabbay, 1992). Twin, family, and adoption studies are the conventional methods used in behavioral genetic studies; basically, the trait under study is measured and correlations between related persons of varying degrees are determined. In twin studies, heritability is estimated as twice the difference between identical and same-sex fraternal twin correlations for a given trait. As identical twins share 100% of the same genes and fraternal twins share only 50%, one would expect higher correlations for identical twins if genetic factors influence a trait, and this is typically observed for many measured physical and psychological traits. In fact, Turkheimer and Gottesman (1991) posed the question of whether null hypotheses in psychology should even assume heritability estimates of zero.

As noted, heritability estimates apply to genetic and environmental variation within a group or sample; they cannot and should not be used to explain between-group differences. Even if a trait has high heritability in two different groups, this does not indicate that between-group differences in the trait are genetic in origin. Jensen (1969) confounded within- and between-group heritability with his claim that Black-White IQ differences were genetic in origin. Block (1995) used an analogy to explain the flaws in Jensen's logic:

> Suppose you buy a bag of ordinary seed corn from a hardware store. This is genetically variegated (not cloned) corn. You grow one handful of it in a carefully controlled environment in which the seeds get uniform illumination and uniform nutrient solution. The corn plants will vary in height and since the environment is uniform, the heritability of height will be 100%. Now take another handful of corn from the same bag which you grow in a similarly uniform environment but with a poor nutrient solution. The plants will vary in height again but all will be stunted. The heritability of height in both groups is 100%, but the difference in height between the groups is entirely environmentally caused. So heritability can be *total* within groups even if there is no genetic difference between groups. (pp. 110–111).

This example distinctly applies to race differences in IQ; even if IQ scores are highly heritable among both Blacks and Whites, the difference in IQ scores between the two scores may be entirely environmental in origin.

Also, heritability is not a constant; it varies as a function of both genetic and environmental variance in a population. If environmental variance is low (i.e., if all of the individuals in a sample are experiencing very similar environments) and genetic variance is high (individuals under study are not closely related and therefore show much genetic variability), then heritability will also be high. Conversely, if environmental variance is high and genetic variance is low within the given sample, heritability will be low. Therefore, heritability estimates only yield information about the current variance within the sample; they may change if new genetic variance (individuals with differing genotypes) or new environmental variance (interventions or other influences) are introduced. As Bronfenbrenner and Ceci (1994) noted, heritability only estimates actualized genetic potential under the given environmental conditions; nonactualized genetic potential, which might be expressed under different conditions, is not measured or considered. However, heritability is often misrepresented as a static, unalterable entity (e.g., Herrnstein & Murray, 1994).

Conceptualization of Environment and Gene-Environment Interaction

Data regarding the heritability of traits merely partition variance into genetic and environmental components. Unfortunately, research in behavioral genetics often does not extend much further in its conceptualization of genetic and environmental interactions in human development. Wachs (1983) noted the different ways in which behavioral geneticists and environmentally oriented researchers think about and measure environmental influences. For environmentally oriented researchers, direct measure of environmental influences, either through observation or by experimental manipulation, is a basic principle (Wachs, 1983). Typically, a variety of measures are used, including self and observer reports, demographic variables, and social, cultural, political, and historical data. Environment is conceptualized as a multidimensional, dynamic entity that cannot be subsumed under single conceptual scheme. Moreover, emphasis is placed on the transactional nature of the environment (i.e., the interaction between the individual and the environment [Lewin, 1935]). The notion of context, as Dannefer (1992) and Van Oers (1998) discussed, aims to capture the complexity of this interaction.

In contrast, behavioral genetic studies usually treat environment as an unmeasured remainder term, thus violating the basic principle of direct measurement (Wachs, 1983). Because environment is treated as a single term, or perhaps as two terms if divided into shared and nonshared components (e.g., Plomin & Daniels, 1987), as indicated, there is no consideration of the multidimensional, dynamic, transactional influences that mediate environmental influences on human development. Moreover, because environmental influence is usually not directly measured but rather inferred, it is also confounded with error of measurement (Bock & Zimowski, 1987). Even behavioral genetic studies that do include some basic measures of parenting and family environment (e.g., Deater-Deckard, Fulker, & Plomin, 1999; O'Connor, Deater-Deckard, Fulker, Rutter, & Plomin, 1998; Reiss,

2001) do not take into account the multiple, interacting levels of context through which environmental influences are filtered.

Also, interactions between genetic and environmental influences are often not considered in behavioral genetic research. Even when these interactions are taken into account, the relationship between nature and nurture is oversimplified; thus the processes that are involved in these interactions are not well delineated. For example, Scarr and McCartney (1983) contended:

> Development is indeed the result of nature *and* nurture but … genes drive experience. Genes are components in a system that organizes the organism to experience its world …. A good theory of the environment can only be one in which experience is guided by genotypes that both push and restrain experiences. (p. 425)

In their conceptualization of gene-environment interaction, Scarr and McCartney (1983) note three types of such interactions defined by Plomin, DeFries, and Loehlin (1977; see Table 3.1). First, there are passive genetic effects, in which the genetic makeup of others, such as parents and peers, can influence one's environment. For example, parents who are introverts will not only pass on genes for introversion to their children; due to their own proclivities, they may also create particular environments where introversion can be expressed more readily.

TABLE 3.1
Types of Gene-Environment Interaction

Genetic Effects	Impact on Environment
Passive	Genetic makeup of parents, peers, and other salient individuals influence the child's environment, e.g., parents who are introverts may create less social environments for their children.
Active	Individuals seek out environments that match their genetic makeup, e.g., sensation-seeking individuals may actively seek more high risk environments.
Evocative	Traits may evoke particular responses from others, e.g., individuals who are taller and physically larger than average may evoke more fear than smaller individuals.

Note. From "Genotype-environment Interaction and Correlation in the Analysis of Human Behavior," by R. Plomin, J. C. DeFries, and J. C. Loehlin, 1977, *Psychological Bulletin, 84,* p. 309–322; and "How People Make Their Own Environments: A Theory of Genotype-environment Effects," by S. Scarr and K. McCartney, 1983, *Child Development, 54,* p. 424–435.

Passive effects may also take the opposite form; for example, parents who know their children are vulnerable for a particular outcome, such as reading disability, may make a more conscious effort to create an environment which mitigates this vulnerability (Scarr, 1988). Active genetic effects are those in which individuals actively seek out environments that match their genetic makeup. For example, a person who is genetically predisposed to exhibit introversion may seek out a solitary environment; this is due indirectly to the person's genetic makeup. Therefore, any of the person's characteristics attributed to the solitary environment are partly genetically based. In addition, people of similar genetic makeup are likely to evoke similar responses from the environment. For example, if a child is genetically predisposed to be introvertive, his/her introversion will evoke a particular response from parents and peers. As such, treatment by parents and peers, which is traditionally thought to be an environmental measure, can be actually influenced by genetic factors. This is called an evocative genetic effect.

Scarr and McCartney (1983; Scarr, 1988) contended essentially that because these types of effects create a predictable relationship between genotypes and environments, it is more appropriate to think of genotype-environment correlations rather than interactions. Because genotypes are the antecedent variable in this relationship, Scarr and McCartney (1983; Scarr, 1988) attributed primary causality to them. Scarr (1988) stated that most differences among people arise from genetically determined differences in the experiences to which they are attracted and that they evoke (pp. 233–234)."

The framework proposed by Plomin et al. (1977) and extended by Scarr and McCartney (1983; Scarr, 1988) is interesting and valid to an extent; however, like much behavioral genetic research, it is decidedly oversimplified and misleading. For example, evocative effects of genes may primarily reflect societal biases. An individual's race is an inherited feature, and, particularly for Black youth, race may evoke negative responses from individuals such as teachers and law enforcement officers (Spencer, 1999). It is critical to acknowledge that any physical feature, such as height, body type, or weight, is heritable and could evoke positive or negative responses from parents, teachers, and/or peers. These responses could reflect societal biases concerning body types and could vary substantially among ethnic groups, regions, and societies and be additionally influenced by gender. For example, early maturing Black and White boys may evoke very different responses from teachers and become, in fact, academic risk factors for Blacks but enhancements for Whites (see Spencer, 1999, 2000).

Experiences may differ as a function of identifiability. Given the importance of societal biases in determining and characterizing evocative effects, it seems inappropriate, at best, to speak of genes evoking responses; the causality could equally be attributed to societal biases—which are environmental effects. Thus, additional theoretical and methodological perspectives must be employed to clarify the nature of evocative effects.

To demonstrate a passive effect, racial minority parents may understand their children's vulnerability to racist environmental effects and may use racially relevant strategies to mitigate the impact. Parental temperament may influence their methods of transmission; for example, those who are more introverted may plan solely to use Historically Black Colleges and Universities [HBCUs] for cultural socialization. Parents who know that their response style is extremely extroverted may prefer to live in Black neighborhoods, to use cultural socialization techniques, and to use HBCUs as the major post secondary college option for their offspring. This strategy might infer parental analysis that their own children's (assumed) extroversive demeanor will evoke more positive and less racist responses from racially homogeneous environments. Thus, there may be an interaction between passive and evocative effects.

Given that a majority of Black professionals in the medical and dental fields have obtained their undergraduate instruction at HBCUs, as a research question, it would be insightful to obtain data on parental personal, childhood and adolescent childrearing strategies and post-secondary college experiences. Also, passive genetic effects (i.e., introvertive parents creating environments of solitude) are affected by social and economic opportunities available to parents and by cultural influences.

Additionally, the notion of active genetic effects assumes that individuals have the opportunity to select environments of their liking. Many economically disadvantaged youth do not have much choice in the environments they encounter. Accordingly, given low economic resources, they must learn to cope with the environments in which they live and must navigate. While these coping processes, as reactive coping strategies, may certainly reflect the genetic makeup of these youth, again it seems inappropriate to attribute causality to genetic factors. For example, let us assume that a trait such as leadership ability is highly heritable. The same individual who becomes a gang leader in one environment (which she/he played little role in creating) may become an entrepreneur in another. In either case, the individual's genetic makeup plays a significant role in the developmental outcome; yet, the respective outcomes and their consequences are quite different and dependent upon the available environments. This difference, then, is due purely to environmental factors, even though the given individual may have actively sought out leadership positions because of his/her genetic makeup.

Thus, results regarding genetic effects could easily be misinterpreted. While we have noted shortcomings, we do consider the ideas of Plomin et al. (1977) and Scarr and McCartney (1983) interesting and useful. In fact, Scarr (1988) did briefly allude to some of the same limitations, although she did not expound on them and appears to have minimized their importance. In later sections, we revisit these ideas in conjunction with the work of Bronfenbrenner (1979, 1989, 1993) and with our own proposed framework.

Another major finding in behavioral genetic research, reviewed by Plomin and Daniels (1987), is that studies show that very little variance on most psychological measures is attributable to shared family environments. Through twin and adoption designs, behavioral genetic researchers have found that most of the environmental variance on cognitive and personality measures is due to nonshared environments—the unique experiences of the individual and not the overall characteristics of the families. Nonshared influences included differential parental treatment, different relationships with peers and members outside the family, and individual experiences such as accidents or illness. Plomin and Daniels (1987) suggested that researchers should focus on differences within families rather than differences between families.

The findings Plomin and Daniels (1987) cited are certainly interesting and are considered in our proposed framework. Once again, however, the concepts and conclusions drawn from this work are oversimplified, and the terminology is misleading. Environment is not directly measured; a more appropriate terminology would refer to shared and nonshared experiences as opposed to environments (or perhaps similar and different experiences to be even more accurate). The effects of nonshared environment are confounded with measurement error (Bock & Zimowski, 1987). Also, generalizations about shared and nonshared environmental influences are drawn from rather homogeneous and limited twin and adoption studies. In her commentary on Plomin and Daniel's (1987) review, Scarr (1987) noted that families of low socioeconomic status are not included in the cited studies and that the conclusions should be qualified appropriately. Some (e.g., Jensen, 1987), however, have erroneously taken these studies to mean that only idiosyncratic experiences matter and that socioeconomic factors and cultural influences are not important in developmental outcomes.

Because of the relatively homogeneous and skewed samples of twin and adoption studies and the oversimplified conceptualization of environment, issues of social, cultural, political, and historical context are typically ignored in behavioral genetic studies. Though research in behavioral genetics is useful, it has the unfortunate potential to be misunderstood and misapplied if these broader issues are not taken into account.

EXTENDING THE BEHAVIORAL GENETIC PARADIGM: REFRAMING HERITABILITY AND ENVIRONMENT

As noted by several commentators (e.g., Bronfenbrenner & Ceci, 1993, 1994; Wachs, 1983), behavioral genetic research does not address the question of how nature and nurture interact to yield developmental outcomes. The focus on heritability and mere partitioning of variance (e.g., as shared and nonshared environments) neglects the salient processes involved in human development. It is critical to elucidate these processes to afford their application to developmental and prevention research and to interventions for the betterment of society. Accordingly, in this section, we begin to build the bridge between behavioral genetic research and a process-oriented approach to human development, focusing on Bronfenbrenner & Ceci's (1993, 1994) bioecological model and Bronfenbrenner's (1979, 1993) ecological systems theory. This analysis parallels the previous section in that the bioecological model contextualizes the concept of heritability, while ecological systems theory provides a multidimensional, dynamic, and transactional framework for examining the environment, and both shed light on the interaction of genetic and environmental influences in human development.

The Bioecological Model

Bronfenbrenner and Ceci (1994) presented four distinguishing attributes of the bioecological model. First, they defined measurable mechanisms, known as proximal processes, through which genetic influences are actualized into observable phenomena. Thus, the processes that mediate genetic and environmental influences on human development are a fundamental component of the model. Second, Bronfenbrenner and Ceci (1994) highlighted the aforementioned variability of heritability, noting that the bio-ecological model, "stipulates system variation in heritability as a joint function of proximal processes and characteristics of the environment in which these processes take place" (p. 570).

With this second feature, the bioecological model provides for a measure—heritability—which ironically is the same measure used in most behavioral genetic studies. Within the model, heritability is interpreted as the proportion of variance attributable to actualized genetic potential (Bronfenbrenner & Ceci, 1993, 1994), as opposed simply to genetic influences. Bronfenbrenner and Ceci (1994) noted that heritability can make its most important contribution in social science when researchers focus on its variability. The variation in heritability allows a linkage between heritability and developmental functioning, with the proximal processes defined in the first feature serving as the conceptual bridge between the two.

The third characteristic of the bioecological model is that it considers variation in heritability as it relates to particular developmental outcomes, and the fourth is that the model simultaneously evaluates heritability and absolute level of developmental competence. The features of Bronfenbrenner and Ceci's (1994) model are summarized in the following list.

1. Proximal processes are defined as measurable mechanisms through which genetic influences are actualized into observable phenomena (e.g., parent-child interactions).
2. Heritability is interpreted as the proportion of variance attributable to actualized genetic potential. Heritability varies as a function of proximal processes and environment.
3. Variation in heritability is considered as it relates to particular developmental outcomes.
4. Heritability and absolute level of developmental competence are evaluated simultaneously.

Bronfenbrenner and Ceci (1994) postulated that improving the quality of proximal processes will lead to both higher levels of heritability and to elevated levels of developmental functioning (Fig. 3.1). The reason for the latter is readily apparent; heritability will increase because as proximal processes improve in quality for individuals in a given population, these individuals will maximize their genetic potentials, and observed differences in the population will be due to these differing genetic potentials.

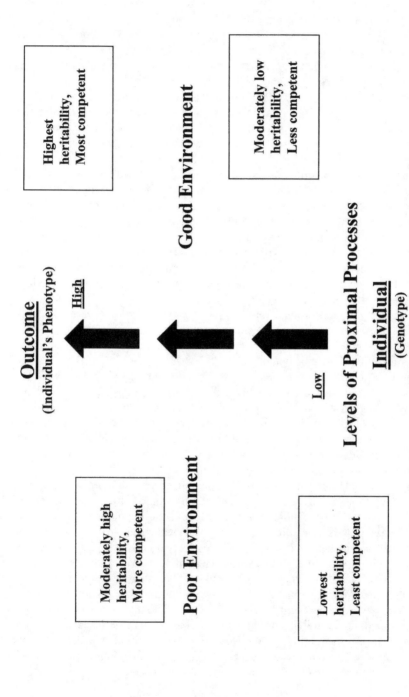

FIG. 3.1. The bioecological model. Heritability as a function of environment and proximal processes. Adapted with permission from Bronfenbrenner and Ceci (1994), Figure 3, p. 581. Copyright © 1994 by the American Psychological Association.

Bronfenbrenner and Ceci (1994) derived three propositions from their bio-ecological model, which they use to formulate hypotheses. The first proposition delineates the person-environment interaction in human development, stating that human development takes place through processes of progressively more complex reciprocal interaction between an active, evolving biopsychological human organism and the persons, objects, and symbols in its immediate environment (p. 572).

Bronfenbrenner and Ceci (1994) noted that this interaction must be consistent over time to effectively facilitate development. Consistent patterns of interaction are the proximal processes defined earlier. Examples of proximal processes include a child's interactions with parents and peers, development of competencies and problem solving skills, and acquisition of knowledge.

The second proposition of the bioecological model states that the form, power, content, and direction of the proximal processes effecting development vary systematically as a joint function of the characteristics of the developing person, of the environment—both immediate and more remote—in which the processes are taking place, and of the nature of the developmental outcomes under consideration (p. 572). With this precept, Bronfenbrenner and Ceci introduced the factors—attributes of the person and the environment and the character of developmental outcomes being analyzed—that govern proximal processes and their impact.

With the third proposition, Bronfenbrenner and Ceci (1994) restated that proximal processes transform genetic potentials into actualized outcomes (phenotypes). They noted that the factors that govern proximal processes dictate their power to actualize genetic potentials.

From these three propositions, Bronfenbrenner and Ceci (1994) derived three hypotheses. First, they restated the view, noted earlier, that effective proximal processes will increase heritability by increasing the proportion of variation attributable to actualized genetic potential. Second, they proposed that in actualizing genetic potentials, proximal processes work to both enhance competence and reduce dysfunction, increasing heritability in both cases. The implications that follow from this hypothesis are: (a) Proximal processes have more power to actualize genetic potentials for positive developmental outcomes within organized, advantaged environments than in inconsistent, disadvantaged environments, and (b) Proximal processes have more power to buffer genetic potentials for negative developmental outcomes within inconsistent, disadvantaged environments than in organized, advantaged environments. These first two hypotheses essentially state that heritability, defined in terms of variance attributable to actualized genetic potential, varies as a direct function of the quality of both proximal processes and the environment. Bronfenbrenner and Ceci's (1994) third hypothesis is that proximal processes have a greater ability to actualize genetic potentials for positive developmental outcomes for individuals living in more inconsistent and disadvantaged environments if interventions (e.g., Head Start) are provided that: 1. Supply additional developmental resources, and 2. Enhance proximal processes beyond what is experienced in other settings.

Bronfenbrenner and Ceci (1994) cited a few studies that they interpret as supporting their first two hypotheses (Fischbein, 1980; Riksen-Walraven, 1978; Scarr-Salapatek, 1971), and they noted the obvious implications for intervention of the third hypothesis, which is derived from the first two. The authors, however, also note that the model still needs to be tested extensively.

Ecological Systems Theory

While the bioecological model lays out the relationship between genetic influences, heritability, and proximal processes as they take place in particular environments, ecological systems theory (Bronfenbrenner, 1979, 1989, 1993) focuses on characterizing levels of environmental influence in terms of dynamic, interactive, systems of person-environment relationships (Fig. 3.2). Ecological systems theory is organized hierarchically, involving interactive systems of increasing complexity embedded in the framework of human development. Bronfenbrenner (1979, 1993) began by transforming Lewin's (1935) formulation that behavior is a coupled function of the person and the environment; he substituted development for behavior, stating that development is also a function of the person and the environment over time.

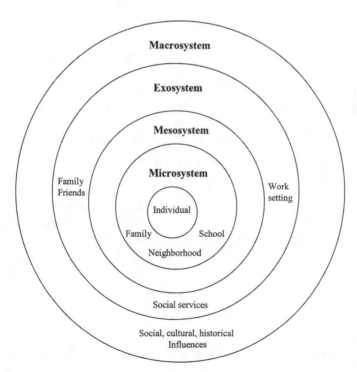

FIG. 3.2. Bronfenbrenner's ecological systems theory. Levels of context that impact human development (Bronfenbrenner, 1989, 1993).

Also noted is the temporal contingence of developmental function; each successive developmental period is dependent on all previous periods of development.

Bronfenbrenner (1993) noted that through most of developmental psychology, theoretical constructs devised to describe the characteristics of the person have not considered issues of context; developmental qualities of individuals are conceived without reference to the environments in which they are occurring (see Table 3.2). Examples of such qualities include standardized psychological measures such as personality and IQ tests. This type of analysis reflects the personal attributes model (Bronfenbrenner, 1989) and has a narrow focus on the individual, assuming that findings from standardized measures can be generalized without attention to context. Bronfenbrenner (1993) questioned the assumptions of environment generalizability that underlie the personal attributes model; he did recognize that these standardized measures are useful, but he argued that research designs must simultaneously consider issues of social, cultural, and historical context and incorporate context-oriented measures.

Conversely, the social address model (Bronfenbrenner, 1989), which is the most common approach, considers only environmental factors, such as social class, family size, and other demographic variables. The specific characteristics of

TABLE 3.2
Types of Theoretical Models in Human Development

Type of Model	Description	Shortcomings
Personal attributes model	Focus on definition and measurement of individual characteristics.	Ignores effects of context; assumes generalizability.
Social address model	Focus on demographic characteristics (e.g. Social class, family size, etc.).	Ignores impact of specific contextual characteristics and activities within particular environments.
Person-context model	Examines both individual and context.	Does not delineate developmental processes.
Process-person-context model	Highlights variability within developmental processes as a function of the person and the environment.	N.A.

Note. From "Ecological Systems Theory," by U. Bronfenbrenner, 1989, *Annals of Child Development,* pp. 187–248.

the environment, activities that occur in particular environments, and the impact of these activities on individuals are all neglected in the social address model (Bronfenbrenner & Crouter, 1983). The person-context model examines both the individual and the context but does not analyze the processes involved in development. This model is able to specify ecological niches (Bronfenbrenner, 1989), but it does not delineate the processes by which developmental outcomes are attained.

Bronfenbrenner's (1979, 1989, 1993) ecological systems theory, in contrast, is a process-person-context model that, like the bioecological model, highlights variability within developmental processes as a function of the characteristics of the person and the environment.

Ecological systems theory is organized in terms of four levels of environment that mediate person-environment interaction: microsystem, mesosystem, exosystem, and macrosystem. The first level of Bronfenbrenner's model, the microsystem, involves the interaction of the person with the immediate social and physical environment; examples include home, family, and school settings. All of the levels of environmental influence are filtered through microsystems, where actual experiences take place. Proximal processes, earlier defined in the bioecological model as the mechanisms through which genetic influences are actualized into observable phenomena (Bronfenbrenner & Ceci, 1994), are essentially patterns of person-environment interactions within microsystems; these change during the development of the person (Bronfenbrenner, 1979, 1989, 1993). The mesosystem describes interactions between the various microsystems in a person's life; it essentially constitutes the network of interpersonal relationships that overlap across the various settings. The exosystem entails more distal influences, including the structure of the community where the person resides and settings where the person is not directly involved. Finally, the macrosystem is comprised of the larger societal institutions, such as government, economy, media, and so forth, which lay the social and historical context for development (Bronfenbrenner, 1979, 1989, 1993).

Ecological systems theory provides a dynamic, contextually sensitive framework from which to analyze environments and gene-environment interactions. It can be applied to shed light on behavioral genetic theorizing noted earlier. For example, to the extent that they can occur, the active and passive effects of gene-environment correlation noted earlier (Plomin et al., 1977; Scarr & McCartney, 1983) primarily involve the lower levels of the model. Individuals may have some ability to shape their own environments and those of their relatives (perhaps based on their genetic makeups) at the level of the microsystem, and perhaps even at the mesosystem. However, individuals are by definition not involved in their exosystems of development, and notwithstanding a few extraordinary examples (e.g., Dr. Martin Luther King and Mahatma Gandhi), few can influence the macrosystem. Broad, societal influences such as structural racism (Spencer, Harpalani, & Dell' Angelo, 2002) and racial stereotyping (Harpalani, 1999) are filtered through macrosystems to impact the development and experiences of minority youth; regardless of their genetic makeup, individuals can do little to eliminate these factors. Even more mundane situations of stress—such as being ignored in commercial venues (e.g., not provided service) or followed in a store and are experienced as cumulative "microoppression," can have a significant impact on stigmatized groups such as African Americans (e.g., Carroll, 1998).

In addition to the uncontrollable effects of the macrosystem and their impact on everyday experiences, the ability to shape immediate environments is limited for many youth. For example, Stevenson (1997) describes how African American youth are "missed" and "dissed" by mainstream American society, and how this treatment in conjunction with neighborhood factors relates to African American youth becoming "pissed" while managing their anger. Black youth are "missed" as stereotypical media-based images distort the meanings of their social and affective displays—usually in negative terms. Hence, these unique cultural displays are devalued and viewed with insolence—dissed. These are effects of the macrosystem that cannot be regulated by individuals. In conjunction with these misrepresentations, many Black youth reside in high-risk contexts where anger display may be an appropriate coping mechanism. Anger may indeed become a form of competence for social and emotional viability in certain high-risk contexts, such as neighborhoods, which are microsystems. These displays may also be misconstrued or constitute inappropriate behavior in other microsystems, such as school settings. Hence, misrepresentation, disrespect, and hazardous contextual factors at various ecological levels interact in creating the anger of Black youth (i.e., pissed). Phelan, Davidson, and Cao (1991) also discuss how dissonance between various microsystems—hence at the level of the mesosystem, can impinge on resiliency and healthy development.

Before moving on to present our phenomenological variant of Bronfenbrenner's (1979, 1989, 1993) ecological systems theory, it may be useful to consider the role of the genotype in ecological systems theory. Ecological systems theory focused on delineating environmental influences rather than genetic influences. The genotype (i.e., genetic makeup), is an implicit component that Bronfenbrenner obviously considers but does not identify explicitly in his model. This is probably because the genotype involves only the person and not person-environment interaction; it is not changed by environmental influences. Indeed, focus on the genotype in part leads behavioral geneticists to often take a rather static view of human development. However, the important component in development is not the genotype itself, but rather its expression (i.e., phenotype). The expression of the genotype is dependent on environmental interaction, and this expression cannot be determined accurately without observing the particular genotype being expressed in the given environment (Gottlieb, 1995). Therefore, while the genotype is an important and measurable component in developmental analysis, its expression (and thus its true impact) should be considered in conjunction with environmental influences and developmental processes.

PHENOMENOLOGICAL VARIANT OF ECOLOGICAL SYSTEMS THEORY: A PROCESS-ORIENTED MODEL TO ANALYZE NATURE–NURTURE INTERACTION IN HUMAN DEVELOPMENT

Bronfenbrenner's (1979, 1989, 1993) ecological systems theory provides an ideal tool to describe and examine the effects of various levels of social, cultural, political, and historical context on human development. Bronfenbrenner (1979, 1989, 1993; Bronfenbrenner & Ceci, 1993, 1994) also denotes proximal processes as mechanisms by which genotypes are transformed into phenotypes; this occurs through patterns of interactions within microsystems that involve both the genetic makeup of individuals and the various layers of contextual influences described earlier.

With the Phenomenological Variant of Ecological Systems Theory (PVEST; Spencer, 1995), we integrate a phenomenological perspective with Bronfenbrenner's ecological systems theory (1989), linking context with life course identity formation. In doing so, we extend the bioecological/ecological systems paradigm of nature–nurture interaction in two ways. First, PVEST centers on describing individual identity formation unfolding over time rather than on context. Although both our work and that of Bronfenbrenner (1979, 1989, 1993) and Bronfenbrenner and Ceci (1993, 1994) take into account issues of identity formation and context, we believe that our focus on describing identity formation in a life course framework allows for a more comprehensive explanation of human development. Second, in the PVEST model, we delineate several developmental processes, in addition to the proximal processes described in the bioecological model and ecological systems theory, which facilitate identity formation and human development. Each of these processes involves gene-environment interaction, with a focus on how individuals make meaning of their experiences in context.

Thus, PVEST utilizes an Identity-focused Cultural Ecological (ICE) perspective, integrating issues of social, historical, and cultural context with individual human development (see Spencer 1995; Spencer, Dupree, & Hartmann, 1997; Dupree, Spencer, & Bell 1997). Though Scarr (1988) correctly argued that "the phenomenology of experiences is ... correlated with the genotype of the individual perceiver and processor" (p. 241), we believe that this view is far too simplistic; in the mold of much of the behavioral genetic research we have reviewed, it is an accurate but oversimplified statement. We submit that delineating the processes involved, rather than a mere statement of obvious correlation, is necessary for an understanding of nature–nurture interaction in human development. In fact, a fuller understanding of process and context is necessary to understand how the genotype impacts development. As such, our treatment of the genotype is similar to Bronfenbrenner's; it is an important and influential aspect of human development, however, it is the expression of the genotype, in context, that is actually a component of the developmental system.

Components of PVEST

As a systems theory, PVEST consists of five components linked by bi-directional processes (Fig. 3.3); it is a cyclic, recursive, temporally contingent model that describes identity development throughout the life course. The first component, net risk/vulnerability level, consists of linked factors that may either buffer against or predispose individuals to a particular vulnerability level to adverse outcomes. Risks include genetic makeup and maturational processes, family structure, socioeconomic conditions such as poverty, sociocultural expectations such as race, sex and gender stereotypes, assumptions of privilege (or their absence), sociohistorical processes including racial subordination and discrimination, and myriad other contextual factors. The risks, of course, may be offset by protective factors that can potentially buffer the individual (e.g., nurturing families, cultural capital, "just" social policies). In fact, the genotype may be viewed as series of risk contributors and protective factors, with two critical caveats: (a) The exact components of the genotype that predispose and/or buffer individuals from adverse outcomes may vary with context; and (b) The genotype itself is not bidirectionally influenced; it does not change with new experiences (although gene expression, which as noted is the actual variable in the developmental system, does change with context).

Linking risk contributors and protective factors with actual experiences are proximal processes, which in our model are defined in essentially the same way that Bronfenbrenner (1979, 1989, 1993) and Bronfenbrenner and Ceci (1993, 1994) used them. Proximal processes actualize genotypes into observable phenomena and are patterns of interaction in the immediate settings of development. Thus, they link risk contributors and protective factors with net stress engagement, the second component of PVEST. The level of net stress engagement refers to the actual net experience of situations which challenge one's psychosocial identity as well as psychological and physical well-being; these are essentially risk contributors that are actually encountered and manifested as challenges in everyday life and may be offset or balanced by available supports. Experiences of discrimination, violence, and negative feedback are salient stressors for minority youth, while adult supports can serve as protective factors for these experiences. On the other hand, for European American youth, assumptions of privilege may interfere with healthy development in an increasingly diverse America (see Spencer et al., 2001). Cultural pluralist parental socialization strategies, instead, might serve as a protective factor for such youth. Net stress engagement is impacted not only by genetic propensities but also by the layers of contextual factors described in ecological systems theory.

The encounter of stress facilitates primary (reactive) coping processes, and reactive coping methods, the third component of PVEST, and are employed to resolve dissonance-producing situations. Normative cognitive maturation makes awareness of dissonance unavoidable and acute. Primary (reactive) coping processes are immediate or in the moment responses that include strategies to solve

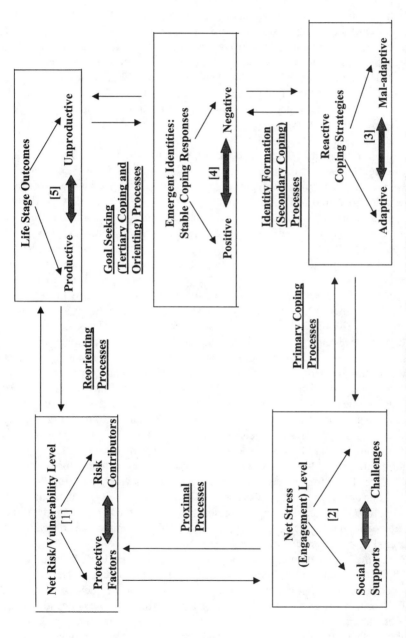

FIG. 3.3. Spencer's Phenomenological Variant of Ecological Systems Theory (PVEST). Cyclic integration of context, experience, coping, identity, outcomes, and the processes of human development.

71

problems that can lead both to either adaptive or maladaptive solutions. In addition, a solution may be adaptive in one context, such as neighborhood, and maladaptive in another, such as school (see Stevenson, 1997). Or for others, because of consistency of experience across settings (i.e., maximized self-context fit), psychic energy is preserved and available for proactive use (e.g., academic "on task" behavior is enhanced). Again, coping methods are influenced by genetic factors such as temperamental traits, but these are filtered through the actual experiences of stress and the supports that are available to deal with this stress. As particular stresses and supports may be present or lacking in particular contexts of development, the observed expressions of genotype, manifested as coping responses, may vary across contexts.

Self-appraisal is a key factor in coping and identity, and how individuals view themselves depends on their perceptions of contextual conditions, expectations, and processes. As coping strategies are employed, self-appraisal continues, and those strategies yielding desirable results for the ego are preserved. Accordingly, through identity formation (as secondary coping) processes, stable coping responses develop, and coupled together yield emergent identities—the fourth component of PVEST. Emergent identities provide psychosocial stability across time and space and, thus, define how individuals view themselves within and between their various contextual experiences as manifested across the life course. This process is also influenced by genetic makeup, filtered not only through particular experiences of stress and available supports, but also through coupling of primary (reactive) coping responses across various contexts. The combination of cultural/ethnic identity, sex role understanding, self and peer appraisal, and other factors (e.g., primary language competencies and immigration status), all combine to define individual identity, including sense of efficacy.

Identity lays the foundation for future perception and behavior, such as goal seeking, as one copes with and engages the environment in the pursuit of competence and a sense of efficacy. Goal seeking processes continue along with ongoing (tertiary) coping processes that lead to adverse or productive life-stage outcomes, the fifth component of PVEST. Productive outcomes include good health, positive relationships, and self-efficacy, while adverse outcomes include poor health, incarceration, low competence, and self-destructive behavior. Most studies of the nature–nurture issue tend to link genotype directly with life stage outcomes, neglecting the coping and identity processes that mediate the two. Again, the influence of genotype is apparent throughout the PVEST framework; however, it is mediated by ongoing developmental processes.

As a function of the particular stage of development, each life stage outcome yields new risk contributors, stressors, and so forth, which occur through reorienting processes as individuals move through the next phase of development. The PVEST framework recycles and recourses through the life course as individuals balance these new risks against protective factors, engage new stress levels, given challenges potentially offset by supporters, try different coping strategies, and redefine how they and others view themselves.

New genetic influences are also encountered with maturation, and the expression of the genotype also changes with the impact of previous experiences, coping, identity formation, goal seeking, and reorienting. For example, the expression of personality traits, which usually has a genetic component, will yield different behaviors depending on the situation encountered and the impact of events and developmental processes in the previous developmental cycle. Thus, though the genotype remains the same, its expression may change with context and developmental history.

Implications and Applications of PVEST in Research on the Nature–Nurture Question

PVEST has several implications for findings in behavioral genetic research. The life-course framework readily allows an analysis of nature–nurture interactions and suggests possibilities for further elucidating the mechanisms involved in creating individual differences. For example, with PVEST, one can readily examine Plomin and Daniel's (1987) question of why siblings are so different. Plomin and Daniel's (1987) noted that this is due to nonshared environment, and utilizing the PVEST can shed light on how nonshared experiences of siblings can yield different coping strategies that lead to differential identity formation processes and outcomes. This creates varying sets of risk factors, as divergence continues through the lifespan. Thus, PVEST is an ideal theoretical tool to clarify the specific factors and processes involved in non-shared environment.

PVEST also shows both the validity and limitation of Scarr and McCartney's (1983; Scarr, 1988) theory of genotype causality of environment. The impact of genetic influences is apparent at every level of PVEST but only in conjunction with numerous other factors, including varying phenomenological processes, experiences of stress, available support, and developmental history. PVEST can also aid the identification of other factors, such as race and ethnicity, which shape experiences encountered between groups and, thus, should be considered when analyzing how people "make their own environments." Some individuals and groups have many more options in this realm than others, and ignoring or minimizing this fact will only lead to more misunderstanding and misinterpretation of evidence. The very framing of the issue as analyzing how people make their own environment, given unaddressed discrimination practices and stereotypes, only exaggerates between-group tensions and unacknowledged environmental hazards. The main point here is that the major role of social, cultural, political, and historical contexts in development must be considered. PVEST provides an identity-focused cultural ecological (ICE) perspective that readily affords the necessary integration and analysis as mediating processes.

Also, by using a process-oriented approach and adding several developmental processes to Bronfenbrenner's work, we hope to not only elucidate human development but also to suggest multiple points for intervention and prevention opportunities. Application of PVEST can help the identification of resiliency-promoting factors for vulnerable youth and demonstrate how these factors fit into a developmental, life course framework (Spencer, Harpalani, & Dell' Angelo, 2002). Moreover, with the integration of various biological, contextual, and support variables, in conjunction with developmental history, PVEST can help identify profiles of resiliency and vulnerability for individuals with different characteristics and from different backgrounds.

Ultimately, with the completion of the Human Genome Project, variation at specified genetic loci and the interaction of these loci, rather than behavioral genetic designs such as twin and adoption studies, will be used to investigate the nature–nurture question. PVEST can readily accommodate this advance, as particular alleles can be treated as risk contributors and/or protective factors within the framework. These can be studied in conjunction with other risk and protective factors and relevant experiences of stress and support to see how these factors combine to yield coping strategies and facilitate identity formation and life outcomes. Moreover, in line with Gottlieb's (1995) suggestion, rather than making generalizations about the expression of genotypes across environmental settings, PVEST allows genotype expression to be analyzed within particular contexts. This kind of analysis can also be applied to test Bronfenbrenner and Ceci's (1994) hypotheses regarding the variability of heritability across environments.

CONCLUSION

With the PVEST framework, we have attempted to provide a process-oriented model, using an identity-focused cultural ecological (ICE) perspective, to shed light on the question of "How?" posed by Anastasi (1958) and Bronfenbrenner and Ceci (1993). Our model is structured in terms of the actual human life course and takes into account both the genetic makeup of individuals and the particular contexts in which development occurs. Moreover, our focus on process speaks directly to the question of how nature and nurture interact in human development.

Kurt Lewin once asserted, "There is nothing so practical as a good theory." Human development has long needed a theoretical framework from which to test ideas but which is also flexible enough to accommodate the vast diversity in contexts and identity formation that characterize the human experience. We believe that PVEST can provide such a model for human development, both in theory and in practice. An examination of the "How?" question is a critical step in this process.

ACKNOWLEDGMENT

Resources for the preparation of this draft were awarded to the first author from NIMH, OERI/FIS, NSF, and the Ford and Kellogg Foundations, and to the second author from the Spencer Foundation.

REFERENCES

Anastasi, A. (1958). Heredity, environment, and the question "How?" *Psychological Review, 65,* 197–208.

Block, N. (1995). How heritability misleads about race. *Cognition, 56,* 99–128.

Bock, R. D., & Zimowski, M. F. (1987). Contributions of the biometrical approach to individual differences in personality measures. *Behavioral and Brain Sciences, 10*(1), 17–18.

Bronfenbrenner, U. (1979). *The ecology of human development: Experiments by nature and design.* Cambridge, MA: Harvard University Press.

Bronfenbrenner, U. (1989). Ecological systems theory. In R. Vasta (Ed.), *Annals of Child Development* (pp. 187–248). Greenwich, CT: JAI Press.

Bronfenbrenner, U. (1993). The ecology of cognitive development: Research models and findings. In R. H. Wozniak & K. W. Fischer (Eds.), *Development in context: Acting and thinking in specific environments* (pp. 3–44). Hillsdale, NJ: Lawrence Erlbaum Associates.

Bronfenbrenner, U., & Ceci, S. J. (1993). Heredity, environment, and the question "How?"—A first approximation. In R. Plomin & G. E. McClearn (Eds.), *Nature, nurture, and psychology* (pp. 313–324). Washington, DC: American Psychological Association.

Bronfenbrenner, U., & Ceci, S. J. (1994). Nature–nurture reconceptualized in developmental perspective: A bioecological model. *Psychological review, 101*(4), 568–586.

Bronfenbrenner, U., & Crouter, A. C. (1983). The evolution of environmental models in developmental research. In P. H. Mussen (Series Ed.) & W. Kessen (Vol. Ed.), *Handbook of child psychology: Vol. 4. History, theory, and methods* (pp. 357–414). New York: Wiley.

Carroll, G. (1998). Mundane extreme environmental stress and African American families: A case for recognizing different realities. *Journal of Comparative Family Studies, 29*(2), 271–283.

Dannefer, D. (1992). On the conceptualization of context in developmental discourse: Four meanings of context and their implications. In D. L. Featherman, R. M. Lerner, & M. Perlmutter (Eds.), *Life-span development and behavior.* Hillsdale, NJ: Lawrence Erlbaum Associates.

Deater-Deckard, K., Fulker, D. W., & Plomin, R. (1999). A genetic study of family environment in the transition to early adolescence. *Journal of Child Psychology and Psychiatry, 40*(5), 769–775.

Dupree, D., Spencer, M. B., & Bell, S. (1997). The ecology of African-American child development: Normative and non-normative outcomes. In G. Johnson-Powell & Y. Yamamoto (Eds.), *Transcultural child psychiatry: A portrait of America's children* (pp. 237–268). New York: Wiley.

Fischbein, S. (1980). IQ and social class. *Intelligence, 4,* 51–63.

Gabbay, F. H. (1992). Behavior-genetic strategies in the study of emotion. *Psychological Science, 3*(1), 50–55.

Gottlieb, G. (1995). Some conceptual deficiencies in "developmental" behavior genetics. *Human Development, 38,* 131–141.

Harpalani, V. (1999). *Research on racial stereotyping: Developmental consequences and considerations.* Unpublished manuscript, University of Pennsylvania, Philadelphia, PA.

Herrnstein, R. J., & Murray, C. (1994). *The bell curve: Intelligence and class structure in American life.* New York, NY: Free Press.

Jensen, A. R. (1969). How much can we boost IQ and scholastic achievement? *Harvard Educational Review, 39,* 1–123.

Jensen, A. R. (1987). Unconfounding genetic and nonshared environmental effects. *Behavioral and Brain Sciences, 10*(1), 26–27.

Lewin, K. (1935). *A dynamic theory of personality.* New York: McGraw-Hill.

O'Connor, T. G., Deater-Deckard, K., Fulker, D., Rutter, M., & Plomin, R. (1998). Genotype-environment correlations in late childhood and early adolescence: Antisocial behavioral problems and coercive parenting. *Developmental Psychology, 34*(5), 970–981.

Phelan, P., Davidson, A. L., & Cao, H. T. (1991). Students' multiple worlds: Negotiating the boundaries of family, peer, and school cultures. *Anthropology & Education Quarterly, 22,* 224–250.

Plomin, R. (1990). *Nature and nurture: An introduction to human behavioral genetics.* Pacific Grove, CA: Brooks/Cole Publishing Company.

Plomin, R. (1996). Beyond nature versus nature. In L. L. Hall (Ed.), *Genetics and mental illness: Evolving issues for research and society* (pp. 29–50). New York: Plenum Press.

Plomin, R., & Daniels, D. (1987). Why are children in the same family so different from one another? *Behavioral and Brain Sciences, 10*(1), 1–60.

Plomin, R., DeFries, J. C., & Loehlin, J. C. (1977). Genotype-environment interaction and correlation in the analysis of human behavior. *Psychological Bulletin, 84,* 309–322.

Plomin, R., DeFries, J. C., McClearn, G. E., & McGuffin, P. (2001). *Behavioral genetics.* New York: Worth Publishers.

Reiss, D. (2001). *Genes, family subsystems and adjustment.* Paper presented at Brown University Center for Study of Human Development conference, "Genetic Influences on Human Behavior and Development," Providence, RI.

Riksen-Walraven, J. M. (1978). Effects of caregiver behavior on habituation rate and self-efficacy in infants. *International Journal of Behavioral Development, 1,* 105–130.

Scarr, S. (1987). Distinctive genotypes depend on genotypes. *Behavioral and Brain Sciences, 10*(1), 38–39.

Scarr, S. (1988). How genotypes and environments combine: Developmental and individual differences. In N. Bolger, A. Capsi, G. Downey, & M. Moorehouse (Eds.), *Persons in context: Developmental processes* (pp. 217–244). New York: Cambridge University Press.

Scarr, S., & McCartney, K. (1983). How people make their own environments: A theory of genotype-environment effects. *Child Development, 54,* 424–435.

Scarr-Salapatek, S. (1971). Race, social class, and IQ. *Science, 174,* 1285–1295.

Spencer, M. B. (1995). Old issues and new theorizing about African American Youth: A phenomenological variant of ecological systems theory. In R. L. Taylor (Ed.), *Black youth: Perspectives on their status in the United States* (pp. 37–70). Westport, CT: Praeger.

Spencer, M. B. (1999). Social and cultural influences on school adjustment: The application of an identity-focused cultural ecological perspective. *Educational Psychologist, 34,* 1, 43–57.

Spencer, M. B. (2000). Identity, achievement orientation and race: "Lessons learned" about the normative developmental experiences of African American males. In W. Watkins, J. Lewis, & V. Chou (Eds.), *Race and education* (pp. 100–127). Needham Heights, MA: Allyn & Bacon.

Spencer, M. B., Dupree, D., & Hartmann, T. (1997). A phenomenological variant of ecological systems theory (PVEST): A self-organization perspective in context. *Development and Psychopathology, 9,* 817–833.

Spencer, M. B., Harpalani, V., & Dell' Angelo, T. (2002). Structural racism and community health: A theory-driven model for identity intervention. In W. Allen, M. B. Spencer, & C. O'Connor (Eds.), *New perspectives on African American education: Race, achievement, and social inequality* (pp. 259–282). Oxford, UK.: Elsevier Science.

Spencer, M. B., Silver, L. J., Seaton, G., Tucker, S. R., Cunningham, M., & Harpalani, V. (2001). Race and gender influences on teen parenting: An identity-focused cultural-ecological perspective. In T. Urdan & F. Pajares (Eds.), *Adolescence and Education* (Vol. I, pp. 231–268). Greenwich, CT: Information Age Publishers.

Stevenson, H. C. (1997). "Missed, Dissed, and Pissed": Making meaning of neighborhood risk, fear and anger management in urban Black youth. *Cultural Diversity and Mental Health, 3*(1), 37–52.

Turkheimer, E. (1998). Heritability and biological explanation. *Psychological Review, 105*(4), 782–791.

Turkheimer, E., & Gottesman, I. I. (1991). Is $H^2 = 0$ a null hypothesis anymore? *Behavioral and Brain Sciences, 14*(3), 410–411.

Van Oers, B. (1998). From context to contextualizing. *Learning and Instruction, 8*(6), 473–488.

Wachs, T. (1983). The use and abuse of environment in behavior-genetic research. *Child Development, 54,* 396–407.

4 Commentary

Anne Fausto-Sterling
Brown University

The interests that bring me to this topic include my own training and background in developmental biology, that is, the development of embryos from fertilization to birth, and my interest in systems theory and questions of embodiment, which come from the work I've done on two aspects of gender. My interests in gender can, in turn, be subdivided into the individual and the institutional. Individual aspects of gender often include the development of what people call sex differences. I define these as the set of cultural attributes or overlapping, but somewhat average, differences that appear between boys and girls and men and women as they work their way through the life cycle. Thinking institutionally about sex differences, however, leads me to examine how those characteristics emerge in the context of gender as many feminist theorists define gender—as a set of power relationships and a set of cultural attributes. So, gender has multiple meanings, which require definition at the beginning of any interdisciplinary discussion of the topic. Unless we make clear how we are using the word, there is enormous slippage from one level of social organization to another.

Gender has to do with power dynamics, and it can have expression in economics and the law as Felton Earls suggested in the context of his own work. Gender can have cultural expressions. Feminist humanists study these cultural expressions—for example, the portrayal of women and men in advertisements or on television. But, interestingly, a particular style of portrayal can have effects at the level of what one might call embodiment. The images, for example, of models or movie actresses or TV stars have changed over a period of years from the more voluptuous mode to the more anorexic mode; accompanying this change one finds 5-year-old girls who are saying that their legs are too fat. How do we move from

79

that set of cultural images to individual body images? How do children incorporate such changing ideals of beauty? That is an aspect of embodiment that I think about in the course of my work that is relevant to the discussions presented here.

Another path that has drawn me to questions of systems theory concerns the various explanations of human sexuality, including the development of sexual identity and sexual orientation, and somewhat separately, questions of sexual behavior. In the arena of sexuality studies, theories range from heavy reliance on biological explanations to almost exclusive reliance on cultural interactions. In between, we find what sometimes gets called psychology or "the mind." None of these theoretical approaches are innocent. For example, what you believe about the development of sexual orientation can be very important if you're trying to overturn a statute in the state of Colorado that suggests that homosexuals do not have or ought not to have the right to certain kinds of protection under the law. In this example, biodeterminist arguments are marshalled to support gay rights, while cultural determinists on the religious right maintain that sexuality is a matter of choice and, thus, justly subject to the moral condemnation of certain religious groups.

As I've thought about work on sexuality and gender, and, as I've particularly tried to join my background in biology with my cultural, feminist analysis of human development, I find myself turning and more and more to a systems approach to understanding what's happening. I began to outline these interests in my most recent book, *Sexing the Body: Gender Politics and the Construction of Sexuality* (Fausto-Sterling, 2000). My stance toward both 100% biological and 100% psychological models of the development of gender, gender identity, human sexuality, and sexual identity has been pretty antagonistic. The argument has all too often been posed in a dualistic fashion. It's unfortunate that psychologists, who have worked on questions of development of gender, gender identity, sex roles, and so forth seem divided into two camps. On one side, some maintain a rigid culturalist point of view. This contrasts with others who think of themselves as biopsychologists. Biopsychologists argue, more or less, that all sex differences and gender attributes emerge as a result of differential prenatal exposures to certain kinds of hormone. I believe that both positions are impoverished in some pretty deep ways and that they both provide caricatures of one another. Biological psychologists present caricatures of feminist positions, while feminists present caricatures of biological positions.

I would like us to find a way out of this unproductive conflict. One of the things I'd like us to think about is the way in which certain concepts we employ are interrelated but not quite the same. First, let's think through the idea of a systems theory or a systems approach to development (and by development I mean everything from the moment of fertilization until death). Second, let's think about process oriented explanations. As noted in several of the chapters, the process oriented investigator tries to figure out how something comes into being rather than how much of statistical variance is explained by a certain component. Process orientation seems to me of most interest if we're trying to understand the development of human behaviors, both ones we think are good and ones we think are maladaptive. Third, let's talk about embodiment (as discussed in several chapters in this book). Overton showed us a drawing by M. C. Escher of two hands drawing each other to illustrate looking at a relational concept. The Escher prints that most represent how I understand systems theories are the ones in which he does multiple animals. Escher represents two or three kinds of animals in repetitions across the woodcut. If one looks, one sees, for example, swans flying, and then, if one looks differently, one sees fish. The border of the swan is also the border of the fish. I like these woodcuts because they represent repeated elements in which each element is formed by the other. If the shape of the swan is changed, so too is the shape of the fish. If we think about nature and nurture as each being 100%, organisms are 100% nature and 100% nurture. Just as when Escher changes the outline of the swan and, therefore, automatically alters the fish, changing either nature or nurture reverberates in the entire system. I think it is interesting that a number of us have turned to this one artist who has provided a way to visualize some of the ideas that we're thinking about.

With the above background, let me pose six questions: First what are the research programs that are implied, especially from the more theoretical chapters by Lerner and Spencer? Luckily, I think that we have one beautiful, very specific example in Stephen Suomi's chapter. His work shows one way in which a research program might cash out from a developmental systems perspective. Although I think it's one quite exciting way, it's not the only way, because research progress will depend on what phenomena we are interested in studying in the first place. We need to think how to develop specific research programs that directly test the interplay between genes and environment. We're all in this because we want to understand something better, and if we don't have a research program, we won't have a future for this approach to looking at the world.

For the second question, I would also like to ask the reader to contrast and/or unpack the concepts of embodiment and compare them with concepts from developmental systems theories. The concept of embodiment (see Overton's chapter) is not exactly the same thing as developmental systems theory, and yet the same sorts of people tend to talk about these two sets of concepts. I would like us to think a little bit more about how they relate to one another and how they're different and also how they might be implemented in similar or different ways in terms of research programs.

The third question, and this is a really big one but I think it's one that requires some serious strategic thought, is: How might we integrate research programs with different perspectives from different disciplines, focused on different dimensions of organization, from the cellular to the legal and economic? Furthermore, how do we work at the interstices or the intersections of different levels of analyses and find areas of linkage? We can see in Stephen Suomi's chapter an example of the movement from studies at the subcellular level to studies at the level of social organization. In studies of humans, we might be talking about everything from the legal system to the frontal lobe.

But we are not all equally expert at studying everything all at once. And, it seems to me that projects must be developed collaboratively. We should combine the expertise of a cultural critic, a psychologist, and a molecular biologist. That is not an easy task, but it seems critically important. Although I don't believe that every research project need always be completely integrative, I do think that really good research that's within a particular level of organization (such as molecular biology) needs to be connected to other research projects done at other levels of organization (such as psychosocial behavior). Think again of those intersecting circles. How can we make this happen? Do we need experts who are able to translate between groups? Do we need institutes like the Santa Fe Institute, which looks at the operation of complex systems at a variety of different levels but mostly by computational and mathematical approaches? How can we implant avenues of interdisciplinary collaboration as a structure into our psychology departments, or our education departments, or our molecular biology departments? If we're really going to begin to understand how an individual develops throughout a lifetime, then we need to integrate everything from what's going on inside the cell to what's going on in the legal system, then we need to think about how to collaborate and integrate. That's a big challenge.

My fourth question is about developmental systems theory. Obviously, developmental systems theory is one of those phrases that is applied in all sorts of different settings. It is used in the field of international relations by economists who are studying sales, by neuroscientists, and by evolutionary biologists (among others). In each case, it's a way of thinking about large, complex systems. Do systems that operate at different levels of organization have different functional or lawful characteristics? In other words, if we're interested as theorists in the laws under which systems operate, are different kinds of systems governed by different kinds of laws? Or, do we have to think about shifting gears each time we change levels of organization? When we ask how the image of an ultrathin actress becomes embodied as an ideal of beauty in the minds (and eating habits) of teenage girls, are we asking about the same metaprocess as when we try think about a cell—a collection of 100 or a 1,000 genes pumping out their gene products all at once and coming up with some specific, stable differentiated state? These are equally complex systems, but can they be explained on the basis of the same general laws? Can we use the same logic, the same thought processes to understand them?

My fifth question is can we have general accounts of psychology or, if we're talking about process oriented explanations, do we end up with the same number of accounts as there are individual people in the world? In other words, does every individual develop differently or are there ways to generalize? I have wrestled with this question in terms of theories of development of sexual orientation, because most attempts to theorize sexual orientation are attempts to generalize, and they are ones that generally wipe out differences of individual experience. I haven't been able to think of a way out of this quandary except to say that the specific paths that lead to a particular adult sexual orientation at a particular time in one's life cycle have got to differ to some degree for every individual. The question is: Does that conclusion make it impossible to have a general theory for the development of different forms of sexuality?

Finally, I want to challenge everyone to ask who's going to start applying these ideas to the development of gender and sexual identities. It seems to me that developmental psychologists interested in developmental systems approaches shy away from addressing the question of the development of sex differences. Historically, more social psychologists have studied this issue but have not taken advantage of the exciting potential in the kind of work that's been presented here. I urge people who have the kind of imagination that allows them to apply dynamic systems theory to development to think about how it would cash out in terms of the development of boys and girls and men and women. That does mean getting mired into areas where one might get accused of being politically incorrect, and obviously, I've been down this road myself. But if we stay away from it for fear of stepping on toes or for fear of being politically incorrect, we leave the field open mostly to those who, from my point of view, *are* politically incorrect. Therefore, I challenge everyone here to begin thinking with all of the important ideas that they've presented about how these ideas could be applied in constructive ways to understanding the development of gender, sexuality, and sexual expression.

REFERENCES

Fausto-Sterling, A. (2000). *Sexing the Body: Gender Politics and the Construction of Sexuality.* New York: Basic Books.

5 Normally Occurring Environmental and Behavioral Influences on Gene Activity: From Central Dogma to Probabilistic Epigenesis

Gilbert Gottlieb
University of North Carolina at Chapel Hill

The new discipline of the genetics of behaviour, to judge by some recent books, is caught in the dogmas of Mendelian genetics without regard to developments in modern genetics during the last ten years, and to modern experimental approaches to the genetic roots of behaviour. Books on the subject usually begin with an account of the principles of Mendelian genetics. The material on behaviour deals mainly with mutated animals and their observed changes in behaviour. That is exactly what genetic principles predict. If an important mutation should not be followed by a change in behaviour—then geneticists would have to worry about the validity of the principles.

What these books fail to pay attention to is the trend in modern genetics which deals with the activation of gene areas, with the influence of external factors on the actualization of gene-potentials and their biochemical correlates in behaviour. I would venture to guess that, apart from the dogma, the main reason for this silence is the fear of even the slightest suspicion that one might misinterpret such facts to mean that a Lamarckian mechanism were at work. (Hydén, 1969, pp. 114–115)

In the ensuing decades since Hydén made the above observation, things have not changed very much. A virtual revolution has taken place in our knowledge of environmental influences on gene expression that has not yet seeped into the social sciences in general and the behavioral sciences in particular. Aside from the feared misinterpretation of Lamarckian mechanisms at work, there is an explicit dogma, formulated as such, that does not permit environmental influences on gene activity: The Central Dogma of Molecular Biology, first enunciated by Crick in 1958.

Though the central dogma may seem quite remote from psychology, I think it lies behind some psychological and behavioral theories that emphasize the sheerly endogenous construction of the nervous system and early behavior (e.g., Elman et al., 1996; Spelke & Newport, 1998), and the "innate foundation of the psyche" (e.g., Tooby & Cosmides, 1990), independent of experience or functional considerations: The essentially dichotomous view that genes and other endogenous factors construct part of the organism and environment determines other features of the organism. The present chapter attempts to show how genes and environment necessarily cooperate in the construction of organisms; specifically, how genes require environmental and behavioral inputs to function appropriately during the normal course of individual development.

PREDETERMINED AND PROBABILISTIC EPIGENESIS

In earlier articles, I described two concepts of epigenetic development: predetermined and probabilistic epigenesis (Gottlieb, 1970, 1976). In these early formulations, the difference between the two points of view hinged largely on how they conceived of the structure-function relationship. In predeterminism, it was unidirectional (S –> F), whereas in probabilism, it was bidirectional (S <–> F). Subsequently, I (Gottlieb, 1983, p. 13; 1991, p. 13) extended the uni- and bidirectionality to include genetic activity:

Predetermined Epigenesis

Unidirectional Structure–Function Development

Genetic activity (DNA –> RNA –> Protein) –>

structural maturation –> function, activity, or experience

Probabilistic Epigenesis

Bidirectional Structure–Functional Development

Genetic activity (DNA <–> RNA <–> Protein) <–>

structural maturation <–> function, activity, or experience

As applied to the nervous system, structural maturation refers to neurophysiological and neuroanatomical development, principally the structure and function of nerve cells and their synaptic interconnections. The unidirectional structure-function view assumes that genetic activity gives rise to structural maturation that then leads to function in a nonreciprocal fashion, whereas the bidirectional view holds that there are reciprocal influences among genetic activity, structural maturation, and function. In the unidirectional view, the activity of genes and the maturational process are pictured as relatively encapsulated or insulated, so that they are uninfluenced by feedback from the maturation process or function, whereas the bidirectional view assumes that genetic activity and maturation are affected by function, activity, or experience. The bidirectional or probabilistic view applied to the usual unidirectional formula calls for arrows going back to genetic activity to indicate feedback serving as signals for the turning on and turning off of genetic activity. The usual view, as we shall see below in the central dogma of molecular biology, calls for genetic activity to be regulated by the genetic system itself in a strictly feed-forward manner. In this chapter, I (a) present the central dogma as a version of predetermined epigenesis and (b) elaborate on the prior description of probabilistic epigenesis to bring it up to date on what we now know about the details of the bidirectional effects among genetic activity, structural maturation, neural and behavioral function, and experience.

THE CENTRAL DOGMA

The central dogma asserts that "information" flows in only one direction from the genes to the structure of the proteins that the genes bring about through the formula DNA –> RNA –> Protein. (Messenger RNA [mRNA] is the intermediary in the process of protein synthesis. In the lingo of molecular biology, the DNA –> RNA is called transcription, and the RNA –> Protein is called translation.) After retroviruses were discovered in the 1960s—in which RNA reversely transcribes DNA through the enzyme reverse transcriptase—Crick wrote a postscript to his 1958 paper in which he congratulated himself for not claiming that reverse transcription was impossible: "In looking back I am struck not only by the brashness which allowed us to venture powerful statements of a very general nature, but also by the rather delicate discrimination used in selecting what statements to make" (1970, p. 562). He then went on to consider the central dogma formula, DNA –> RNA –> Protein, in much more explicit detail than in his earlier paper. In particular, he wrote: " These are the three [information] transfers which the central dogma postulates never occur:

Protein –> Protein

Protein –> DNA

Protein –> RNA." (p. 562)

I suppose if one is going to be brash about making proposals in largely unchartered waters, it stands to reason one might err, even given the otherwise acknowledged insight of the author regarding other scientific issues. In the present case, Crick was wrong in two of the three central-dogmatic postulates described above. Regarding protein-protein interactions, it is now known that in neurodegenerative disorders such as Creutzfeldt-Jakob disease, prions (abnormally conformed proteins) can transfer their abnormal conformation to other proteins

(=Protein –> Protein transfer of information), without the benefit of nucleic acid participation (RNA or DNA; Telling et al., 1996). The strength of the dogma that nucleic acids are required for information transfer is so compelling that some people believe there must be something like an RNA transforming virus that brings about the changed protein conformation, even though there is no evidence for such a virus (Chesebro, 1998; Grady, 1996).

Regarding Protein –> DNA transfer, there has long been recognized a class of regulative proteins that bind to DNA, serving to activate or inhibit DNA expression (i.e., turning genes on or off; reviews in Davidson, 1986, and Pritchard, 1986).

With respect to the third prohibited information transfer (Protein –> RNA), which would amount to reverse translation, to my knowledge that phenomenon has not yet been observed.

Any ambiguity about the controlling factors in gene expression in the central dogma was removed in a later article by Crick, in which he specifically says that the genes of higher organisms are turned on and off by other genes (Crick, 1982, p. 515). Figure 5.1 shows the central dogma of molecular biology in the form of a diagram.

The Genome According to Central Dogma

The picture of the genome that emerges from the central dogma is (a) one of encapsulation, setting the genome off from supragenetic influences, and (b) a largely feedforward informational process in which the genes contain a blueprint or master plan for the construction and determination of the organism. In this view, the genome is not seen as part of the developmental-physiological system of the organism, responsive to signals from internal cellular sources such as the cytoplasm of the cell, cellular adhesion molecules (CAMs), or to extracellular influences such as hormones, and certainly not to extraorganismic influences such as stimuli or signals from the external environment. Witness the well-known biologist Ernst Mayr's (1982) view "that the DNA of the genotype does not itself enter into the developmental pathway but simply serves as a set of instructions" (p. 824). Mae-Wan Ho (1984) characterized this view of the genes

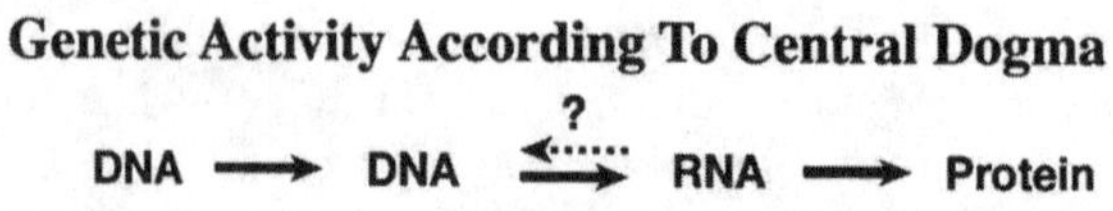

Genetic Activity According To Central Dogma

$$?$$
$$DNA \longrightarrow DNA \xleftarrow{\;\;\cdots\;} RNA \longrightarrow Protein$$

FIG. 5.1. Central dogma of molecular biology. The right-going arrows represent the central dogma. The discovery of retroviruses (represented by the left-going arrow from RNA to DNA) was not part of the dogma but, after the discovery, was said by Crick (1970) not to be prohibited in the original formulation of the dogma (Crick, 1958).

as the unmoved movers of development and the masters of the cellular slave machinery of the organism. Ho's own work on the transgenerational effects of altered cytoplasmic influences seriously faults this view, as does the research reviewed by Jablonka & Lamb (1995).

Genes are conserved during evolution so some of the same genes are found in many different species. What this has shown us is that there is not an invariable association between the activity of a specific gene and the part of the body in which it is active. One of the nicest demonstrations is the activity of the so-called *Hox* genes that are found in a number of species (Grenier, Garber, Warren, Whitington, & Carroll, 1997). As shown in Fig. 5.2, in fruit flies the *Hox* genes are active only in the abdominal segment of the body, whereas in centipedes the same *Hox* genes are active in all segments of the body except the head. And, in a related worm-like creature, Onychophora, the *Hox* genes are active only in a single segment of the organism, in its hindmost region. Because these are not homologous parts of these three species, this demonstrates that the specific developmental contribution of the same genes varies as a consequence of the developmental system in which they find themselves. Genes that play a role in the abdominal segment of fruit flies are active in virtually all the bodily segments of centipedes but only in a single segment in Onychophora.

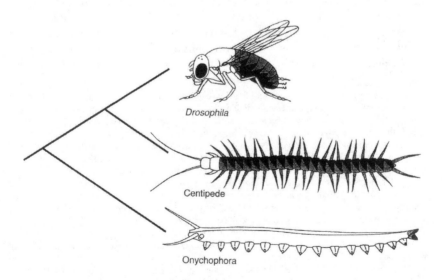

FIG. 5.2. Darkened areas indicate different parts of the body in which the same Hox genes are active in three species: abdominal segment in Drosophila, virtually the entire body in Centipede, and only the single hindmost segment in Onychophora. Modified from Grenier et al., 1997, with permission.

The main point of the present chapter is to extend the normally occurring influences on genetic activity to the external environment, thereby further demonstrating that the genome is not encapsulated and is, in fact, a part of the organism's general developmental-physiological adaptation to environmental stresses and signals: Genes express themselves appropriately only in responding to internally and externally generated stimulation. Further, in this view, while genes participate in the making of protein, protein is also subject to other influences (Davidson, 1986; Pritchard, 1986), and protein must be further stimulated and elaborated to become part of the nervous system (or other systems) of the organism, so genes operate at the lowest level of organismic organization and they do not, in and of themselves, produce finished traits or features of the organism.[1] Thus, there is no correlation between genome size and the structural complexity of organisms (reviewed in Gottlieb, 1992, pp. 154–157), nor is there a correlation between numbers of genes and numbers of neurons in the brains of a variety of organisms (Table 5.1). The organism is a product of epigenetic development, which includes the genes as well as many other supragenetic influences. Because this latter point has been the subject of numerous contributions (reviewed in Gottlieb, 1992, 1997), I will not deal with it further here but, rather, restrict this chapter to documenting that the activity of genes is regulated in just the same way as the rest of the organism, being called forth by signals from the normally occurring external environment, as well as the internal environment (Nijhout, 1990; Pritchard, 1986). Though this fact is not well known in the social and behavioral sciences, it is surprising to find that it is also not widely appreciated in biology proper (Strohman, 1997). In biology, the external environment is seen as the agent of natural selection in promoting evolution, not as a crucial feature of individual development (van der Weele, 1995). Many biologists subscribe to the notion that "the genes are

---

[1]Among the most scholarly, early critiques to make this point was that of G. Stent (1981), who wrote "For the viewpoint that the structure and function of the nervous system of an animal is specified by its genes provides too narrow a context for actually understanding developmental processes and thus sets a goal for the genetic approach that is unlikely to be reached. Here too 'narrow' is not to mean that a belief in genetic specification of the nervous system necessarily implies a lack of awareness that in development there occurs an interaction between genes and environment, a fact of which all practitioners of the genetic approach are certainly aware. Rather, 'too narrow' means that the role of the genes, which, thanks to the achievements of molecular biology, we now know to be the specification of the primary structure of protein molecules, is at too many removes from the processes that actually 'build nerve cells and specify neural circuits which underlie behavior' to provide an appropriate conceptual framework for posing the developmental questions that need to be answered." (pp. 186–187)
Stent's critique was taken a step further by Nijhout (1990), who wrote in a general way about the importance of interactions, above the genetic level, in the internal environment of the organism to bring about growth and differentiation (morphogenesis). Nijhout's point was that "genes do not ... 'cause' or 'control' morphogenesis; they enable it to take place" (p. 443). Even more pertinent to the theme of the present essay, Nijhout wrote that "the genes whose products are necessary during development are activated by stimuli that arise from the cellular and chemical processes of development. Thus the network or pattern of gene activation does not constitute a program, it is both the consequence of, and contributor to, development" (p. 443). In the present chapter, I extend this point of view to the external environment.

TABLE 5.1
Approximate Number of Genes and Neurons in the Brains
of Organisms in Different Lineages

Lineage	Genes	Neurons
Chordates		
Mus musculus	70,000	40 million
Homo sapiens	70,000	85 billion
Nematodes		
Caenorhabdhitis elegans	14,000	302
Arthropods		
Drosophila melanogaster	12,000	250,000

Note.   From G. L. Gabor Miklos, unpublished. Reprinted by permission. The exact number of neurons in the brain of C. elegans is known to be 302.

safely sequestered inside the nucleus of the cell and out of reach of ordinary environmental effects" (Wills, 1989, p. 19).

NORMALLY OCCURRING ENVIRONMENTAL INFLUENCES ON GENE ACTIVITY

As can be seen in Table 5.2, a number of different naturally occurring environmental signals can stimulate gene expression in a large variety of organisms from nematodes to humans. The earliest demonstration of this regularly occurring phenomenon that I could find in intact organisms is the work of H. Hydén (Hydén & Egyházi, 1962). In this rarely cited study, hungry rats had to learn to traverse a narrow rod from an elevated start platform to an elevated feeding platform—a veritable balancing act. The nuclear base ratios in their vestibular nerve cells were then compared with an untrained control group and a control group given passive vestibular stimulation. The RNA base ratios in the experimental groups differed from both the control groups, and there was no difference between the control groups.

TABLE 5.2
Normally Occurring Environmental and Behavioral Influences
on Gene Activity

Species	Environmental Signal or Stimulus	Result (alteration in)
Nematodes	Absence or presence of food	Diminished or enhanced neuronal *daf*-7 gene mRNA expression, inhibiting or provoking larval development
Fruit flies	Transient elevated heat stress during larval development	Presence of proteins produced by heat shock and thermotolerance (enhanced thermal regulation)
Fruit flies	Light-dark cycle	Presence of PER and TIM protein expression and circadian rhythms
Various reptiles	Incubation temperature	Sex determination
Songbirds (canaries, zebra finches)	Conspecific song	Increased forebrain mRNA
Hamsters	Light-dark cycle	Increased pituitary hormone mRNA and reproductive behavior
Mice	Acoustic stimulation	Enhanced c-*fos* expression, neuronal activity, organization of the auditory system
Mice	Light-dark cycle	C-*fos* mRNA expression in hypothalamus, circadian locomotor activity
Rats	Tactile stimulation	Enhanced c-*fos* expression and increased number of somatosensory (sense of touch) cortical neurons
Rats	Learning task involving vestibular system	Change in nuclear RNA base ratios in vestibular nerve cells
Rats	Visual stimulation	Increased RNA and protein synthesis in visual cortex
Rats	Environmental complexity	Increased brain RNA diversity

Rats	Prenatal nutrition	Increase in cerebral DNA (increased number of brain cells)
Rats	Infantile handling (brief separation from mother)	Increased hypothalmic mRNAs for corticotropin-releasing hormone throughout life
Cats	Visual stimulation	Increased visual cortex RNA complexity (diversity)
Humans	Academic examinations taken by medical students (psychological stress)	Reduced mRNA activity in interleukin 2 receptor (immune system response)

Note.   mRNA = messenger RNA; PER and TIM are proteins arising from activity of *per* (*period*) and *tim* (*timeless*) genes; activity of c-*fos* genes leads to production of c-FOS protein. References documenting the findings listed can be found in Gottlieb (1998, Table 2).

I think the Hydén & Egyházi study is rarely cited because the results not only did not fit into any existing paradigm, but they also seemed to raise the Lamarckian spectre mentioned by Hydén in the opening quotation.[2] If that is the case, there is an elementary misunderstanding. First, environmental stimulation of gene activity in the organ of balance does not mean the genes were necessarily *altered* in the process, or second, if they were altered, there is no reason to assume that the alteration was passed on to the progeny, as would be required by the way Lamarck used the notion of the inheritance of acquired characters in his theory of evolution.[3] In the Hydén and Egyházi study, the most conservative and acceptable explanation is that genes (DNA) were turned on in the experimental group in a way that they were not turned on in the control groups, resulting in an alteration of RNA base ratios in the experimental group.

---

[2]Due to the great advances in molecular techniques since 1962, some present-day workers may question the results of Hydén and Egyházi on methodological grounds.

[3]Although it is not a popular idea, and it is a separate question, genes can be altered by internal (reverse transcription, for example) and external events during development and, under certain conditions, the activities of these altered genes can persist across generations (Campbell & Perkins, 1983; Campbell & Zimmerman, 1982; Holliday, 1990; Jablonka & Lamb, 1995).

To understand the findings summarized in Table 5.2, the nongeneticist will need to recall that the sequence of amino acids in proteins is determined by the sequence of nucleotides in the gene that "codes" for it, operating through the intermediary of mRNA. So there are three levels of evidence of genetic activity in Table 5.2: protein expression or synthesis, mRNA activity, and genetic activity itself. A difference in number of brain cells as a consequence of environmental influences, as in the Mack and Mack and Zamenhof and van Marthens studies, means that DNA activity has been turned on by the environmental stimulation. In the case of the more recent Mack and Mack (1992) study, they were able to measure *fos* activity as well as count the number of cortical cells, whereas in the earlier Zamenhof and van Marthens (1978) study, they were able only to count the number of cerebral cells as evidence of DNA activity.

As noted in Table 5.2, there are important neural and behavioral correlations to genetic activity, even though the activity of the genes is quite remote from these effects. The posttranslational expression of genes beyond the initial synthesis of protein involves the intervention of many factors before the end product of gene activity is realized (review in Pritchard, 1986, p. 179).

The fact that normally occurring environmental events stimulate gene activity during the usual course of development in a variety of organisms means that genes and genetic activity are part of the developmental-physiological system and do not stand outside of that system as some biologists and others have assumed on the basis of the central dogma. The mechanisms by which environmental signals turn on genetic activity during the normal course of development is being actively explored in a number of laboratories. The interested reader is referred to the reviews by Campbell and Zimmermann (1982), Holliday (1990), Morgan and Curran (1991), Rosen and Greenberg (1994), Curran, Smeyne, Robertson, Vendrell, and Morgan (1994), and Jablonka and Lamb (1995). Psychologists may be particularly interested in the fact that environmentally provoked gene expression is thought to be required for long-term memory (review in Goelet, Castellucci, Schacher, & Kandel, 1986).

FROM CENTRAL DOGMA OF MOLECULAR BIOLOGY TO PROBABILISTIC EPIGENESIS

The main purpose of this essay is to place genes and genetic activity firmly within a developmental-physiological framework, one in which genes not only affect each other and mRNA but are affected by activities at other levels of the system, up to and including the external environment. This developmental system of bidirectional, coactional influences is captured schematically in Fig. 5.3. In contrast to the unidirectional and encapsulated genetic predeterminism of the central dogma, a probabilistic view of epigenesis holds that the sequence and outcomes of development are probabilistically determined by the critical operation of various endogenous and exogenous stimulative events (Gottlieb, 1970, p. 111; recent review in Gottlieb, 1997). The probabilistic-epigenetic framework presented in Fig.

BIDIRECTIONAL INFLUENCES

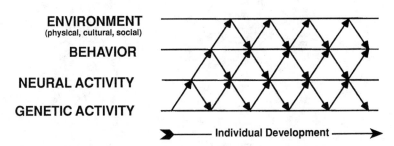

ENVIRONMENT
(physical, cultural, social)

BEHAVIOR

NEURAL ACTIVITY

GENETIC ACTIVITY

➤———— Individual Development ————➤

FIG. 5.3. Probabilistic-epigenetic framework: Depiction of the completely bidirectional and coactional nature of genetic, neural, behavioral, and environmental influences over the course of individual development. From *Individual Development and Evolution: The Genesis of Novel Behavior* by Gilbert Gottlieb. Copyright © 1992 by Oxford University Press, Inc. Used by permission of Oxford University Press, Inc.

5.3 is based not only on what we now know about mechanisms of individual development at all levels of analysis but also derives from our understanding of evolution and natural selection. As is well known, natural selection serves as a filter and preserves reproductively successful phenotypes. These successful phenotypes are a product of individual development and, thus, are a consequence of the adaptability of the organism to its developmental conditions. Therefore, natural selection has preserved (favored) organisms that are adaptably responsive to their developmental conditions, both behaviorally and physiologically. Organisms with the same genes can develop very different phenotypes under different ontogenetic conditions, as witness the two extreme variants of a single parasitic wasp species shown in Fig. 5.4 and identical twins reared apart in the human species (Fig. 5.5).[4]

Because the probabilistic- epigenetic view presented in Fig. 5.3 does not portray enough detail at the level of genetic activity, it is useful to flesh that out in comparison to the previously described central dogma of molecular biology. As shown in Fig. 5.6, the original central dogma explicitly posited one-way traffic from DNA –> RNA –> Protein and was silent about any other flows of information (Crick, 1958).

---

[4]This great amount of phenotypic variation observed in identical twins (sharing the same genotype) coordinates well with the enormous degree of phenotypic variation in the human species, in which there is in fact only a very small degree of individual genetic variation at the level of DNA. DNA is composed of two base pairs of nucleotides. There is such a small amount of variation in these base pairs in the human population that any two individuals selected at random from anywhere on earth would exhibit differences in only three or four base pairs out of 1000 base pairs (i.e., .3% or .4%!; Cann, 1988; Merriwether et al., 1991).

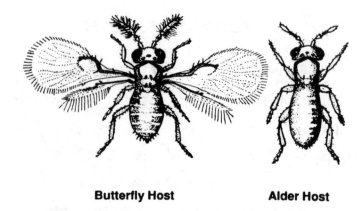

Butterfly Host   **Alder Host**

FIG. 5.4. Two very different morphological outcomes of development in the minute parasitic wasp, depending on the host (butterfly or alder fly) in which the eggs were laid. The insects are of the same species of parasitic wasp (*Trichogramma semblidis*). Modified after Wigglesworth, 1964.

Later, after the discovery of retroviruses (RNA –> DNA information transfer), Crick (1970) did not claim to have predicted that phenomenon but, rather, that the original formulation did not expressly forbid it. In the bottom of Fig. 5.6, probabilistic epigenesis, being inherently bidirectional in the horizontal and vertical levels (Fig. 5.3), has information flowing not only from RNA –> DNA but between Protein <–>

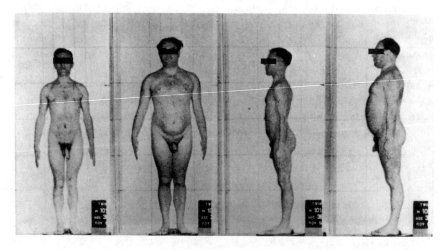

FIG. 5.5. Remarkable illustration of the enormous phenotypic variation that can result when monozygotic (single egg) identical twins are reared apart in very different family environments from birth. From Tanner, 1978, based on Shields, 1962.

Genetic Activity According To Central Dogma

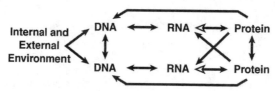

Genetic Activity According To Probabilistic Epigenesis

FIG. 5.6. Different views of influences on genetic activity in the central dogma and probabilistic epigenesis. The filled arrows indicate documented sources of influence, while the open arrow from Protein back to RNA remains a theoretical possibility in probabilistic epigenesis and is prohibited in the central dogma (as are Protein <-> Protein influences). Protein -> Protein influences occur when (1) prions transfer their abnormal conformation to other proteins and (2) when, during normal development, proteins activate or inactivate other proteins as in phosphorylation example described in text. The filled arrows from Protein to RNA represent the activation of mRNA by protein as a consequence of phosphorylation, for example. DNA <-> DNA influences are termed "epistatic," referring to the modification of gene expression depending on the genetic background in which they are located. In the central dogma genetic activity is dictated solely by genes (DNA -> DNA), whereas in probabilistic epigenesis internal and external environmental events activate genetic expression through proteins (Protein -> DNA), hormonal, and other influences. To keep the diagram manageable, the fact that behavior and the external environment exert their effects on DNA through internal mediators (proteins, hormones, etc.) is not shown; nor is it shown that the protein products of some genes regulate the expression of other genes. Further discussion in text.

Protein and DNA <-> DNA. The only relationship that is not yet supported is Protein -> RNA, in the sense of reverse translation (Protein altering the structure of RNA), but there are other influences of Protein on RNA activity (not its structure) that would support such a directional flow. For example, a process known as phosphorylation can modify proteins such that they activate (or inactivate) other proteins (Protein -> Protein) which, when activated, trigger rapid association of mRNA (Protein -> RNA activity). When mRNAs are transcribed by DNA, they do not necessarily become immediately active but require a further signal to do so. The consequences of phosphorylation could provide that signal (Protein -> Protein ->

mRNA activity –> Protein). A process like this appears to be involved in the expression of "fragile X mental retardation protein" under normal conditions and proves disastrous to neural and psychological development when it does not occur (Weiler et al., 1997).[5] (An excellent overview of the various roles of phosphorylation in the nervous system is provided by Hyman & Nestler, 1993, chap. 4.)

Amplifying the left side of the bottom of Fig. 5.6, it is known that gene expression is affected by events in the cytoplasm of the cell, which is the immediate environment of the nucleus and mitochondria of the cell wherein DNA resides, and by hormones that enter the cell and its nucleus. This feed-downward effect can be visualized thusly:

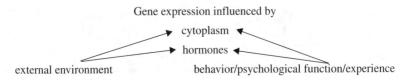

Gene expression influenced by

cytoplasm

hormones

external environment   behavior/psychological function/experience

According to this view, different proteins are formed depending on the particular factors influencing gene expression. Concerning the effect of psychological functioning on gene expression we have the evidence in Table 5.2 of heightened interleukin 2 receptor mRNA, an immune system response, in medical students taking academic examinations (Glaser et al., 1990). More recently, in an elegant study that traverses all levels from psychological functioning to neural activity to neural structure to gene expression, Cirelli, Pompeiano, and Tononi (1996) showed that genetic activity in certain areas of the brain is higher during waking than in sleeping in rats. In this case, the stimulation of gene expression was influenced by the hormone norepinephrine flowing from locus coeruleus neurons that fire at very low levels during sleep, and at high levels during waking and when triggered by salient environmental events. Norepinephrine modifies neural activity and excitability, as well as the expression of certain genes. So, in this case, we have evidence for the interconnectedness of events relating the external environment

---

[5]The label of "fragile X mental retardation protein" makes it sound as if there is a gene (or genes) that produces a protein that predisposes to mental retardation whereas, in actual fact, it is this protein which is missing (absent) in the brain of fragile X mental retardates and, thus, represents a failure of gene (or mRNA) expression rather than a positive genetic contribution to mental retardation. The same is likely true for other genetic disorders, whether mental or physical: These most often represent biochemical deficiencies of one sort or another due to the lack of expression of the requisite genes and mRNAs to produce the appropriate proteins necessary for normal development. Thus, the search for candidate genes in psychiatric or other disorders is most often a search for genes that are not being expressed, not for genes that are being expressed and causing the disorder. So-called cystic fibrosis genes and manic-depression genes, among others, are in this category. The instances that I know of in which the presence of genes causes a problem are Edward's Syndrome and trisomy 21 (Down Syndrome), wherein the presence of an extra, otherwise normal, chromosome 18 and 21, respectively, causes problems because the genetic system is adapted for two, not three, chromosomes at each location. In some cases, it is of course possible that the expression of mutated genes can be involved in a disorder, but in my opinion, it is most often the lack of expression of normal genes that is the culprit.

and psychological functioning to genetic expression by a specifiable hormone emanating from the activity of a specific neural structure whose functioning waxes and wanes in relation to the psychological state of the organism.

IMPORTANCE OF BEHAVIORAL AND NEURAL ACTIVITY IN DETERMINING GENE EXPRESSION, ANATOMICAL STRUCTURE, AND PHYSIOLOGICAL FUNCTION

Many, if not all, of the normally occurring environmental influences on genetic activity summarized in Table 5.2 involve behavioral and neural mediation. In the spirit of this chapter, I want to emphasize the contribution of events above the genetic level (the whole organism and environmental context) by way of redressing the balance to the way many think about the overriding importance of molecular biology. The earliest synaptic connections in the embryonic and fetal nervous system are created by spontaneous activity of nerve cells (review in Corner, 1994, and Katz & Shatz, 1996). This early, exuberant phase produces a very large array of circuits which is then pared down by the organism's encounters with its prenatal and postnatal environment. In the absence of behavioral and neural activity (e. g., experimentally induced paralysis), cells do not die and circuits do not become pruned in an adaptive way that fits the organism to the demands of its physical, social, and cultural environments (Pittman & Oppenheim, 1979). A recent review of the development and evolution of brain plasticity may be found in Black and Greenough (1998).

Sometimes one reads the perfectly reasonable-sounding suggestion that, though genes don't make anatomical, physiological, or behavioral traits, they constrain the outer limits of variation in such traits. It is of course the developmental system, of which the genes are a part (Fig. 5.3), and not solely the genes that constrain development. It is not possible to predict in advance what the outcome of development will be when the developing organism is faced with novel environmental or behavioral challenges never before faced by the species or strain of animal. This has been known since 1909, when Woltereck did the first experiments that resulted in the open-ended concept of the norm of reaction, an idea that has been misunderstood by some behavior geneticists who think of genes as setting up a too-narrow range of reaction (reviews in Gottlieb, 1995; Platt & Sanislow, 1988).

A very striking example of the role of novel behavior bringing about an entirely new anatomical structure can be seen in Fig. 5.7: Slijper's (1942) goat. This animal was born with undeveloped forelimbs and adopted a kangaroo-like form of locomotion. As a result, its skeleton and musculature became modified, with a pelvis and lower spinal column like that of a biped instead of a quadruped (Fig. 5.7). Thus, while there can be no doubt that genes and other factors place constraints on development, Slijper's goat shows that it is not possible to know the limits of these constraints in advance, though it might seem quite reasonable to assume, in advance of empirical inquiry, that a quadruped is not capable of bipedality. While an open-ended, empirically based norm of reaction can accommodate Slijper's goat,

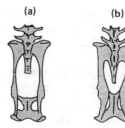

FIG. 5.7. Modification of pelvic and spinal anatomy consequent to bipedalism. (a) Pelvis and lower spine of a normal quadrupedal goat. (b) Pelvis and lower spine of a goat born without forelimbs and which adopted a form of locomotion similar to a kangaroo. From Pritchard, 1986, after Slijper, 1942. Used by permission of Dorian Pritchard.

a narrowly constrained, rationally based range of reaction cannot, no matter how reasonable it seems. It may very well be that all quadruped species can not adapt bipedally, but we can't know that without perturbing the developmental system.

SUMMARY AND CONCLUSIONS

While it is tempting to show the nice link between probabilistic epigenesis and an epigenetic behavioral theory of evolution, that topic has been reviewed in depth in several recent publications (Gottlieb, 1992, 1997), so I will forego that temptation here in favor of sticking to the main point of the chapter. The central dogma lies behind the persistent trend in biology and psychology to view genes and environment as making identifiably separate contributions to the phenotypic outcomes of development. Quantitative behavior genetics is based on this erroneous assumption. It is erroneous because animal experiments have shown again and again that it is not possible to identify the genetic and environmental components of any phenotype, whether behavioral, anatomical, or physiological (extensive review in Wahlsten & Gottlieb, 1997).[6] While genes no doubt play a constraining role in development,

---

[6]This is not the same as saying one can't pinpoint the participation of specific genes and specific environments in contributing to phenotypic outcomes. However, because genes and environments always collaborate in the production of any phenotype, it is not possible to say that a certain component of the phenotype was caused exclusively by genes (independent of environmental considerations) and some other component was caused exclusively by environment (independent of a genetic contribution). An understanding of developmental phenomena demands a relational or coactive concept of causality as opposed to singular causes acting in supposed isolation (discussed at length in Gottlieb, 1991, 1997). Overton (1998) presented an historical overview on the topic of dualistic conceptions of causality versus the more recent relational or coactive concept of causality. Further, with respect to the erroneous separation of hereditary and environmental contributions to the phenotype by quantitative behavior geneticists, Wahlsten (1990) has shown that the absence of heredity-environment interaction is a statistical artifact stemming from the insufficient power of the ANOVA to detect such interactions, not the empirical absence of such gene-environment interactions.

the actual limits of these constraints are quite wide and, most important, cannot be specified in advance of experimental manipulation or accidents of nature as documented in Figs. 5.4, 5.5, and 5.7. (The prenatal environment also plays a constraining role that can not be known in advance of experimental or manipulative inquiry; Gottlieb, 1971, 1997.) There is no doubt that development is constrained at all levels of the system (Fig. 5.3), not only by genes and environments.

The theoretical crux of this chapter is that the internal and external environments supply the necessary signals to the genes that instigate the eventual production of the requisite proteins under normal as well as unusual conditions of development. There is no genetic master plan or blueprint that is self-actualized during the course of development as was assumed by the central dogma. Undoubtedly, there are unusual developmental conditions to which genes can not respond adaptably, but the range of possible adaptable genetic responses to strange environmental conditions is truly astounding, as when bird oral epithelial cells mixed with mouse oral mesenchyme cells result in the production of a fully enameled molar tooth (Kollar & Fisher, 1980). The saying "scarce as a hen's tooth" is based on the fact that bird oral epithelial cells never produce teeth when in conjunction with bird oral mesenchyme cells, as would be the case under normal conditions of development. If this finding is "clean" (no mouse oral epithelial cells accidentally contaminating the mix), it involves the appropriate reactiviation of a genetic combination that had been latent for 80 million years when birds' last toothed ancestor existed (Pritchard, 1986, pp. 308–309). Also, the finding that a crucial nutriment experimentally deleted from the environment of bacterial cells could lead to the production of that nutriment by a genetic recombination (adaptive mutation) caused a storm of disbelief in the biological community until it could be shown that there was indeed a molecular basis for this "theoretically impossible" finding (Harris, Longerich, & Rosenberg, 1994; Thaler, 1994).

It will be interesting to see how probabilistic epigenesis becomes modified in the ensuing years as more information accrues through the necessarily interdisciplinary and multidisciplinary efforts of future researchers. The contrasting ideas of predetermined and probabilistic epigenesis were first put forward in Gottlieb (1970). While the central dogma as depicted in Fig. 5.6 is consistent with the formulation of predetermined epigenesis, it is too much to claim that the contrasting formulation of probabilistic epigenesis in 1970 predicted all the details of the relationships in the lower half of Fig. 5.6. One can only say that those relationships are consistent with the bidirectional influences stated in the probabilistic formula *genetic activity <–> structure <–> function* presented in Gottlieb (1976, p. 218) and elaborated in Gottlieb (1991, see especially appendix, p. 13). As I have described in detail elsewhere (e.g., Gottlieb, 1992, 1997), the formulation of probabilistic epigenesis built on the writings of Z.-Y. Kuo (1976), T. C. Schneirla (1960), D. S. Lehrman (1970), and Ashley Montagu (1977).

Finally, in response to a concern raised by colleagues who have read this chapter in manuscript form, I do hope that the emphasis on normally occurring environmental influences on gene activity does not raise the spectre of a new, subtle

form of environmentalism. If I were to say organisms are often adaptably responsive to their environments, I don't think that would label me an environmentalist.
So, by calling attention to genes being adaptably responsive to their internal and
external environments, I am not being an environmentalist but merely including
genetic activity within the probabilistic-epigenetic framework that characterizes
the organism and all of its constituent parts (Fig. 5.3). The probabilistic-epigenetic view follows the open-systems view of development championed
by the biologists Ludwig von Bertalanffy (1962), Paul Weiss (1939/1969), and
Sewall Wright (1968). Their writings were based on a highly interactive conception of embryology, and the central dogma simply overlooked this tradition of biological theorizing, resulting in an encapsulated formulation of gene activity at
odds with the facts of embryological development. (The current reductionistic
theoretical stance of molecular biology continues to disregard epigenetic considerations [Strohman, 1997]). Building on the insights of von Bertalanffy, Weiss,
and Wright, the probabilistic-epigenetic view details the cooperative workings
of the embryological open systems view at the genetic and neural levels, prenatal
and postnatal behavior, and the external environment. This view fleshes out at
the prenatal and intraorganismic levels of analysis various other approaches in
developmental psychology: ecological (Bronfenbrenner, 1979), transactional
(Sameroff, 1983), contextual (Lerner & Kaufman, 1985), interactional or holistic (Johnston, 1987; Magnusson, 1988), individual-sociological (Valsiner,
1997), structural-behavioral (Horowitz, 1987), dynamic systems (Thelen &
Smith, 1994), and, most globally speaking, interdisciplinary developmental science (Cairns, Elder, & Costello, 1996).

ACKNOWLEDGMENT

The author's research and scholarly activities are supported in part by NIMH Grant
MH-52429 and National Science Foundation Grant BCS-0126475. I have benefited
from discussions with Jaan Valsiner and other members of the Carolina Consortium
of Human Development, as well as from the comments of Dorian Pritchard, Lynda
Uphouse, Richard C. Strohman, Kathryn Hood, and Nora Lee Willis Gottlieb on
earlier drafts of the manuscript. James Black and William Greenough made very
helpful substantive suggestions for which I am most grateful. Ramona Rodriguiz
provided generous bibliographic assistance. This chapter is abstracted from G.
Gottlieb (1998), with the permission of the American Psychological Association.

REFERENCES

von Bertalanffy, L. (1962). *Modern theories of development: An introduction to theoretical
    biology.* New York: Harper.
Black, J. E., & Greenough, W. T. (1998). Developmental approaches to the memory pro-
    cess. In J. L. Martinez & R. P. Kesner (Eds.), *Learning and memory: A biological view*
    (3rd ed., pp. 55–88). NY: Academic Press.

Bronfenbrenner, U. (1979). *The ecology of human development: Experiments by nature and design.* Cambridge, MA: Harvard University Press.

Cairns, R. B., Elder, G. H., & Costello, E. J. (Eds.). (1996). *Developmental science.* New York: Cambridge University Press.

Campbell, J. H. & Perkins, P. (1983). Transgenerational effects of drug and hormonal treatments in mammals: A review of observations and ideas. *Progress in Brain Research, 73,* 535–553.

Campbell, J. H., & Zimmermann, E. G. (1982). Automodulation of genes: A proposed mechanism for persisting effects of drugs and hormones in mammals. *Neurobehavioral Toxicology and Teratology, 4,* 435–439.

Cann, R. L. (1988). DNA and human origins. *Annual Review of Anthropology, 17,* 127–143.

Chesebro, B. (1998). BSE and prions: Uncertainties about the agent. *Science, 279,* 42–43.

Cirelli, C., Pompeiano, M., & Tononi, G. (1996). Neuronal gene expression in the waking state: A role for locus coeruleus. *Science, 274,* 1211–1215.

Corner, M. A. (1994). Reciprocity of structure-function relations in developing neural networks: The Odyssey of a self-organizing brain through research fads, fallacies, and prospects. *Progress in Brain Research, 102,* 3–31.

Crick, F. (1958). On protein synthesis. *Symposia of the Society for Experimental Biology, no. 12. The biological replication of macromolecules,* pp. 138–163. Cambridge, UK: Cambridge University Press.

Crick, F. (1970). Central dogma of molecular biology. *Nature, 227,* 561–563.

Crick, F. (1982). DNA today. *Perspectives in Biology and Medicine, 25,* 512–517.

Curran, T., Smeyne, R., Robertson, L., Vendrell, M., & Morgan, J. I. (1994). FoslacZ expression: A transgenic approach to gene activation in the brain. In S. Zalcman, R. Scheller, & R. Tsien (Eds.), *Molecular neurobiology: Proceedings of the Second NIMH Conference* (pp. 165–172). Rockville, MD: National Institute of Mental Health.

Davidson, E. H. (1986). *Gene activity in early development.* Orlando, FL: Academic Press.

Ehret, G., & Fisher, R. (1991). Neuronal activity and tonotopy in the auditory system visualized by *c-fos* gene expression. *Brain Research, 567,* 350–354.

Elman, J. L., Bates, E. A., Johnson, M. H., Karmiloff-Smith, A., Parisi, D., & Plunkett, K. (1996). *Rethinking innateness: A connectionist perspective on development.* Cambridge, MA: MIT Press.

Glaser, R., Kennedy, S., Lafuse, W. P., Bonneau, R. H., Speicher, C., Hillhouse, J., & Kiecolt-Glaser, J. K. (1990). Psychological-stress-induced modulation of interleukin 2 receptor gene expression and interleukin 2 production in peripheral blood leukocytes. *Archives of General Psychiatry, 47,* 707–712.

Goelet, P., Castellucci, V. F., Schacher, S., & Kandel, E. R. (1986). The long and short of long-term memory—a molecular framework. *Nature, 322,* 419–422.

Gottlieb, G. (1970). Conceptions of prenatal behavior. In L. R. Aronson, E. Tobach, D. S. Lehrman, and J. S. Rosenblatt (Eds.), *Development and evolution of behavior: Essays in memory of T. C. Schneirla* (pp. 111–137). San Francisco: Freeman.

Gottlieb, G. (1971). *Development of species identification in birds: An inquiry into the prenatal determinants of perception.* Chicago: University of Chicago Press.

Gottlieb, G. (1976). Conceptions of prenatal development: Behavioral embryology. *Psychological Review, 83,* 215–234.

Gottlieb, G. (1983). The psychobiological approach to developmental issues. In M. M. Haith & J .J. Campos (Eds.), *Handbook of child psychology: Infancy and developmental psychobiology* (Vol. 2, 4th ed., pp. 1–26). NY: Wiley.

Gottlieb, G. (1991). Experiential canalization of behavioral development: Theory. *Developmental Psychology, 27,* 4–13.

Gottlieb, G. (1992). *Individual development and evolution: The genesis of novel behavior.* New York: Oxford University Press.

Gottlieb, G. (1995). Some conceptual deficiencies in "developmental" behavior genetics. *Human Development, 38,* 131–141.

Gottlieb, G. (1997). *Synthesizing nature-nurture: Prenatal roots of instinctive behavior.* Mahwah, NJ: Lawrence Erlbaum Associates.

Gottlieb, G. (1998). Normally occurring environmental and behavioral influences on gene activity: From central dogma to probabilistic epigenesis. *Psychological Review, 105,* 792–802.

Grady, D. (1996). Ironing out the wrinkles in the prion strain problem. *Science, 274,* 2010.

Grenier, J. K., Garber, T. L., Warren, R., Whitington, P. M., & Carroll, S. (1997). Evolution of the entire arthropod *Hox* gene set predated the origin and radiation of the onychophoran/arthropod clade. *Current Biology, 7,* 547–553.

Harris, R. S., Longerich, S., & Rosenberg, S. M. (1994). Recombination in adaptive mutation. *Science, 264,* 258–260.

Ho, M.-W. (1984). Environment and heredity in development and evolution. In M.-W. Ho & P. T. Saunders (Eds.), *Beyond neo-Darwinism: An introduction to the new evolutionary paradigm* (pp. 267–289). San Diego, CA: Academic Press.

Holliday, R. (1990). Mechanisms for the control of gene activity during development. *Biological Reviews, 65,* 431–471.

Horowitz, F. D. (1987). *Exploring developmental theories: Toward a structural/behavioral model of development.* Hillsdale, NJ: Lawrence Erlbaum Associates.

Hydén, H. (1969). Afterthoughts. In A. Koestler & J. R. Smythies (Eds.), *Beyond reductionism: New perspectives in the life sciences* (pp. 114–117). London: Hutchinson.

Hydén, H., & Egyházi, E. (1962). Nuclear RNA changes of nerve cells during a learning experiment in rats. *Proceedings of the National Academy of Sciences, USA, 48,* 1366–1373.

Hyman, S. E., & Nestler, E. J. (1993). *The molecular foundations of psychiatry.* Washington, DC: American Psychiatric Press.

Jablonka, E., & Lamb, M. J. (1995). *Epigenetic inheritance and evolution: The Lamarckian dimension.* Oxford: Oxford University Press.

Johnston, T. D. (1987). The persistence of dichotomies in the study of behavioral development. *Developmental Review, 7,* 149–182.

Katz, L. C., & Shatz, C. J. (1996). Synaptic activity and the construction of cortical circuits. *Science, 274,* 1133–1138.

Kollar, E. J., & Fisher, C. (1980). Tooth induction in chick epithelium: Expression of quiescent genes for enamel synthesis. *Science, 207,* 993–995.

Kuo, Z.-Y. (1976). *The dynamics of behavior development* (enlarged ed.). NY: Plenum.

Lehrman, D. S. (1970). Semantic and conceptual issues in the nature–nurture problem. In L. R. Aronson, E. Tobach, D. S. Lehrman, & J. S. Rosenblatt (Eds.), *Development and evolution of behavior: Essays in memory of T. C. Schneirla* (pp. 17–52). San Francisco: Freeman.

Lerner, R. M., & Kaufman, M. B. (1985). The concept of development in contextualism. *Developmental Review, 5,* 309–333.

Mack, K. J., & Mack, P. A. (1992). Induction of transcription factors in somatosensory cortex after tactile stimulation. *Molecular Brain Research, 12,* 141–147.

Magnusson, D. (1988). *Individual development from an interactional perspective: A longitudinal study.* Hillsdale, NJ: Lawrence Erlbaum Associates.

Mayr, E. (1982). *The growth of biological thought.* Cambridge, MA: Belknap Press of Harvard University Press.

Merriwether, D. A., Clark, A. G., Ballinger, S. W., Schurr, T. G., Soodyall, H., Jenkins, T., Sherry, S. T., & Wallace, D. C. (1991). The structure of human mitochondrial DNA variation. *Journal of Molecular Evolution, 33,* 543–555.

Montagu, A. (1977). Sociogenic brain damage. In S. Arieti and G. Chrzanowski (Eds.), *New dimension in psychiatry: A world view* (Vol. 2, pp. 4–25). NY: Wiley.

Morgan, J. I., & Curran, T. (1991). Stimulus-transcription coupling in the nervous system: Involvement of the inducible proto-oncogenes *fos* and *jun. Annual Review of Neurosciences, 14,* 421–451.

Nijhout, H. F. (1990). Metaphors and the role of genes in development. *BioEssays, 12,* 441–446.

Overton, W. F. (1998). Developmental psychology: Philosophy, concepts, and methodology. In R. M. Lerner (Ed.), *Handbook of child psychology: Theoretical models of human development* (Vol. 1, 5th ed., pp. 107–189). New York: Wiley.

Pittman, R., & Oppenheim, R. W. (1979). Cell death of motoneurons in the chick embryo spinal cord. IV. Evidence that a functional neuromuscular interaction is involved in the regulation of naturally occurring cell death and the stabilization of synapses. *Journal of Comparative Neurology, 187,* 425–446.

Platt, S. A., & Sanislow, C. A. (1988). Norm-of-reaction: Definition and misinterpretation of animal research. *Journal of Comparative Psychology, 102,* 254–261.

Pritchard, D. J. (1986). *Foundations of developmental genetics.* London: Taylor and Francis.

Rose, S. P. R. (1967). Changes in visual cortex on first exposure of rats to light: Effect on incorporation of tritiated lysine into protein. *Nature, 215,* 253–255.

Rosen, L. B., & Greenberg, M. E. (1994). Regulation of *c-fos* and other immediate-early genes in PC-12 cells as a model for studying specificity in neuronal signaling. In S. Zalcman, R. Scheller, & R. Tsein (Eds.), *Molecular Neurobiology: Proceedings of the Second NIMH Conference* (pp. 203–216). Rockville, MD: National Institute of Mental Health.

Sameroff, A. J. (1983). Developmental systems: Contexts and evolution. In W. Kessen (Ed.), *Handbook of child psychology: History, theory, and methods* (Vol. 1, 4th ed., pp. 237–294). NY: Wiley.

Schneirla, T. C. (1960). Instinctive behavior, maturation—Experience and development. In B. Kaplan & S. Wapner (Eds.), *Perspectives in psychological theory—Essays in honor of Heinz Werner* (pp. 303–334). New York: International Universities Press.

Shields, J. (1962). *Monozygotic twins.* London: Oxford University Press.

Slijper, E. J. (1942). Biologic-anatomical investigations on the bipedal gait and upright posture in mammals, with special reference to a little goat, born without forelegs. II. *Proceedings Series C Biological and Medical Sciences: Koninklijke Nederlandse Akademie van Wetenschappen Amsterdam, 45,* 407–415.

Spelke, E. S., & Newport, E. L. (1998). Nativism, empiricism, and the development of knowledge. In R. M. Lerner (Ed.), *Handbook of child psychology: Theoretical models of human development* (Vol. 1, 5th ed., pp. 275–340). New York: Wiley

Stent, G. (1981). Strength and weakness of the genetic approach to the development of the nervous system. *Annual Review of Neuroscience, 4,* 163–194.

Strohman, R. C. (1997). The coming Kuhnian revolution in biology. *Nature Biotechnology, 15,* 194–200.

Tanner, J. M. (1978). *Fetus into man: Physical growth from conception to maturity.* Cambridge, MA: Harvard University Press.

Telling, G. C., Parchi, P., DeArmond, S. J., Cortelli, P., Montagna, P., Gabizon, R., Mastrianni, J., Lugaresi, E., Gambetti, P., & Pruisner, S. B. (1996). Evidence for the conformation of the pathologic isoform of the prion protein enciphering and propagating prion diversity. *Science, 274,* 2079–2082.

Thaler, D. S. (1994). The evolution of genetic intelligence. *Science, 264,* 224–225.

Thelen, E., & Smith, L. B. (1994). *A dynamic systems approach to cognition and action.* Cambridge, MA: MIT Press.

Tooby, J., & Cosmides, L. (1990). The past explains the present: Emotional adaptations and the structure of ancestral environments. *Ethology and Sociobiology, 11,* 375–424.

Valsiner, J. (1997). *Culture and the development of children's action: A theory of human development* (2nd ed.). NY: Wiley.

Wahlsten, D. (1990). Insensitivity of the analysis of variance to heredity-environment interaction. *Behavioral and Brain Sciences, 13,* 109–120; open peer commentary, 121–161.

Wahlsten, D., & Gottlieb, G. (1997). The invalid separation of nature and nurture: Lessons from animal experimentation. In R. J. Sternberg & E. Grigorenko (Eds.), *Intelligence, heredity, and environment* (pp. 163–192). New York: Cambridge University Press.

van der Weele, C. (1995). *Images of development : Environmental causes in ontogeny.* Unpublished doctoral dissertation, Vrije University, Amsterdam.

Weiler, I. J., Irwin, S. A., Klintsova, A. Y., Spencer, C. M., Brazelton, A. D., Miyashiro, K., Comery, T., Patel, B., Eberwine, J., & Greenough, W. T. (1997). Fragile X mental retardation protein is translated near synapses in response to neurotransmitter activation. *Proceedings of the National Academy of Sciences USA, 94,* 5395–5400.

Weiss, P. (1939). *Principles of development: A text in experimental embryology.* New York: Holt, Rinehart & Winston. (Reprinted in 1969 by Hafner.)

Wigglesworth, V. B. (1964). *The life of insects.* Cleveland, OH: World Publishing Co.

Wills, C. (1989). *The wisdom of the genes: New pathways in evolution.* New York: Basic Books.

Wright, S. (1968). *Evolution and the genetics of population: Vol. 1. Genetic and biometric foundations.* Chicago: University of Chicago Press.

Zamenhof, S., & van Marthens, E. (1978). Nutritional influences on prenatal brain development. In G. Gottlieb (Ed.), *Early influences* (pp. 149–186). New York: Academic Press.

6
Beyond Heritability: Biological Process in Social Context

Richard Rende
Brown Medical School and The Miriam Hospital

INTRODUCTION

As an undergraduate student in the early 1980s, I became interested in the disorder autism. I received an opportunity to become involved in research on this condition, much of which involved direct observation of children and adolescents who were living in a residential facility. Over the course of 3 years of direct contact with these youngsters, the profound mystery of their condition overwhelmed me. Essentially all of them had parents who did not show evidence of psychiatric disorder, and many of them had healthy siblings. There was no evidence of parental mistreatment or trauma, and in most cases no known etiological event. Yet all of them demonstrated profound difficulties in relating to others, and many clearly had severe cognitive and developmental delays.

Working directly with individuals with autism made me curious about the history of the disorder. I became aware that the modern conceptualization of this disorder could be traced back to a 1943 article by the child psychiatrist Leo Kanner. In that paper, Kanner (1943) presented his clinical observations of a number of children whose behavior could not be captured by the prevailing diagnostic categories. He noted that these children showed profound difficulties in relating to others, including their parents, as well as a number of other notable interruptions in the developmental process. Based on parental report and retrospection, it appeared that these children had demonstrated impairment in social relatedness from a very early age, even during infancy. Kanner also noted that some of the parents seemed to have particular personality characteristics (such as aloofness and coldness) and tended to work in specific types of employment.

Kanner's proposition in that paper was that these children suffered from a syndrome labeled *autism*, which was characterized by an innate (biological) inability to form normal social relationships. Although his clinical and diagnostic observations have in essence been supported and enhanced over the past 60 years, more controversy surrounded his speculations on etiology. Some of the controversy was due to his choice of the term *autism*, which implied historically a withdrawal from the social world even though he emphasized the potentially innate aspect of the syndrome. A corresponding invitation to speculation arose from his observation on the personality characteristics of some of the parents of his clinical sample. Pulling these two threads together led to environmental theories of autism, some of which focused on the construct of the refrigerator mother. In such theories, the cold, uncaring mother made infants withdraw into a world of their own, thereby accounting for the lack of social bonding typical of autism. A good example of this approach was provided in a book by Bettelheim (1967), as evidenced by the following excerpt: "stories about autistic children being unresponsive from birth on do not, in and by themselves, suggest an innate disturbance. Because it may be a very early reaction to their mothers that was triggered during the first days and weeks of life" (p. 399).

Theories such as the one Bettelheim offered were taken seriously by the scientific community and subject to empirical testing. Overall, during the 1970s, a number of lines of evidence did not support psychodynamic theories of autism, including: (a) the direct study of parents with children with autism (most if not all had relationships with other children that were clearly within the normal boundaries), (b) the recognition of indicators of compromised neurodevelopment in autism such as epileptic seizures (consistent with the notion of autism as a biological disorder), and (c) the demonstration of cognitive deficits in autism (such that it became clear that autism was not simply an emotional reaction to the psychosocial world but rather involved a broad array of cognitive disabilities). The 1970s also gave rise to twin studies of autism that suggested that the biological root of the syndrome could involve genetic factors (for a brief review of the early studies see Rutter, Macdonald, Le Couteur, Macdonald, & Simonoff, 1990).

Returning to my own professional development, my exposure to children with autism convinced me of the potential effects that biology could have on development. I was also somewhat surprised by the notion that environmental theories could be as misleading and potentially damaging as the inappropriate use of biological frameworks. I decided to receive training in behavior genetics to get a solid grounding in this approach, persuaded to no small degree by the increasing attention being paid to genetic theories of autism at that time (now speaking of the late 1980s).

My training in behavioral genetics was conducted within a broader training in human development and especially the then emerging discipline of developmental psychopathology. As such, I was struck by the increasing enthusiasm for genetic research in psychiatry, fueled by reports of single genes that caused schizophrenia and bipolar disorder, which led to speculations that our entire system of classifying psychiatric disorders would be revamped based on genetic findings (see Rende & Plomin, 1995). Although I had no trouble conceptualizing autism as a genetic disorder, I found it difficult to consider most psychiatric disorders as purely genetic diseases. Clearly genetics would be critical pieces in the etiological puzzle for most forms of psychopathology, but suspecting that common disorders such as depression would be due solely to genetics seemed as absurd as claiming that autism was due to refrigerator mothers.

It is now over a decade later, and of course there has been extraordinary change in the way in which genetics is studied. From my perspective, behavior genetic paradigms have been extremely useful in placing research priorities at the intersection of genes and environments, avoiding the pitfalls of both extreme geneticism and environmentalism. My goal in this chapter is to provide a personal window into behavioral genetic research and methodology, to uncover what it does, what it cannot due, and what it can do better. The window I am looking through is the study of psychopathology, and rather than provide any type of systematic review of the literature, I propose to share the perception I have evolved (and continue to evolve) about behavior genetics.

BEHAVIOR GENETICS: A "CRITIQUE-BASED" OVERVIEW

Let me start with a disclaimer. I am not writing this chapter to say that behavior genetics is a perfect and in fact ultimate way to dissect human behavior. It is not. It is a way to begin to uncover the developmental dance between biological process and social context. It is also, perhaps surprisingly to some of its harshest critics, a way to provide the strongest evidence that both genes and environments are critical components to etiological theories of psychopathology.

Why would this claim by surprising to critics of the approach? Most criticisms of the behavior genetic paradigm (BG for short) would argue a number of points, such as:

1. BG creates an artificial distinction between genetic and environmental influence, especially by modeling each as separable main effects;
2. The methodology used to estimate the critical component of the BG model, the construct of heritability, is flawed and biologically meaningless; and
3. The methodology used to estimate environmental influence is flawed, because the environment is not actually measured but is treated essentially as a residual term after accounting for genetic effects.

Let's take these each in turn.

BG Creates an Artificial Distinction Between Genetic and Environmental Influence, Especially by Modeling Each as Separable Main Effects

The short response here is: I agree. BG does create such an artificial distinction. However, I think the behavioral sciences as a whole would crumble if we required that our paradigms did not rely on artificial distinctions! Empirical forays into complex territory will not get very far without them. It would be nearly impossible to begin to model interactive effects without some initial empirical guidance as to the main effect variables.

The issue I believe is not if a paradigm relies on artificial distinctions but, rather, if the artificial distinctions will promote our understanding of the phenomena. Has the BG oversimplification of the influences on human development enhanced our understanding of behavior? I would argue in the affirmative here. Many critics would argue that the oversimplification has promoted a limited and potentially harmful view of genetic influence, carrying the connotation that heritable factors determine large portions of variance in behavioral outcomes which are unaffected (and hence unable to be affected) by environmental influences. Although in the past I have trotted out the typical BG response to such criticism, including the usual disclaimers about heritability being a descriptive statistic and hence being the "what is" and NOT the "what could be" (see, e.g., Rende & Plomin, 1995), I take these criticisms seriously and worry that BG could in fact be easily misconstrued in this way and in fact misused. I would urge critics to allow for environmental terms in this artificial distinction and consider the next idea.

BG Models Have Profoundly Affected the Conception of Genetic Influence in the Broader Scientific Community, Especially the Segment That Actually Searches for Genomic Regions Associated With Disease.

For many years, genetic models were models of single-gene disorders. Disorders of suspected but undetermined genetic origin would be investigated using statistical genetic methods (e.g., segregation analysis) that presumed the existence of a single-locus allelic variation that either led to, or did not lead to, disease. This model worked extraordinarily well for diseases that could indeed be traced to a single locus. In the behavioral realm, the earliest and perhaps most influential success of this approach was the identification of a genetic marker for Huntington's Disease (HD) in 1983 (Gusella et al., 1983). It made sense to claim that the presumed underlying allelic variation led to disease/no disease in this enticingly "simple" manner: The allelic site provided both the necessary and sufficient agent for disease (or no disease). Such a finding started in part the revolution in psychiatry that genetic models could be applied to diseases affecting human behavior and in fact lead to discovery in the laboratory of actual locations on the genome.

Be reminded of my earlier observation that some factions within psychiatry took this notion to the extreme in the late 1980s: The HD model became THE model of how genetics would work. As noted earlier, there were initial reports of success in psychiatric genetics in isolating the genomic regions linked to schizophrenia

(Sherrington et al., 1988) and bipolar disorder (Egeland, Gerhard, Pauls, Sussex, & Kidd, 1987). Though it became clear pretty rapidly that these findings would not be replicated (see Plomin & Rende, 1991), the enthusiasm for the approach did not diminish. Such enthusiasm flew in the face of evidence that most if not all psychiatric disorders did not show patterns of familial aggregation consistent with single-loci origins (in contrast to HD); most were very difficult to diagnose, especially because of the absence of any notable confirming pathophysiology; and in many cases they were simply too common in the population to be due to a single locus on the genome. Some of these difficulties could be swiped away in genetic models with fudge factors such as incomplete penetrance (the idea being that a single-locus effect could be somewhat diminished for unspecified reasons); others could be used to justify single-gene approaches (e.g., the problem would not be with the genetic model but rather with the limitations of psychiatric diagnosis such that once diagnostic approaches improved the genetic models would work).

It is more than a decade later and changes have occurred in the search for genes in psychiatry. The genetic model used to study HD is no longer the dominant model. Indeed, the bustling field of genetics devoted to psychiatric disorders now routinely uses phrases such as "susceptibility genes," thus reflecting that the search is for not one but multiple sites of allelic variation that confer only vulnerability to (rather than causation of) disorder. One notable example of the change in perspective is a paper published during the mid 1990s that argued for genetic strategies aimed at identifying susceptibility genes for complex disorders such as psychiatric disorders (Risch & Merikangas, 1996). Why was this paper important? It provided detailed genetic models for such susceptibility genes that assumed (a) that there would be multiple genes implicated for any disorder, (b) that such genes conferred vulnerability to disease, and (c) these genes would interact in some way with key environmental factors to confer risk for disease. Although intuitively appealing to developmentalists, such a publication was, in my view, a landmark because it summarized, using the language of genetics, the legitimacy of etiological models that embraced probabilistic (rather than deterministic) genetic effects within a broader framework of risk that included nongenetic factors. Such models are starting to take shape in current genetic research. Returning to the example of autism, recent studies have revealed evidence for multiple regions in the genome associated with autism (Alarcon, Cantor, Liu, Gilliam, & Autism Genetic Research Exchange Consortium, 2002; Collaborative Linkage Study of Autism, 2001), a far cry from a single-gene model, and one that required substantial conceptual and methodological adjustment by molecular geneticists.

Why would the community of genetic researchers be willing to alter their thinking and, more important, invest the time and effort to modify the techniques and statistics used in genomic research? Why would they be willing to acknowledge that genes could convey only probabilistic risk for disorder, that many such genes may exist, and that they become expressed within a broader context of nongenetic influence, when such an admission would make their work much harder to conduct? I contend that BG research was a critically important (and perhaps the most critical) factor underlying this paradigm shift. For two decades, BG studies supported the contention that genetic factors were implicated in the etiology of nearly all psychiatric disorders. These same studies, however, also supported the contention that genes were not a necessary and sufficient condition for the expression of disease. Simply put, the inclusion of latent environmental categories in genetic models allowed for the demonstration that "genetic effects" (or "heritability," but more on this later!) were always LESS THAN ONE HUNDRED PERCENT! Even for the most "genetic" disorders such as autism, schizophrenia, and bipolar disorder, identical or monozygotic (MZ) twins were never 100% concordant. For schizophrenia, in fact, concordance rates were typically reported at about 50%, meaning that half the time, identical twins were discordant for schizophrenia, which meant that a simple model of inheritance, based on a single necessary and sufficient disease locus, was not plausible. It should be noted that, for a classic single-locus disease, MZ twins would have a 100% concordance rate.

Before moving on to what BG models end up modeling, then, it is my contention that BG models had a tremendous impact on genomic research by providing convincing evidence that there are multiple probabilistic genes that contribute to complex diseases with high prevalence rates in the population such as those encountered in psychiatry as well as other branches of medicine (see Risch & Merikangas, 1996). The artificial cleavage of etiology into genetic and nongenetic sources of variation, at the very least, had the important effect of demonstrating that it made conceptual sense to model nondeterministic genetic influence as well as nongenetic influence, including environmental factors as typically conceptualized by developmental researchers.

The Methodology Used to Estimate the Critical Component of the BG Model, the Construct of Heritability, Is Flawed and Biologically Meaningless

Thus far, I have suggested that the artificial cleavage of nature and nurture in the prototypical BG approach had heuristic value by at least allowing for nurture in the omnibus model. Now I will take on one of the corollary concerns with the BG approach, which involves what is estimated as the nature part of this cleavage. This brings us to the construct of heritability, which serves as a useful statistical indicator to some, a rather meaningless index to others, and a potentially harmful, biased, and even blatantly incorrect calculation to the harshest critics.

First, a bit of review of the historical context from which the heritability construct emerged, at least the one used in modern BG. As reviewed elsewhere (e.g., Rende, 1996, 1999; Rende & Plomin, 1995), BG has relied on both a theory and methods which date to the early 1900s. The theory, quantitative genetic theory (QGT), postulated that individual differences in complex traits (such as human behavior) could be due to both genetic and nongenetic factors; that genetic factors involved the expression of not just one but multiple genes; that the same held true for nongenetic factors (i.e., there could be many nongenetic risk factors); and that the hypothesized multiple genetic and nongenetic factors acted together in an additive fashion to produce individual differences in traits. As such, QGT offered not just a polygenic model to contrast with Mendelian (single locus –> single trait) models of inheritance but also explicitly allowed for and in fact embraced nongenetic influences, leading to a multifactorial framework.

Was this breakdown of genetic and nongenetic sources of variance arbitrary and perhaps awkward in terms of reflecting how genes become expressed in environmental contexts? Yes, it was. However, considering the historical context in the early 1900s, when a Mendelian approach to traits was *the* model for geneticists, QGT was critical in showing, in genetic terms, how polygenic and nongenetic influence could arise given what was understood about genetics at the time. In addition, because I am now focusing on the heritability part of the equation, it should be appreciated that QGT could take credit for introducing the idea of polygene influences that were probabilistic and also not monopolistic (i.e., nongenetic influences were important too).

Finally, it is critical to emphasize that the arbitrary and awkward demarcation between genetic and environmental influence reflected a theoretical model postulating sources of individual differences in traits, not individual development (e.g., Rende, 1999, 2000; Rende & Plomin, 1995). Although it is often pointed out, correctly, in critiques of BG that genes are expressed under environmental conditions, QGT argued, somewhat convincingly from my perspective, that "G" and "E" could theoretically be teased apart in an initial main effects model of individual differences. Consider those rare single-gene disorders that follow Mendelian patterns of inheritance, such as HD. There is a certain truth in saying that an individual develops HD via the expression of a disease causing locus within the more inclusive environment, including the biological environment. However, there is also a certain truth in saying that, from an individual differences perspective, the reason that some people in the population develop HD and others do not is not due to an intractable connection between genetic and environmental risk factors; overall, the individual differences in HD in the population can be accounted for statistically by the presence or absence of the allelic polymorphism associated with the disease.

Given the framework of QGT, two other developments occurred that led to modern BG. One development was in methodology, namely the recognition and exploitation of experiments provided by nature (the twin paradigm) or human conditions (the adoption paradigm); the other relates to the use of the construct of heritability. Beginning with methodology, I focus here on the history of the twin method as it is instructive as to what inspired researchers to even consider doing this. Although the twin method is often traced to Galton, the actual proposition of the essence of the twin method (the comparison of the similarity of monozygotic [MZ] twins and dizygotic [DZ] twins) was not proposed until the 1920s (1924 to be exact; see Rende, Plomin, & Vandenberg, 1990). At that time, the recognition and acceptance in biology that there were in fact two types of twins led to the independent statement of the classical twin method in America and Germany. Hermann Siemens, the German dermatologist who made one of the propositions, argued the essence of the method: If heritable factors contributed to disease, then

MZ twins should be more similar than DZ twins for a given disorder (see Rende et al., 1990). This statement did not refute nongenetic (or environmental) influence but merely suggested a litmus test for detecting evidence for genetic effects on a disease of unknown etiology. Notice that it also did not prescribe that there should be, or had to be, genetic influence on disease; rather the twin comparison would inform on the likelihood that genes were part of the etiology.

I believe that the modest goal of the twin method Siemens presented was a reasonable and rationale proposition relating to the search for clues for the contributing factors to diseases of unknown etiology. It was not foolproof—it was an indirect way of obtaining evidence in favor of genetic influence, and overall it certainly lacked precision and control as one would expect from a natural experiment. However, it was at least a method capable of generating a hypothesis and also yielding data suitable to testing the hypothesis. As such, it adhered to the same basic principles that would guide any epidemiological investigation of a disease of unknown etiology and would provide data that would have to be evaluated in the manner appropriate to the level of data collected (one way of saying that observing statistical associations in noncontrolled experiments can lead only to speculations about causation). Also, note that the twin method used a framework that did not require single gene causation of disease and thus helped promote the idea of nondeterministic polygenic contributions (with the possibility of nongenetic influences being accepted as well).

Taking the twin method at face value, I would certainly have a problem with harsh critiques of the essence of the approach. It is a limited way of providing a crude initial test of the hypothesis that genes affect disease after acknowledging multiple caveats about the limitations of the method. Nothing more, nothing less. Was it useful? Jumping ahead in history, this fundamental application of the twin method was indeed quite influential in providing support for the idea that autism may be due to genetic factors rather than adverse rearing conditions such as refrigerator mothers (e.g., see Rutter et al., 1990). Treating twin data as a first, not last, step, researchers have followed through on the implications drawn from twin studies of autism with an exciting and extraordinary identification of actual genomic regions linked to this baffling disease (Alarcon et al., 2002; Collaborative Linkage Study of Autism, 2001) more than 20 years after the first twin study of autism was published (Folstein & Rutter, 1977).

The second aspect to the development of modern BG involved an extension of the twin method (and adoption method as well although I will continue to use the twin method as an example) and is arguably the more controversial aspect to this work. I refer here to heritability. What exactly is it? Technical definitions of heritability abound and have been debated, but the often overlooked point I want to stress here is that, in the most fundamental sense, heritability is nothing more than an indicator (just one and not the only one) of the effect size of the hypothetical genetic influence included in multifactorial models. Let's break this down in simple terms, taking as an example the initial presentation of the classical twin method. It was argued that comparing the similarity of MZ and DZ twins could provide one test of the hypothesis that genetic factors contribute to the etiology of a disease. This approach could be formalized in statistical terms by saying that it would be important to test if there were statistically significant differences between the similarity indicator for MZ and DZ twins. Say we are discussing disease, as Siemens was in 1924. The similarity indicator would be concordance for the disease. Thus, one would compare statistically the concordance rates of MZ and DZ twins and test to see if they are indeed different. Now suppose the phenotype is a continuous trait, rather than a categorical one such as disease status. The similarity indicator would then be a correlation, and the correlations of MZ and DZ twins would be compared statistically by a method such as Fisher's z-test. In either case (concordance rates or correlations), it would be also be possible to make a statement as to the magnitude of difference between the similarity indicator for MZ and DZ twins. Considering this magnitude would be, then, in one sense a statistical way of determining how confident we could be in inferring that a genetic effect was present (i.e., simply different from zero) in regard to the differences in a distribution (not within any person in the sample comprising the distribution).

If the past two or three decades of BG research had presented such a metric, would there have been the same level of controversy that has surrounded the heritability statistic? If there would be opposition to this approach, the basis would have to be the argument that natural experiments (rather than the calculation of heritability) are not meaningful, as carrying through the comparison of MZ and DZ twins would simply be a statistical way of translating the essence of the twin method. Certainly useful information could be provided without going beyond these basic statistical techniques. For example, the twin research on autism showed much higher concordance rates in MZ twins as compared with DZ twins. However, the concordance rate for MZ twins was never 100%. Based on these two pieces of data, it could be argued that a hypothesis could be formed (not proven but rather generated by the twin comparison): Genetic influence would be important for autism, but it would not represent the effects of a single deterministic allelic variation (which is the picture emerging from the most recent molecular investigations).

The rationale for calculating a statistic such as heritability is simply, from my perspective, to provide a quantitative indicator of the effect size of genetic influences on individual differences in susceptibility to disease. It is not the only way one could do this. For example, in a 1997 report from a National Institute of Mental Health workgroup devoted to the genetics of mental disorders ("Genetics and Mental Disorders: Report of the NIMH Genetics Workgroup"), the heritability statistic was not used or even mentioned. The potential importance of genetic factors was inferred by calculating recurrence risk ratios (lamdas) from published twin, adoption, and family studies of psychiatric disorders. What is lamda? It is the risk of disorder to relatives divided by the disorder's lifetime prevalence, a rather non-controversial statistical indicator in the field of genetic epidemiology. Using the twin method as an example, lamdas would be calculated separately for MZ and DZ twins and then compared to determine if they were different. The magnitude of the MZ/DZ difference would then be used to determine the likelihood of genetic influence on the disorder. Thus, in the NIHM report, autism, schizophrenia, and bipolar disorder were hypothesized to be disorders in which genes played a substantial role in etiology, whereas many other disorders were assumed to have much smaller genetic contributions. These inferences are made with the caveat that the available data come from natural experiments, but that is essentially the state of the art for disorders of unknown etiology. It seems reasonable to try to capitalize on such natural experiments to give us some handle on the likelihood of genetic contribution to disease, especially as the stakes are now quite high since the issue becomes determining if it is worthwhile to conduct genomic search strategies for disorders.

Opposition to this overall approach would thus have to focus on some form of dislike of searching for genetic effects on disease rather than a specific issue with the calculation of the heritability statistic. Heritability, the way it is calculated and used in BG studies, does not have to be used at all to perform one of the basic goals of BG paradigm, which is to determine the likelihood of genetic contribution to disease. Why bother with this determination? Why not simply assume that genes play a role in all diseases? To repeat myself, the stakes are now quite high, as the issue is whether genomic search strategies should be pursued. As discussed earlier, the search for genes now involves a consideration of susceptibility loci that only represent vulnerability to a disorder as a part of the overall risk. This task is daunting, given the number of genes that could be involved and their relatively small effect size (e.g., Risch & Merikangas, 1996). As such, some empirical guidance would be necessary to select rationally phenotypes that would be good candidates for genotypic analysis, and this is where BG studies have been of importance and may greatly enhance our ability to isolate genetic risk factors. Again returning to autism as an example, twin studies were highly influential in suggesting that the candidate phenotype for genetic studies should be broadened well beyond the classic diagnostic boundaries of this disorder to include a host of language and cognitive disabilities (see Rutter et al., 1990). Importantly, this suggestion has begun to pay off in molecular genetic studies of autism as the focus is on such a broader candidate phenotype, with an emerging finding being that specific aspects of the language disability associated with autism may be associated with one of multiple loci involved in the pathogenesis of the disease (Collaborative Linkage Study of Autism, 2001).

In my own work, I have in fact used prototypical BG models that have yielded estimates of heritability, as typically reported in the BG literature. I have always interpreted them, and tried to present them, as effect size indicators of a basic litmus test to determine if genetic factors played an important role in the etiology of a given form of psychopathology. However, despite the numerous descriptions of BG and specifically heritability provided in the literature over the past two decades, I can still understand how there could be misinterpretation of this statistic. Let's focus on what it is not:

Heritability is *not* an indicator of the number of genes involved for a trait.

Heritability is *not* an indicator of what proportion of an individual's risk is due to genetic make-up.

Heritability is *not* a fixed determination of the overall effect of genes on a trait.

What, then, is heritability? As mentioned earlier, it is most fundamentally a descriptive statistic. It is a way of formalizing the test for genetic effects in natural experiments such as the twin design. It is a descriptive statistic that gives an estimate of effect size for a latent trait of genetic influence based upon a particular population measured in a particular way at a particular moment in time. It provides a statistical indicator that speaks to the confidence that one might have in inferring that genetic differences among individuals account for more than zero of the reliable variance in a trait (again measured in a particular way in a particular population at a particular moment in time). It can also, however, provide a quasi- (or psuedo-) precise estimate of the magnitude of genetic effects that can be quite misleading, if all the appropriate caveats concerning heritability are ignored.

Given the advances in biometrical model fitting in the literature and also the prototypical language used in BG, the highly limited scope of heritability is most times not highlighted in the literature and in fact typically ignored. What readers generally see is statements that "disorder X is Z% heritable." I've been guilty of using this shorthand myself. Indeed, I acknowledge that the language and methods of BG have probably contributed to the misunderstanding and in fact dislike of the heritability statistic in some circles. It certainly reads more like a static absolute measure of genetic causation, especially given the precision of biometrical model fitting used in many current BG studies.

I would suggest that critics of the BG approach evaluate for themselves whether their discomfort arises from the way in which heritability is described and used in the BG literature, or whether, as argued earlier, they simply don't like the idea of conducting natural experiments. There is a critical difference here. Confusing one byproduct of BG research with the overall intent and execution of BG research will not bring clarity to this area. I would argue strongly that, for disorders of unknown etiology (including most behavioral and psychiatric conditions), natural experiments offer some promise for pointing us in the proper direction. Almost without exception, these natural experiments (and in fact the heritability construct itself) have suggested that while genes are important for most forms of psychopathology, the genetic effect is less than one, and thus nongenetic effects need to be included in etiological models. This has been an empirical finding based on a number of natural experiments and not just a theoretical assumption. This empirical finding, again, stands in contrast to classic genetic models of disease that assumed genes represented the necessary and sufficient condition for disorder. BG research, and the heritability statistic, have really opened the door for more complicated models that focus on etiology at the intersection of genetic and nongenetic influence. However, I would also add that I would like to see (and perhaps should do myself) more user-friendly explanations of what heritability is and is not in papers, especially those intended for broad audiences that are only acquainted with BG research and hence are not necessarily informed on the pure meaning of heritability.

The Methodology Used to Estimate Environmental Influence Is Flawed, Because the Environment Is Not Actually Measured but Is Treated Essentially as a Residual Term After Accounting for Genetic Effects

This is, in many ways, a fairly accurate statement. Referring again to the history of the twin method as an example, the proposition to compare MZ and DZ twins was not made to capture the impact of the environment on diseases or traits. It was designed to detect evidence of genetic influence. Within the twin paradigm, the genetic coefficient is the only one that varies in the fundamental biometric model: There is a residual environmental component (shared environment or common environment) that accounts for similarity of twins that is independent of zygosity, and there is a residual environmental component that reflects the degree to which twins are not similar (unique environment or nonshared environment). In this model, even the term "environment" is something of a misnomer, as it has the very specific meaning of influence that is not heritable.

Of course, a slightly different scenario exists for adoption studies, in which direct effects of rearing environment not confounded with genetic similarity may be observed. Although adoption studies played a large role in behavior genetics for a number of years, they have declined greatly because of pragmatic difficulties relating to the adoptive process, especially in the United States. Thus, for many readers of the BG literature, the vast majority of studies use the twin paradigm, with the corresponding limitations to detect environmental influence.

One implication of this limitation is that when environmental effects are found, it may be that they are especially potent and worthy of attention. For example, over a decade ago sibling interaction was reported to show large effects of common environmental influences, especially when observed via videotaped interaction (Rende, Slomkowski, Stocker, Fulker, & Plomin, 1992). This effect was most notable for behaviors relating to warmth between siblings and was shown using data on biological and adoptive siblings in the Colorado Adoption Project (CAP). Over the next decade, a comprehensive analysis of sibling warmth in a combined twin-sibling design that included a broad range of genetic relatedness (the Nonshared Environment in Adolescent Development project or NEAD) revealed again extraordinary evidence for shared environmental influences (Reiss, 2000). This work dovetails with an emerging story that sibling influence on deviant behavior in adolescence is potent, as having a warm relationship with a delinquent older sibling is a strong predictor of an increase in deviancy through adolescence (Slomkowski, Rende, Conger, Simons, & Conger, 2001). In this example, a theoretical model postulating sibling effects on deviant behavior as a form of social learning is buttressed by the repeated observation that both sibling interaction and deviant behavior show high levels of common environmental influence (e.g., Slomkowski et al., 2001). Although one could argue that sibling effects on deviancy are epiphenomena due to their common genetic relatedness, BG paradigms have been very influential in refuting this proposition, because the common environmental effects on sibling behavior and its link to deviancy are observed after controlling for possible genetic effects (e.g., Reiss, 2000).

A similar argument is currently being made for sibling effects on smoking. A number of studies of smoking in adolescence have consistently shown that common environmental influences are robust, especially for initiation of smoking (e.g., Slomkowski & Rende, 2001). Our work in this area is beginning to demonstrate that such common environmental influences are attributable, in part, to warmth between siblings: Siblings with warm relationships (characterized by high social contact, mutual friends, overt feelings of affection for each other) tend to be highly similar on smoking behavior (Slomkowski & Rende, 2001; Slomkowski, Rende, & Niaura, 2002). This finding has also been reported in twin studies of adults, as frequency of social contact between twins is associated with twin similarity for smoking, even after accounting for zygosity (e.g., Kendler et al., 1999).

Another example of a replicated common environmental effect is depression in adolescence. Nearly a decade ago I reported that high levels of depressive symptoms showed a robust common environmental effect, using data from the NEAD study introduced earlier (Rende, Plomin, Reiss, & Hetherington, 1993). This was accomplished using a modification of the standard BG model that is designed to analyze extreme scores in a distribution of individual differences. There are now three studies that have replicated this finding (Deater-Deackard, Reiss, Hetherington, & Plomin, 1997; Eley, 1997; Rice, Harold, & Thapar, 2002), and our current work is also supporting this basic finding (Rende, Slomkowski, & Niaura, 2002).

I present these examples of detecting common environmental influences on a range of important behaviors and dimensions in adolescence—sibling interaction, deviancy, smoking, and depressive symptoms—to demonstrate that it is possible to elicit evidence of nongenetic influence, or more specifically family-wide common environmental influence, in the prototypical BG model. Again, these findings may be especially notable, because I do agree in part with the critique that the BG paradigms and models—especially when applied in the classic twin design—are not well positioned to reveal environmental effects (see Dick & Rose, 2002). Considering in more detail potential environmental influences, and how they may be uncovered, should be a challenge for BG researchers, as discussed in more detail later.

BEYOND HERITABILITY: THE FUTURE OF BEHAVIOR GENETICS

I begin this section with a question raised in a recent paper on behavior genetics: "Is behavior genetics, then, a thing of the past, a field whose success makes it obsolete?" (Dick & Rose, 2002, p. 70)

The authors who recently posed this question answered that BG is not a thing of the past. To a degree, I agree with this claim. From my own perspective, I think that there needs to be a gradual transition, fueled by a forceful effort, to move from latent trait models to models that actually measure the "G" and "E" in the BG model, one of the possibilities for BG research highlighted by Dick and Rose (2002). The yield of BG has been, in my view, somewhat mixed. Although it has been extremely successful at providing evidence for a role of genetic influence on virtually all phenotypes of interest to behavioral scientists (e.g., McGuffin, Riley, & Plomin, 2001), the BG paradigm has yielded less in terms of elucidating environmental effects, especially those that reflect influences common to family members. My response to the three critiques I raised earlier was intended to show both this success and lack of success. Taking the broad view on genetic models of disease, and especially the climate with which they were being applied to psychiatric disorders in the late 1980s, BG has achieved a number of accomplishments that should set the stage nicely for a next phase of development for this paradigm. These include the conceptualization of genetic effects as the expression of a number of susceptibility genes of small effect size, which coexist with nongenetic influences, which sometimes are revealed as systematic effects of the environment. However, an overreliance on the latent trait models that have had an impact on the types of genetic models which are used in psychiatric genetics would, I think, start to represent regression in the field. Thus, I would identify three primary goals for future BG research: (a) identifying candidate phenotypes reflective of genetic susceptibility to disorder, (b) using BG designs to elucidate solid evidence for environmental effects, and (c) integrating the "G" and "E" of BG in a meaningful empirical fashion.

Identifying Candidate Phenotypes Reflective of Genetic Susceptibility to Disorder

One of the best uses for traditional BG methods, especially with reference to psychopathology, will be to focus on better indicators of the candidate phenotypes that reflect the genetic susceptibility to psychiatric disorder. BG models of disorder have often applied a liability model of disorder that is conceptually quite appealing and nearly 40 years old (Falconer, 1965). As I have discussed a number of times (e.g., Rende, 1996, 1999; Rende & Plomin, 1995), the liability model makes the good point that what is inherited for complex diseases is not the disease per se but rather some underlying risk factors that convey susceptibility to the disease. For the past decade or so, much of the BG literature on psychiatric disorder has utilized this perspective by fitting quantitative models that assume such a liability and then generate a heritability of this theoretical liability. This is often achieved using sophisticated transformations of categorical data into normal distributions of hypothetical liability to disease. Although I would acknowledge that this technique has been useful—in part because it has shown that heritabilities, while robust, are never 100%—I have also argued on a number of occasions that this approach has overrelied on modeling this latent risk without attempting to measure the underlying vulnerability factors (e.g., Rende, 1999; Rende & Plomin, 1995). This is potentially a problem if BG research becomes lackadaisical about finding what we purport to be of utmost importance, namely underlying indicators of genetic susceptibility, because of too much belief in our latent trait models.

The argument here, which is not a new one in BG or in the study of complex disease, is simply that intensive efforts to measure liability will be necessary to make progress in the identification of susceptibility loci. For many disorders, we do not have serious models of what the liability would be. Let's start with major depressive disorder. What are candidates for underlying liability indicators—often referred to as endophenotypes—for this disorder? There really are none, although a number of candidate domains of behavior could be batted around. Is it sensitivity to life events that would be reflected as an underlying neurocognitive predisposition? Stress reactivity? Temperamental factors? These candidate endophenotypes are just now beginning to make their way in family studies, but I haven't seen (and should note I haven't conducted myself) the requisite studies using BG methodology to test systematically if any of these traits are indeed highly heritable and linked to the heritability of major depressive disorder. I haven't seen (and have not produced myself) a critical mass of papers devoted to discussing what the underlying endophenotypes may be for major depressive disorder. I have seen (and have contributed to) a number of studies suggesting that major depressive disorder is partly heritable, especially if one models liability to depression and then fits the modified BG model that decomposes variance in genetic and nongenetic sources.

This slap on the wrist to BG research can extend to many of the common psychiatric disorders. BG researchers have produced a lot of studies showing that nearly all common disorders are heritable, that the heritability is somewhat robust, and that it is possible to model genetic risk using a liability framework. BG researchers have produced very few studies focused on measuring the hypothesized liability and conducting the requisite tests using BG methods to demonstrate empirically that there is a good endophenotype (or multiple endophenotypes).

Why is this the case? I think in part it is due to the inherent complexity of the etiology of many of the common psychiatric disorders. As a contrast, there is a long tradition, for example, in schizophrenia research on studying endophenotypes, and there are numerous studies examining a number of candidate endophenotypes from a BG perspective such as impaired attention (e.g., Chen & Faraone, 2000; Cornblatt & Malhotra, 2001). I discussed earlier that twin studies were quite useful in broadening the phenotype for autism into more of an endophenotype that is being used in molecular research. Autism and schizophrenia, however, are extreme forms of disability with now obvious neural and cognitive underpinnings, and it could be argued that they are almost studied as neurological disorders. The most common psychiatric disorders do not scream out in terms of what the endophenotypes may be. There are excellent guidelines for what the properties of good endophenotypes would be (e.g., Tsuang, Faraone, & Lyons, 1993; Swan, 1999), but it will take creative thinking and effort to take on, as a priority in BG, the move from measuring heritability of liability to psychiatric disorder to the dedicated search for endophenotypes. One model to follow would be sustained effort to uncover a variety of endophenotypes for alcoholism (e.g., Schuckit, 2001).

The critical void presented by the lack of endophenotypes is, in my view, two-fold: (a) their absence would make the search for actual genetic susceptibility loci nearly impossible (i.e., if we rely on diagnostic categories to guide genomic search strategies, we will be waiting a long time for progress); and (b) even without evidence of underlying susceptibility loci, the existence of believable and well-studied endophenotypes could be integrated with critical environmental risk factors, as discussed later.

Using BG Designs to Elucidate Solid Evidence for Environmental Effects

My second recommendation is one that has received attention from other authors in recent years. The fundamental premise is to utilize BG designs—or genetically informative designs as they are now referred to in such propositions—to control for genetic effects in order to reveal pure environmental effects (Dick & Rose, 2002; Rutter, Pickles, Murray, & Eaves, 2001). This proposition is, in some sense, an attempt to restore some balance in the twin paradigm, which as described earlier, was developed to detect evidence of genetic effects. The especially good aspect to this approach is the suggestion to integrate actual measures of environmental influences on behavior in BG designs and models, with the intention being the possibility of detecting stronger effects of measured environments as compared to residual latent terms in biometrical models.

Dick and Rose (2002) provided a nice illustration of some recent findings using this approach. These include the detection of effects of parental monitoring, home atmosphere, and neighborhood deprivation on behavior problems in childhood. What is interesting here is that the BG paradigm—often maligned for misrepresenting environmental effects—is now being used to offer irrefutable evidence of the importance of environmental risk factors by providing a control for confounding genetic effects. By doing so, it is possible that psychosocial risk factors that may be more easily targeted for preventive interventive strategies could be illuminated using genetically informative designs. Furthermore, from my perspective, one of the critical contributions of using genetically informative designs to highlight the environment could be to elucidate psychosocial risk factors that are specific to disorders versus those that are more diffuse in their effects. Emphasizing the overt measurement of environmental risk in BG designs might promote the development of novel techniques for better capturing indicators of salient nongenetic risk.

Integrating the "G" and "E" of BG in a Meaningful Empirical Fashion

Current thinking in BG is emphasizing, rightly so, the possibility of bringing together the study of genetics and environments, long a goal in BG and most often a methodological complexity not easily solved. For example, Dick and Rose (2002) highlighted strategies for stratifying environmental effects to reveal conditions under which expression of genetic propensity is either enhanced or suppressed, the classic framework of gene-environment interaction. In this approach, one would test for differences in genetic effects under differing environmental contexts.

Although this is an important area of research, most exciting will be eventual strategies for integrating endophenotypes with measured environments in order to move closer to underlying process in the BG framework. Dick and Rose

(2002) used the example of genetic effects on alcohol use differing according to various contextual factors such as urban versus rural environments as one window into gene-environment interaction. In this example, genetic effects referred essentially to heritabilities or the latent genetic liability to alcohol use. As mentioned earlier, given that there are now a number of putative endophenotypes for alcoholism that have emerged from genetic designs (e.g., Schuckit, 2001), it would be fascinating to determine if any of these measured indicators of putative genetic propensity interacted with key social contextual risk factors to produce risk for alcoholism. Similar questions could be asked for other forms of substance use, such as tobacco use, as BG models have shown that environmental factors are most influential for determining initiation of use whereas genetic factors appear to contribute to progression of use to dependence (e.g., Kendler, et al., 1999). Incorporating actual measures of both underlying genetic propensity and social contextual risk could move us much closer to isolating mechanisms by which genes and environments interact.

Dick and Rose (2002) also emphasized the importance of gene-environment correlation, one of the key conceptual advances offered by BG over the past few decades. In contrast to a G-E interaction model, G-E correlation models emphasize the linkages between underlying genetic vulnerability and the creation or shaping of environmental risk. Although G-E interaction may be the most useful theoretical model for substance use phenotypes, G-E correlation may be at the heart of the etiology of many common psychiatric disorders, such as the affective and anxiety disorders. For example, although it had long been recognized that there are linkages between stressful life events and depression, BG designs were quite influential in revealing that the risk for both may be mediated in part by a common thread of individual differences in genetic vulnerability: those at highest risk for depression may also be those at highest risk for creating adverse social contexts. Such a model gets at the interconnectedness of genetic and social risk and the reality of the complexity of the situation for common forms of psychopathology. What BG paradigms could offer for future research would be an impetus to move closer to underlying process by improving our measurement of key mediating factors, both at the level of the individual (endophenotype) and at the level of environment (social context).

SUMMARY: BIOLOGICAL PROCESS IN SOCIAL CONTEXT

There is a "new" BG within "traditional" BG research: behavioral genomics (McGuffin et al., 2001). An extraordinary effort is being undertaken to isolate genomic regions associated with psychopathology, and this effort will undoubtedly intensify in the next decade. I argue that this goal will be dependent to a large degree on our ability to fill in the void between the future of BG— DNA—with the past of BG—the latent construct of heritability. One framework for filling in the void is to move our study in the direction of searching for biobehavioral markers of individual differences of sensitivities to the environment, including biological as well as psychosocial environments. This overall goal of gene chasing will also be rendered meaningless without appropriate attention to the other void in BG—the substitution of latent trait residual environments with measured indicators of social contextual risk.

I argued earlier that, for all its shortcomings, BG research emphasized the need to include both "G" and "E" in our etiological models of psychiatric disorder. Although the complexities that will be offered by genomic search strategies probably cannot even be imagined well at this point, especially when tempered by the corollary attention necessary to address the similar complexity of the environment, it is useful to take this lesson from the past of BG to guide the future of BG: Let's be sure we keep both "G" and "E" in the model. More recent BG paradigms have begun to scratch the surface of how we might begin to bring the study of "G" and "E" together. My hope is that BG will continue in the direction it is moving by attempting to elucidate what the "G" and "E" are and how they intersect.

I would expect, then, that BG will not be dominated by latent trait models or by genomic search strategies. Rather, I would expect that BG will become an example of taking on the empirical challenge of merging the study of biological process with the examination of social context. Even if progress is slow, the conceptual advances will no doubt bode well for our future endeavors, as BG moves beyond heritability to become the multidisciplinary field it has the potential to be.

ACKNOWLEDGMENT

Preparation of this chapter was supported in part by a Research Scientist Development Award (MH01559) from the National Institute of Mental Health.

REFERENCES

Alarcon, M., Cantor, R. M., Liu, J., Gilliam, T. C., Geschwind, D. H., & Autism Genetic Research Exchange Consortium. (2002). Evidence for a language quantitative trait locus on chromosome 7q in multiplex autism families. *American Journal of Human Genetics, 70,* 60–71.

Bettelheim, B. (1967). *The empty fortress: Infantile autism and the birth of the self.* New York: Free Press.

Chen, W. J., & Faraone, S. V. (2000). Sustained attention deficits as markers of genetic susceptibility to schizophrenia. *American Journal of Medical Genetics, 97,* 52–57.

Collaborative Linkage Study of Autism (2001). Incorporating language phenotypes strengthens evidence of linkage to autism. *American Journal of Medical Genetics, 105,* 539–547.

Cornblatt, B. A., & Malhotra, A. K. (2001). Impaired attention as an endophenotype for molecular genetic studies of schizophrenia. *American Journal of Medical Genetics, 105,* 11–15.

Deater-Deackard, K., Reiss, D., Hetherington, E. M., & Plomin, R. (1997). Dimensions and disorders of adolescent adjustment: A quantitative genetic analysis of unselected samples and selected extremes. *Journal of Child Psychology and Psychiatry, 38,* 515–525.

Dick, D. M., & Rose, R. J. (2002). Behavior genetics: What's new? What's next? *Current Directions in Psychological Science, 11,* 70–74.

Egeland, J., Gerhard, D., Pauls, D., Sussex, J., & Kidd, K. (1987). Bipolar affective disorders linked to DNA markers on chromosome 11. *Nature, 325,* 783–787.

Eley, T. C. (1997). Depressive symptoms in children and adolescents: Etiological links between normality and abnormality: A research note. *Journal of Child Psychology and Psychiatry, 38,* 861–865.

Falconer, D. S. (1965). The inheritance of liability to certain diseases, estimated from the incidence among relatives. *Annals of Human Genetics, 29,* 51–76.

Folstein, S. E., & Rutter, M. L. (1977). Infantile autism: A genetic study of 21 twin pairs. *Journal of Child Psychology and Psychiatry, 18,* 297–321.

Gusella, J., Wexler, N., Conneally, P., Naylor, S., Anderson, M., & Tanzi, R. (1983). A polymorphic DNA marker genetically linked to Huntington's disease. *Nature, 306,* 234–238.

Kanner, L. (1943). Autistic disturbances of affective contact. *Nervous Child, 2,* 217–250.

Kendler, K. S., Neale, M. C., Sullivan, L., Corey, L. A., Gardner, C. O., & Prescott, C. A. (1999). A population-based twin study in women of smoking initiation and nicotine dependence. *Psychological Medicine, 29,* 299–308.

McGuffin, P., Riley, B., & Plomin, R. (2001). Toward behavioral genomics. *Science, 291,* 1232–1249.

Plomin, R., & Rende, R. (1991). Human behavioral genetics. *Annual Review of Psychology, 42,* 161–190.

Rende, R. (1996). Liability to psychopathology: A quantitative genetic perspective. In M. Levine, L. Smolak, & R. Streigel-Moore (Eds.), *The developmental psychopathology of eating disorders* (pp. 109–121). Hillsdale, NJ: Lawrence Erlbaum Associates.

Rende, R. (1999). Adaptive and maladaptive pathways in development: A quantitative genetic perspective. In M. LaBuda, E. Grigorenko, I. Ravich-Scherbo, & S. Scarr (Eds), *On the way to individuality: Current methodological issues in behavioral genetics* (pp. 21–42). New York: Nova Science Publishers.

Rende, R. (2000). Emotion and behavior genetics. In M. Lewis & J. M. Haviland-Jones (Eds.), *Handbook of emotions* (2nd ed.). New York: Guilford.

Rende, R., & Plomin, R. (1995). Nature, nurture, and development of psychopathology. In D. Cicchetti & D. Cohen (Eds.), *Developmental psychopathology: Vol. 1. Theory and method* (pp. 291–314). New York: Wiley.

Rende, R., Plomin, R., Reiss, D., & Hetherington, E. M. (1993). Genetic and environmental influences on depression in adolescence: Etiology of individual differences and extreme scores. *Journal of Child Psychology and Psychiatry, 34,* 1387–1398.

Rende, R., Plomin, R., & Vandenberg, S. (1990). Who discovered the twin method? *Behavior Genetics, 20,* 277–285.

Rende, R., Slomkowski, C., & Niaura, R. (2002). *Shared environmental effects on high levels of depressive symptoms in adolescence.* Manuscript submitted for publication.

Rende, R., Slomkowski, C., Stocker, C., Fulker, D., & Plomin, R. (1992). Genetic and environmental influences on maternal and sibling behavior in middle childhood: A sibling adoption study. *Developmental Psychology, 28,* 484–490.

Reiss, D. (2000). *The relationship code.* Cambridge, MA: Harvard University Press.

Rice, F., Harold, G. T., & Thapar, A. (2002). Assessing the effects of age, sex and shared environment on the genetic aetiology of depression in childhood and adolescence. *Journal of Child Psychology and Psychiatry.*

Risch, N., & Merikangas, K. (1996). The future of genetic studies of complex disease. *Science, 273,* 1516–1517.

Rutter, M., Macdonald, H., Le Couteur, A., Macdonald, H., & Simonoff, E. (1990). Genetic factors in child psychiatric disorders: II. Empirical findings. *Journal of Child Psychology and Psychiatry, 31,* 39–82.

Rutter, M., Pickles, A., Murray, R., & Eaves, L. (2001). Testing hypotheses on specific environmental causal effects on behavior. *Psychological Bulletin, 127,* 291–324.

Schuckit, M. A. (2001). Genetics of the risk for alcoholism. *American Journal of the Addictions, 9,* 103–112.

Sherrington, R., Brynjolfsson, J., Petursson, H., Potter, M., Dudleston, K., Barraclough, B., Wasmuth, J., Dodds, M., & Gurling, H. (1988). Localization of a susceptibility locus for schizophrenia on chromosome 5. *Nature, 336,*1 64–167.

Slomkowski, C., & Rende, R. (2001). *Social context of smoking in adolescence in a genetically-informative design.* Paper presented at the Life History Research Society Meeting, St. Michael's, MD.

Slomkowski, C., Rende, R., Conger, K., Simons, R., & Conger, R. (2001). Brothers, sisters, and delinquency: Evaluating social influence from early to middle adolescence. *Child Development, 72,* 271–283.

Slomkowski, C., Rende, R., & Niaura, R. (2002). *Sibling effects on smoking in adolescence: A genetically-informative design.* Manuscript submitted for publication.

Slomkowski, C., Wasserman, G., Shaffer, D., Rende, R., & Davies, M. (1997). Research note: A new instrument to assess sibling relationships in antisocial youth: The Social Interaction Between Siblings (SIBS) interview. *Journal of Child Psychology and Psychiatry, 38,* 253–256.

Swan, G. E. (1999). Implications of genetic epidemiology for the prevention of tobacco use. *Nicotine and Tobacco Research, 1,* S49–S56.

Tsuang, M. T., Faraone, S. V., & Lyons, M. J. (1993). Identification of the phenotype in psychiatric genetics. *European Archives of Psychiatry and Clinical Neuroscience, 243,* 131–142.

7

Uniqueness, Diversity, Similarity, Repeatability, and Heritability

Jerry Hirsch
University of Illinois at Urbana-Champaign

Since the emergence of genetics following the triple rediscovery in 1900 of Mendel's (1866) classic study, there have been attempts to calculate and estimate the number of possible genotypes for a species (Sutton, 1903, pp. 24–39, 231–251). An example of such attempts is Borel (1961), which, according to H. Piéron (1962, p. 12), Borel had made as early as 1941 (see too Corcos & Monaghan, 1993, pp. 188–189; Morgan, 1934, p. 139; Wright, 1932; Snyder, 1949). I too once contributed to this literature (Hirsch, 1963). Re-examination of this work recently has revealed a previously unappreciated complexity.

I made and published the individuality calculation in an invited lead article in *Science* magazine 40 years ago (Hirsch, 1963) and have always been proud that my arithmetic has withstood the test of time. It was and still is correct. Nobody has succeeded in challenging it. But now, I find that I myself must challenge the interpretation that I gave to the calculation at that time, because the calculation does not answer the question I was then asking, however mistakenly at that time we all believed that it did. It answers a different question; however, as you will see, it is a related question.

My purpose now is to explain what formerly has been assumed and what must henceforth be analyzed more carefully. Formerly the situation had been analyzed in the following way: We estimated "the probability that the second offspring born to parents will have exactly the same genotype as their firstborn" to be "less than 1 chance in over 70 trillion," that is $(\frac{1}{2}^{23})^2$ because man, with 23 chromosome pairs, produces gametes with any of $2^{23} = 8,388,608$ alternative genomes. For the second born to be identical to the firstborn, it requires both parents to produce a gamete that replicates the one that each had previously contributed to their firstborn and that these replicates combine once again. Because each individual can produce gametes with any of 2^{23} alternative genomes, the probability of a replicate occurring is $\frac{1}{2}^{23}$ in the case of each parent, independently and separately; and the probability of their joint and simultaneous occurrence in combination was logically inferred to be the product of their separate probabilities, that is $(\frac{1}{2}^{23})^2$, or one chance in over 70 trillion.

The logic is impeccable; we learn it as students in elementary mathematics: The probability of the simultaneous occurrence of two independent events is the product of their separate probabilities. But the actual relationship is different, and we did not appreciate that difference until we started to work with diagrams, which was impossible to do for such large numbers. Certainly, to date, no one else seems to have done so. My 1963 and earlier discussions used words, some genetic symbols, and a few elementary calculations, as others who have considered this problem have done. Under those conditions the complexity remained undetected.

The different picture emerges, however, when we employ the diagrams with which we explain some of elementary genetics to our classes—using numbers small enough so such diagrams are possible. For a species like *Drosophila willistoni*, with only three pairs of chromosomes, the diagram shown in Fig. 7.1 displays the repro-

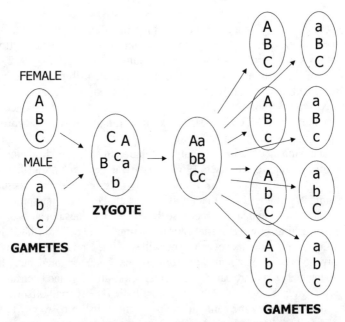

FIG. 7.1.   Recombination, segregation, and independent assortment. Genetic components (chromosomes or genes) are undifferentiated in this exercise except the maternal components are in capital letters and paternal are in lower case to designate which parent contributed what components. Adapted with permission, courtesy of W. S. Sutton (1903) and E. B. Wilson (1924).

ductive cycle from fertilization through gametogenesis for an individual. Two parental gametes (sperm and egg) combine into a zygote on the left and on the right side the resulting individual at gametogenesis produces gametes with $2^3 = 8$ alternative genomes. But, the probability that a given breeding pair will have two identical offspring is not $(\frac{1}{2}^3)^2$. Yes, $\frac{1}{2}^3$ is the probability of the occurrence of a particular gamete from one parent, and the same is true for the other parent. So, why does not its square, that is $(\frac{1}{2}^3)^2 = \frac{1}{64}$, give the probability of a second zygote being identical to the first zygote as we all had previously assumed it does?

The answer can be found by examining the matrix of zygotes (called "Punnett squares" in genetics) produced by arraying along the margins the eight possible male and female gametic genomes where each cell entry is the zygote resulting from the intersection of row and column gametes. This examination is illustrated in Figs. 7.2a and 7.2b. Remember, our examination is being done for the case of a species with three or fewer pairs of chromosomes.

The probability that the second offspring born to parents will be genotypically the same as their firstborn depends upon (a) the number of genotypes that are possible and (b) the relative frequencies of their expected occurrences. Consider the matrices of genotypes produced by gametic genomes arrayed on their margins for some easily illustrated cases, such as 1, 2 and 3 pairs of chromosomes (assuming for simplicity no crossing-over, no mutation, and only two forms [homologues] of each chromosome in a population). Under those assumptions the number of types of gametic genomes on the margins is 2^N, where N is the number of chromosome pairs.

Our collective error has been not to appreciate that when the number of gametic genomes, 2^N is squared, $(2^N)^2$, the result describes the number of cells in the matrix of zygotes, not the number of zygotic genotypes. Figure 7.3 illustrates this issue.

For the two allele case, the number of different genotypes in each matrix is a smaller number, 3^N. In the examples shown, there are $2^1 = 2$, $2^2 = 4$, and $2^3 = 8$ gametic genomes, matrices with $(2^1)^2 = 4$, $(2^2)^2 = 16$, and $(2^3)^2 = 64$ cells but only $3^1 = 3$, $3^2 = 9$, and $3^3 = 27$ different genotypes in the cells for the one, two, and three chromosome-pair cases, respectively. Examination of the matrices reveals, and dramatically so in the off-diagonal, that many genotypes are not uniquely determined by a single combination of maternal and paternal gametes, as our calculation had assumed. In fact, what can be seen in the off-diagonal is that any gamete can enter the multiple heterozygote, if it combines with the appropriate gamete from the opposite sex. Figure 7.4 illustrates the expected occurrences of relative genotype frequencies.

The coefficients in the binomial expansion happen to give the relative frequencies with which the different possible genotypes may be expected to appear in each matrix. In the cases shown there are the frequencies 1:2:1 for (1) a single pair of chromosomes, (2) 1:2:1:2:4:2:1:2:1 for two pairs of chromosomes, and (3) 1:2:1:2:4:2:1:2:1:2:4:2:4:8:4:2:4:2:1:2:1:2:4:2:1:2:1 for three pairs of chromosomes, respectively.

As illustrated in Fig. 7.5, humans, with 23 chromosome pairs, produce gametes with any of $2^{23} = 8,388,608$ possible genomes, and would require a matrix with $(2^{23})^2$

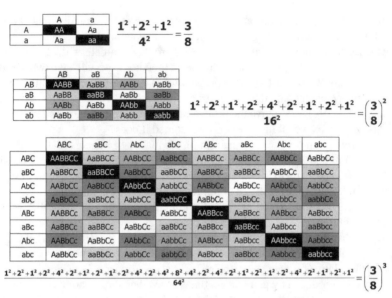

$$\frac{1^2+2^2+1^2}{4^2}=\frac{3}{8}$$

$$\frac{1^2+2^2+1^2+2^2+4^2+2^2+1^2+2^2+1^2}{16^2}=\left(\frac{3}{8}\right)^2$$

$$\frac{1^2+2^2+1^2+2^2+4^2+2^2+1^2+2^2+1^2+2^2+4^2+2^2+4^2+8^2+4^2+2^2+4^2+2^2+1^2+2^2+1^2+2^2+4^2+2^2+1^2+2^2+1^2}{64^2}=\left(\frac{3}{8}\right)^3$$

FIG. 7.2a. Probability of two offspring having identical genotypes illustrated with Punnett squares in which the margins contain genomes and the matrix cells contain zygotic genotypes as the products of matings involving 1, 2, or 3 pairs of chromosomes (represented as upper or lower case letters or both).

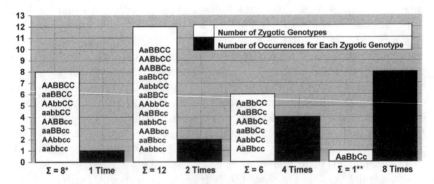

* **Black diagonal in Figure 7.2a = Unique homozygous genotypes**
** **White diagonal in Figure 7.2a = Multiple heterozygous genotype**

FIG. 7.2b. Zygotic genotype frequency of occurrence as shown in the Punnett square of Figure 7.2a involving 3 pairs of chromosomes (represented as upper or lower case letters or both).

Number of Gametic Genomes: $2^1=2$ $2^2=4$ $2^3=8$

Number of Cells in Matrices: $(2^1)^2=4$ $(2^2)^2=16$ $(2^3)^3=64$

Number of different
Zygotic Genotypes: $3^1=3$ $3^2=9$ $3^3=27$

FIG. 7.3.   Number of possible different genotypes in matrices using 1, 2, and 3 pairs of chromosomes. Our collective error has been not to appreciate that when the number of gametic genomes (2^N) is squared ($2^N)^2$, the result describes the number of *cells* in the matrix of zygotes, *not* the number of *zygotic genotypes* (3^N).

$3^1=3$
(1:2:1)

$3^2=9$
(1:2:1:2:4:2:1:2:1)

$3^3=27$
(1:2:1:2:4:2:1:2:1:2:4:2:4:8:4:2:4:2:1:2:1:2:4:2:1:2:1)

FIG. 7.4.   Expected occurrences of relative genotype frequencies in Punnett square matrices with 1, 2, and 3 pairs of chromosomes and 3, 9, and 27 genotypes.

2^{23} = 8,388,608 possible genomes
$(2^{23})^2$ = 70,368,744,177,666 cell matrix
3^{23} = 94,143,178,827 different possible human
    genotypes

FIG. 7.5.   Number of possible human genotypes with 23 chromosome pairs is 94+ billion distributed over a 70+ trillion-cell-matrix. In order to understand the genetic process of reproduction, we present a simplified situation using chromosomes with only two alternative forms in each pair, and without cross-over or breakage occuring. Reality is much more complex.

= 70,368,744,177,666, or over 70 trillion cells, and $3^{23} = 94,143,178,827$, or over 94 billion different possible genotypes distributed over those 70+ trillion cells.

Therefore, the answer to the question about the probability that the second born may have the same genotype as the firstborn requires a different approach. As displayed in Fig. 7.6, starting with the Punnett square in the simplest case of one chro-

For pedalogical reasons we will linearize the Punnett Square for the case of 1 chromosome with 2 homologues:

	A	a
A	AA	Aa
a	Aa	aa

Replication:

- Here heterozygous combinations:

- have twice the frequency of occurrence as homozygous combinations:

- No Replicate Combinations:

	AA	Aa	Aa	aa
AA	Yes	No	No	No
Aa	No	Yes	Yes	No
Aa	No	Yes	Yes	No
aa	No	No	No	Yes

FIG. 7.6.   Probability of replication of heterozygous or homozygous combinations.

mosome pair with two possible homologues, we have four equally likely possibilities (two of them the same) for each individual. Then taking the possible combinations that produce two individuals, we have entered a "yes" when they are identical and a "no" when they are not.

We find agreement occurring in 6 of the 16 cells of this matrix, with the probability of two identical genotypes being $6/16 = 3/8$. More succinctly, instead of duplicating Aa, we could enter the three genotypes on the margins with their respective probabilities: AA – _, Aa – _, aa – _ and notice that a "yes" can occur only when the same entry value defines the row as defines the column. So the reasoning could be abbreviated by recognizing that our 3/8 value is obtained by summing the following terms: the probability of the first genotype multiplied by the probability of an identical second genotype—for AA, Aa, and aa, these are, as shown in Fig. 7.7, respectively:

$$\frac{1^2 + 2^2 + 1^2}{4^2} = \frac{6}{16} = \frac{3}{8}.$$

In general, by a similar line of reasoning we arrive at the values appearing in the table. Note that, where previously we had estimated the probability of two identical children from one couple as 1 in 70 trillion, now we find that it is slightly less than 1 in 160,000—almost a billion times more likely! Our analysis also reveals that the previous estimate was an answer to a question somewhat different from the

Number of Distinct Homologues	P(two children the same) with any parents	P(two children the same) with the same parents
2	3/8	19/32
3	5/27	25/54
4	7/64	103/256
m	$2m-1)/m^3$	$\{(m^3 + 2m^2 + 2m - 1)\}/4m$

Results: m = 2
n = 23

$P\{\text{any parents}\}$ = $(3/8)^{23}$ = $(96/256)^{23}$ = 1.59×10^{-10}
(1 in 6.27 billion)

$P\{\text{same parents}\}$ = $(19/32)^{23}$ = $(152/256)^{23}$ = 6.21×10^{-6}
(1 in 161,107)

Results: m = 4
n = 23

$P\{\text{any parents}\}$ = $(7/64)^{23}$ = $(28/256)^{23}$ = 8.05×10^{-10}
(1 in 1.24 billion)

$P\{\text{same parents}\}$ = $(103/256)^{23}$ = $(103/256)^{23}$ = 3.37×10^{-9}
(1 in 337 million)

FIG. 7.7.   Probability of identical genotypes of two children produced by 1) any parents, or 2) the same parents.

one we had stated, that is, instead of two children from the same parents, it was in fact addressing the question of two identical children from any (same or different) parents in the population. Nevertheless as shown in the table, the answer to the question involving any parents is also grossly different, that is, now seen to be one in 6.27 billion, also a much more likely event.

Furthermore, evidence and analysis also reveal the unrealistic nature of our assumption that there are in a population only two alternative forms of the chromosomes in each pair. In many cases, for example, maximum heterozygosity, both parents were required to have the same genotype—a ridiculous assumption. Whereas that assumption was certainly not concealed, effectively all of us seem to have ignored, or at least failed to appreciate, it.

One might object and raise the "so what" question: that my foregoing discussion has merely shown that, an event once believed to be infinitesimally unlikely, now appears merely very unlikely. At this point reference to the Punnett squares should remind us that our analysis has shown that the populations we study can no longer be considered to comprise almost exclusively unique genotypes. As was illustrated in Figs. 7.2a and 7.2b, there is diversity of genotypes and their frequencies: The figure's main diagonal (upper left to the reader's lower right) contains the unique genotypes, they are homozygotes. The off-diagonal contains N replicates of the single most frequent genotype, the multiple heterozygote. In the cells on both sides of the main diagonal are distributed duplicate to multiple copies of the several homozygote-heterozygote combinations.

Consider the following: Up to this point we have treated the uniformity versus diversity question as an absolute, either two genotypes are identical or they are different. A more realistic approach would be to recognize gradations of similarity from as much alike as monozygotes (identical twins, triplets, etc.) through gradations of partial similarity, that is, varying proportions of shared elements. If two or more individuals are the same with respect to 22 out of our 23 pairs of chromosomes, and differ on one pair of chromosomes, or 21 pairs and differ on two pairs of chromosomes, or 20 pairs and differ on three, and so forth, they will have much in common. Of course, exactly how much will depend on which chromosomes are shared and which are not. Those diagrams show a diversity of genotypes and their frequencies: The main diagonal contains the unduplicated unique genotypes—the homozygotes, the off-diagonal contains N copies of the single and most frequent genotype—the multiple heterozygote. In the cells of the N^2 matrix, exclusive of the two diagonals are distributed duplicate to multiple copies of the several homozygote-heterozygote combinations, which vary in frequency.

In sum, the import of these analyses is not merely to adjust a 40-year-old computation. Rather, it is to underscore the complexity of genetic combinations and to signal the dangers of simplistic approaches to representing genetic variability. For many decades (see Hirsch, 1970, 1997), such dangers have been ignored in several treatments of the concept of heritability.

HERITABILITY IS NOT HEREDITY

After our experience of the last decade with *The Bell Curve*, a best seller by the late Richard Herrnstein of Harvard and Charles Murray (1994), which so badly misused the heritability statistic, and in a recent issue of *Science* devoted to mapping the human genome, an article by Robert Plomin and colleagues (McGuffin, Riley, & Plomin, 2001), which also badly misused the heritability statistic, we should consider the meaning of heritability (see Hirsch, 1997, for analyses and interpretation).

The heritability concept must be distinguished from, rather than confused or conflated with, the heredity concept. Usually, the heritability statistic measures the additive genetic variance of a trait in a population and may be quite different in one population from that in another population of one species. Heredity is our name for the biological system that makes possible the existence and reproduction of each species.

Unfortunately, a recent *Dictionary of Psychology* ignores completely the assumptions under which heritability may be used:

> **heritability.** The extent to which a given characteristic is determined by heredity, usually measured as the proportion of the variance of the characteristic in a given population that can be accounted for by hereditary factors. The heritability will depend both on the variance of the genes and on the variance of the environment; both factors may differ from one population to another within the same species.

heritability ratio (h^2). A measure of heritability, namely $h^2 = V_g/V_t$ where V_g is the variance in a trait accounted for by hereditary factors and V_t is its total variance. (Sutherland, 1996, p. 201)

Heritability was developed in the mid 1930s to predict the outcome of plant and animal breeding studies and was borrowed by some psychologists in the belief that it could be applied to human data, for example, to determine what proportion of IQ is inherited (nature) and how much is acquired through experience (nurture). Analysis of the limitations of heritability reveals its inappropriateness as a measure in human psychology (Hirsch, 1997, pp. 213–214, 220; Jacquard, 1983, p. 476; Kempthorne, 1978, p. 1) where breeding experiments are off limits. Social policy based on inappropriate heritability statistics risks misguided predictions about human psychology in present and future society.

Unfortunately, well-intentioned critics also confounded heredity and heritability: "There exist no data which should lead a prudent man to accept the hypothesis that I.Q. test scores are in any degree heritable" (Kamin, 1974, p. 1), thus like Watson (1914, 1936, 1959), implying the irrelevance of heredity to intelligence as measured by IQ tests. Several comments are relevant here:

1. Merely because the heritability statistic might be inappropriate in a given situation does not permit one automatically to infer environmental causality;
2. The presence of heredity-environment interaction precludes generalization about the effects of both heredity and environment;
3. The presence of interaction is itself evidence that both heredity and environment may be exerting influence, for example, when it appears that the same environmental condition "causes" different phenotypic expressions in different genotypes, that in itself may be evidence of genetic effects; and
4. The detection of interaction usually requires greater statistical power than does the measurement of the effects of the primary variables; attaining that power usually entails relatively large samples (Wahlsten, 1990), that is, if one wants the power to detect an interaction to be 90%, the power to detect the main effects will usually then have to be higher than 90%.

The challenge Cavalli-Sforza made (Cavalli-Sforza & Cavalli-Sforza, 1995) to those he calls "IQ hereditarians, or enthusiasts" is that: In science we all have an obligation to be familiar with the current state-of-the-art and to incorporate previous developments into whatever we do. He showed that the current literature, including his own work, published in good journals yielded much lower heritabilities than those reported by the IQ enthusiasts, who simply go on ignoring the findings of others. I congratulate him on his forthrightness and agree completely with the argument he put forward. But, I go further and say (challenge) directly to him that, by the logic of his very same argument, neither party can ignore the analyses, I now quote below, by the two distinguished statistical geneticists, Oscar Kempthorne and Albert Jacquard, and both published in the well-known and highly respected journal *Biometrics*. They both analyzed the limitations of heritability analysis (it should also be noted that the later publication, by Jacquard, acknowledges with full reference the earlier one in the same journal by Kempthorne that is featured as "A Biometrics Invited Paper;" furthermore, Jacquard [1997, p. 6] now reports that his text has "the approval of the leading American biometrician Oscar Kempthorne" [my translation]):

> The idea that heritability is meaningful in the human mental and behavioral arena is attacked. The conclusion is that the heredity-IQ controversy has been a "tale full of sound and fury, signifying nothing." To suppose that one can establish effects of an intervention process when it does not occur in the data is plainly ludicrous. Mere observational studies can easily lead to stupidities, and it is suggested that this has happened in the heredity-IQ arena. The idea that there are racial-genetic differences in mental abilities and behavioral traits of humans is, at best, no more than idle speculation. (Kempthorne, 1978, p. 1)

> The need for great rigour exists particularly in the case of research projects which have serious implications for us all; this is the case when psychologists study the "heritability of intellectual aptitudes." They should take the precaution of systematically defining in a precise way the sense in which they use the word "heritability"; they should also state whether the assumptions under which this word can be used hold true in their studies. It is highly probable that most of the time this exercise in rigour would lead them to the conclusion that none of the three parameters proposed by geneticists can be of any use in solving their problems. (Jacquard, 1983, p. 476)

The complexity of the widely misunderstood, and so often misused, heritability statistic is further emphasized by the recent posthumous publication of J. B. S. Haldane's discovery of a case of negatively valued heritability. He reported the example "as a warning against the assumption that where a character is mainly determined genetically it will be more frequent in the progeny of those who manifest it than in the progeny of those who do not. This assumption is taken for granted in popular expositions of Darwinism and of eugenics" (Haldane 1996, p. 5). He considered the case to be "not trivial" because some "Other characters may have similar negative heritability" (Haldane, 1996, p. 3; also see accompanying commentary by Woodrow, 1996, who arranged for publication).

With respect to the tragic and widespread confusion about heritability, consider the following: In both *IQ in The Meritocracy* (1973) and *The Bell Curve* (1994), Herrnstein asserted the meritocracy-cognitive elite organization of our society. For the moment, let's act as if he were correct; certainly, he believed that he was. That would mean that he was asserting a correlation between genotype and environment. Genotypes are not randomly distributed over the social environment, they are arranged in his meritocratic hierarchy. Not any randomly selected genotype can be trained at Harvard or other elite schools, because there is an interaction between genotype and environment. Furthermore, our species mates assortatively, not randomly, for example, my wife and I met and married in Paris as American students at the Sorbonne (Sanders, 1996; analogous stories are true of countless colleagues).

Yet, heritability estimation assumes both random mating in an equilibrium population (including therein the equally likely occurrence of every culturally tabooed form of incest) and the absence of either correlation or interaction between heredity and environment. In fact, when one or more of those assumptions are violated, that is, random mating in an equilibrium population, correlation or interaction, heritability is undefined (see Kempthorne, 1997). What must be appreciated is that heritability is not a nature/nurture ratio measuring contributions to individual development and heritability is not heredity—two entirely different concepts that have been hopelessly conflated in *The Bell Curve* and many other texts where most of the hereditarian interpretations have been based on unjustifiable human heritability estimates (see Platt & Bach, 1997). Unfortunately, because of their assonance, when we hear one of the two words, automatically we think the other. Either these authors knew what they were perpetrating and are therefore responsible, or they did not know what they were doing and are therefore irresponsible. It is this level of "scholarship" that Professor Bouchard (1995, p. 418) has recommended as "a superbly written and exceedingly well-documented book.... It deserves the attention of every well-informed and thoughtful citizen."

Herrnstein had neither dark skin nor kinky hair. He was a white, Jewish, Harvard professor. Otherwise, such scholarly incompetence, as has here been revealed, might, if one were to apply his professed "high" standards, have had to be interpreted as an unmistakable sign of his own genetic inferiority.

The problem being considered—the probability of the occurrence of replicate genotypes or replicate components thereof—whether or not it is of particular interest to you, has the advantage of requiring us to recognize the complexity of the genetic system—a reality that intervenes into the consideration of many problems involving genetics.

REFERENCES

Borel, E. (1961). *Les probabilités et la vie, "Que sais-je?"* Le Point de Connaissances Actuelles, No. 91. Paris: Presses Universitaires de France.

Bouchard, T. J., Jr. (1995). Breaking the last taboo [Review of the book *The Bell curve: Intelligence and class structure in American life*]. *Contemporary Psychology, 40,* 415–418.

Cavalli-Sforza, L. L., & Cavalli-Sforza, F. (1995). The great human diasporas: The history of diversity and evolution (first published 1993 in Italy by Arnoldo as *Mondadori editore spa, Milano as chi siamo: La storia della diversita umana,* Sarah Thorne, Trans., English postscript 1995 by Luigi Luca Cavalli-Sforza). Menlo Park, CA: Addison-Wesley Publishing Company.

Corcos, A. F., & Monaghan, F. V. (1993). *Gregor Mendel's experiments on plant hybrids: A guided study.* New Brunswick, NJ: Rutgers University Press.

Haldane, J. B. S. (1996). The negative heritability of neonatal jaundice. *Annals of Human Genetics, 60,* 3–5.

Herrnstein, R. J. (1973). IQ in the meritocracy. Boston: Little Brown.

Herrnstein, R. J., & Murray, C. A. (1994). *The bell curve: Intelligence and class structure in American life.* New York: Free Press.

Hirsch, J. (1963). Behavior genetics and individuality understood: Behaviorism's counterfactual dogma blinded the behavioral sciences to the significance of meiosis. *Science, 142,* 1436–1442.

Hirsch, J. (1970). Behavior-genetic analysis and its biosocial consequences. *Seminar in Psychiatry, 2,* 89–105.

Hirsch, J. (1997). Some history of heredity-vs-environment, genetic inferiority at Harvard(?), and *The* (incredible) *Bell Curve. Genetica, 99,* 207–224.

Jacquard, A. (1983). Heritability: One word, three concepts. *Biometrics, 39,* 465–477.

Jacquard, A. (1997, April). Race, gènes et QI. *La Recherche, 297,* 6.

Kamin, L. J. (1974). *The science and politics of IQ.* Potomac, MD: Lawrence Erlbaum Associates.

Kempthorne, O. (1978). A biometrics invited paper: Logical, epistemological and statistical aspects of nature–nurture data interpretation. *Biometrics, 34,* 1–23.

Kempthorne, O. (1997). Heritability: Uses and abuses. *Genetica, 99,* 109–112.

McGuffin, P., Riley, B., & Plomin, R. (2001). Genomics and behavior: Toward behavioral genomics. *Science, 291,* 1232, 1249.

Mendel, G. (1866). Experiments on plant hybrids. *Verhandlungen des Naturforschenden Vereines in Brünn 4* (1865). *Abhandlungen,* 3–47.

Morgan, T. H. (1934). The mechanism and laws of heredity. In C. A. Murchison (Ed.), *A Handbook of General Experimental Psychology* (pp. 109–154). Worcester, MA: Clark University Press.

Piéron, H. (1962). *La psychologie différentielle* (2nd ed.). Paris: Presses Universitaires de France.

Platt, S. A., & Bach, M. (1997). Uses and misinterpretations of genetics in psychology. *Genetica, 99,* 135–143.

Sanders, J. (1996, December 3). Diversity, '50s style, did us well. *Largo Times,* p. 1.

Snyder, L. H. (1949). *Proceedings of the Eighth International Congress of Genetics,* p. 446.

Sutherland, S. (1996). *The international dictionary of psychology* (2nd ed.). New York: Crossroad.

Sutton, W. S. (1903). The chromosomes in heredity. *Biological Bulletin, 4,* 24–39, 231–251.

Wahlsten, D. (1990). Insensitivity of the analysis of variance to heredity-environment interaction. *Behavioral and Brain Sciences, 13,* 109–120.

Watson, J. B. (1914). *Behavior: An introduction to comparative psychology.* New York: Holt.

Watson, J. B. (1936). John Broadus Watson. In C. Murchison (Ed.), *A history of psychology in autobiography* (Vol. 3, pp. 271–281) Worcester, MA: Clark University Press.

Watson, J. B. 1959. *Behaviorism.* Chicago: University of Chicago Press.

Woodrow, J. C. (1996.) [Comments on J. B. S. Haldane: The negative heritability of neonatal jaundice]. *Annals of Human Genetics, 60,* 7–9.

Wright, S. (1932). The roles of mutation, inbreeding, crossbreeding and selection in evolution. *Proceeding of the Congress of Genetics, 1,* 356–366.

8 Commentary

Lundy Braun
Brown University

The announcement in June 2000 that the human genome has been sequenced (in actuality the genome of Celera's CEO Craig Venter [Weiss 2002]) culminated a long-standing fascination with human inheritance. Since the Human Genome Project (HGP) was launched, claims that genetic research would rescue humanity from the devastation of afflictions such as cancer, diabetes, mental illness, crime, and poverty have been touted by pharmaceutical industry executives, the media, and scientists alike. However, although enthusiasm for such research on the genetics of normal and socially "deviant" behaviors has been tempered by the spectre of eugenics in the United States, the horrors of Nazi Germany, and collective memory of the highly charged, racialized debates over intelligence and inheritance, the application of genetic technologies to social problems was always an explicit goal of early promoters of the HGP. According to Daniel Koshland (1989), a prominent scientist and former editor of *Science*, the new technologies would have the potential to "aid the poor, the infirm, and the underprivileged." Though obviously a hyperbolic comment, the substantial resources currently devoted to research on behavioral genetics indicate that such hopes to solve social problems through scientific research are in reality an integral part of the "new genetics."

The contemporary debate over genetics, environment, and human behavior intersects with other contentious debates over the use of genetic technologies for diagnosis of genetic disease, gene therapy, and human cloning, as well as broader debates over the political economy of health, globalization, and cultural imperialism of western science. Fundamentally, these are debates over the production of scientific knowledge in capitalist societies: What kind of knowledge will be produced by research that privileges genotype? What will be done with this knowledge? What knowledge will NOT be produced as a consequence of the focus on genetics? Who will be involved in decisions about what kind of research will be done? What knowledge could be produced with a different conceptual framework that views genes and environment as inextricably linked and in a dynamic relationship? As molecular genetic research intensifies and what Michael Fortun (2001) refers to as the "bioinfopharmacogenomics" infrastructure expands, it is essential that the political, economic, social, and ethical dimensions of the research enterprise be debated openly among all sectors of the lay public, not just the experts. Central to the debate should be a critical examination of what we mean by biology, what we mean by environment, and how genes and environment work together to shape the life experience of human organisms. By addressing various dimensions of this complex problem, the chapters in this volume make a timely contribution to this much-needed debate.

The controversy over the origin of human traits, whether disease traits or behavioral traits, has been framed historically as one of the relative contribution of "nature versus nurture" or "genes versus environment," and scientists have invested considerable efforts in developing precise quantitative measures to assess each component separately. Given such a dualistic framework, it is not surprising that explanations for variability oftentimes have taken the form of crude genetic or environmental determinism. Building on his important theoretical contributions to the study of human development over the past 30 years, Gilbert Gottlieb critiques the current trend in psychology to privilege genes in his chapter "Normally Occurring Environmental and Behavioral Influences on Gene Activity." Gottlieb locates this trend in James Watson and Francis Crick's formulation of the "central dogma," whereby the flow of "information" is conceptualized as linear from DNA to RNA to proteins. In other words, according to the central dogma, DNA is a blueprint or a set of instructions for cellular and, ultimately, organismal function. In place of this linear model, Gottlieb offers an alternative probabilistic epigenetic framework for behavioral research—a developmentalist approach that views genes in dynamic interaction with the internal and external environment.

Probabilistic epigenesis posits that the external environment "is a crucial feature of individual development" (p. 90), and Gottlieb offers numerous examples from different organisms to support his argument that the external environment influences genetic activity. In particular, he cites studies showing changes in the numbers of cells in the brain due to environment. What is notable is the wide range of environmental influences Gottlieb cites, including physical activities (waking or sleeping), nutrition, heat stress, visual, tactical, and acoustic stimulation. Extrapolated to the human condition, these environmental influences could be termed "life experience." For the study of human behavior, framing environment as life experience opens up new ways of understanding behavior and cautions us that "it is not possible to predict in advance what the outcome of development will be when the developing organisms is faced with novel environmental or behavioral challenges" (p. 99).

In the introduction to his chapter, Gottlieb points out that the dominance of the genetic paradigm is not simply due to a lack of scientific information about cellular pathways: "A virtual revolution has taken place in our knowledge of environmental and behavioral influences on gene expression that has not yet seeped into the social sciences in general and the behavioral sciences in particular" (p. 85). Indeed, there is abundant evidence that DNA cannot be assembled without proteins and that gene expression is regulated by micro- and macroenvironmental influences. No credible biologist would defend the idea that the genome is fully "encapsulated," as the complexity of intracellular and extracellular networks controlling cellular function is well established. For example, it has long been known that intricate positive and negative feedback networks regulate hormone function. Yet, Gottlieb is correct in asserting that the simplistic, static formulation of the central dogma remains a guiding principle in biomedical and behavioral science research and in health policy. Note both the rush to develop genetic databases in the United Kingdom and Iceland and the increasing popularity of molecular epidemiology that attempts to correlate DNA sequences with a wide range of variables, including behavioral variables. Unfortunately, few researchers acknowledge that these variables are culturally produced and that they vary over time and place.

That a Nobel Prize was awarded to Watson and Crick for the discovery of DNA accounts in part for the tenacious hold the simplistic formulation of the central dogma has on the ways in which biology is conceptualized and practiced. Beyond the force of personalities and lure of technological innovation, however, the more fluid and dynamic way of thinking about biological systems that Gottlieb suggests is constrained both by political economic imperatives that over the last decade have generated vast wealth for the scientific elite and by deeply embedded and largely unexamined cultural assumptions about the origins of human difference, whether those differences concern race, class, gender, disease patterns, or behavior. The social world we inhabit shapes the types of scientific experiments we imagine, and recognizing the social nature of science has the potential to open up new and more clarifying avenues of inquiry.

The power of simplistic, unexamined assumptions in science to obscure understanding is demonstrated by Jerry Hirsch in his chapter "Uniqueness, Diversity, Similarity, Repeatability, and Heritability." Here, Hirsch reexamines his earlier calculation published in *Science* in 1963 that demonstrated the probability that two parents would produce genetically identical offspring. Although the calculation was—and is—mathematically correct, Hirsch states, the complexity of genetic variability was not appreciated either by him or by other researchers at the time. This failure to appreciate complexity continues to be reflected in psychologists' use and interpretation of the concept of heritabilty—a concept that was initially developed for animal and plant breeding experiments and subsequently applied to estimate the relative contribution of nature (genes) or nurture (environment) to human intelligence. Hirsch also makes the important point that, in their use of the concept of heritability, both enthusiasts for the dominance of nature and proponents for the primacy of nurture operate from the same conceptual framework that views genes and environment as separable analytical entities, thereby masking the complexity of biological systems. For Hirsch, this is not only problematic from the perspective of scientific understanding but is also dangerous for public policy, as illustrated in the troubling and mean-spirited use of the concept of heritability by Richard Hernstein and Charles Murray in the *Bell Curve.*

Similarly, in "Beyond Heritability: Biological Processes in Social Context," Richard Rende critiques simplistic concepts of heritability and argues that behavioral geneticists need to employ a more nuanced understanding of social context in their research. In this chapter, Rende recounts a short history of behavioral research, which has alternated between environmental and genetic explanations for differences in individual behavior. Rende acknowledges many of the technical and conceptual problems with this research—notably the inadequacy of diagnostic categories for mental illnesses, the problem of definition of behavioral traits, and the limitations of environmentalism or geneticism as explanatory models of disease or deviancy. He is also sensitive to the fact that simplistic understandings, such as the "refrigerator mother" hypothesis of the roots of autism, can harm patients. In relating his own experience as a researcher, Rende says he was "somewhat surprised ... that environmental theories could be as misleading and potentially damaging as the inappropriate use of biological frameworks." Accordingly, he decided to get "a solid grounding" in behavioral genetics, "persuaded to no small degree by the increasing attention being paid to genetic theories of autism at that time" (p. 108).

Rende then goes on to address critics who argue that the models and methodologies used by behavioral geneticists perpetuate artificial distinctions between genes and environment. Though Rende recognizes that distinctions between genes and environment are artificial, he nonetheless makes the case that they are necessary for analytical purposes. It is open to question, however, whether artificial distinctions between genes and environment, even for analytical purposes, will "promote our understanding" as Rende hopes, or close off knowledge that would lead to deeper understanding. Certainly, such a distinction creates conceptual barriers to challenging the dominant genetic paradigm. Even more fundamentally, the distinction takes on a life of its own, and when transformed into data, published in scientific journals, and popularized in the media acquires the authority of objective, neutral, and value-free knowledge.

Nor does Rende's proposal to substitute the notion of "susceptibility" genes for that of dominant genes move us closer to understanding the ways in which genes and environment are mutually constitutive. For inherent to the idea of susceptibility—for both scientists and the public—is the idea of genes as causes. This point is clearly illustrated in a recent article in *The New York Times*, entitled "Schizophrenia May Be Tied to 2 Genes, Research Finds." In this article, the *New York Times* reporter Nicholas Wade (2002) noted that schizophrenia is a complex disorder with a complex etiology. However, Wade went on to state that researchers "have found clues that point to a specific gene as a possible cause of schizophrenia" (p. A11). The hope is that, despite the frustrating history of schizophrenia research marked by reports of the isolation of genes associated with schizophrenia, this discovery "will illuminate the fundamental mechanisms of the disease and might lead to new treatments" (p. A11). Only in the last three-sentence paragraph is the role of the environment even mentioned. This cannot be dismissed as misunderstanding by the media. Wade is an experienced and scientifically sophisticated reporter. Moreover, the editor of the *American Journal of Human Genetics*, where the two papers were published, also expressed the hope that "we might finally be getting close to some genes that predispose people to this important disease." To talk about genes for predisposition in the absence of the context within which those genes operate is to create a powerful rhetorical argument for the genes as primary causes and environment as having "residual" effects—and rhetorical arguments produce knowledge.

One way to begin to move beyond the unproductive debate over nature *versus* nurture is to think more critically about how biological systems function. Genes certainly are one important component of organisms. But, as Gottlieb and others (Fausto-Sterling, 2000; Lewontin, 2000; Oyama, 2000) explicitly noted, genes are always expressed in an environmental context. It is, in other words, impossible to understand human development without taking a conceptual and experimental approach that starts from the premise that biological and environment systems are indivisible. Human—and nonhuman organisms continuously shape and reshape their physical and social environment. Thus, the constructed dualism of genes versus environment has profound consequences for knowledge production and for how knowledge will be used. To understand how culture is embodied, research on human development and disorders of development requires methodologies that allow for the study of genes in the context of the whole organism living in a changing physical and social environment. The genetic paradigm currently holds great appeal for scientists and the public alike. Without doubt, narrow genetic approaches to the study of development, disease, and behavior have generated and will continue to generate detailed molecular knowledge of the genomes of organisms. Unfortunately, because few have taken a systems approach to exploring the dynamic interplay between genes and the environment, understanding human development and disease is destined to remain partial at best.

REFERENCES

Fausto-Sterling, A. (2000). *Sexing the body: Gender politics and the construction of sexuality.* New York: Basic Books.

Fortun, M. (2001). Mediated speculations in the genomic futures market. *New Genetics, 20,* 139–156

Koshland, D. (1989). Sequences and consequences of the human geome. *Science, 146,* 189.

Lewontin, R. (2000). *The triple helix: Gene, organism, and environment.* Cambridge, MA: Harvard University Press.

Oyama, S. (2000). *Evolution's eye: A systems view of the biology-culture divide.* Durham, NC: Duke University Press.

Wade, N. (2002). Schizophrenia may be tied to 2 genes, research finds. *New York Times,* p. A11.

Weiss, R. (2002). Scientists confirm use of own DNA in project: Celera effort included founder's genes. *The Washington Post,* p. A13.

9 Instinct and Choice: A Framework for Analysis

William T. Dickens
The Brookings Institution

Jessica L. Cohen
Massachusetts Institute of Technology

Birds do not need to be taught how to build nests. Evidently the behavior is largely instinctual. Humans need to be taught nearly everything they do (or at least need to learn through other means, such as imitation). Further, our experience of our own behavior is that we make conscious choices—that we are the masters of our own ships. It thus comes as a shock to many people that genetic differences have been shown to be an important determinant of variation in a wide range of human behaviors.

Besides a number of psycho-pathologies,[1] a large and growing list of behaviors—including major measurable aspects of personality (Loehlin 1992), political conservatism (Eaves et. al. 1997), religiosity (Waller, Kojetin, Bouchard, Lykken, & Tellegen, 1990), occupational attitudes (Lykken, Bouchard, McGue, & Tellegen, 1993), social attitudes (Martin et. al. 1986), marital status (Trumbetta et. al. submitted), and even television viewing (Plomin, Corley, DeFries, & Fulker, 1990)—have all been shown to be heritable.[2]

If a trait is heritable, then we know that it is subject to genetic influence. But the vast majority of physical characteristics that are genetically programmed are *not* heritable and the same may be true for behavioral characteristics. Heritability is defined as the fraction of the variance of a trait in a population that is due, directly

---

[1] See Plomin, DeFries, McClearn, & McGuffin (2001) for a review.
[2] This list is incomplete. See Plomin et. al. (1997) for a longer list.

or indirectly, to genetic variation. More precisely, it is the fraction of the variance of a trait in a population facing a particular environment that is explained in a statistical sense by genetic variation. If there is no genetic variation, there can be no heritability. Nearly every human has two hands and five fingers on each hand. This structure is genetically determined, but the traits of having 2 hands or 10 fingers have virtually zero heritability, because the small amount of variation in these traits is due mainly to accidents or developmental defects.

While behavioral geneticists have been documenting the role genes play in behavioral differences, evolutionary psychologists have been developing a research program exploring what role genes may play in determining universal human behaviors.[3] It has been suggested that aspects of our ability to cooperate (Cosmides & Tooby 1992), sexual behavior (Ellis 1992), child rearing (Mann 1992, Fernald 1992), and even aesthetics (Orians & Heerwagen 1992) may result from the operation of specialized evolved psychological mechanisms. Psychologists working in this field have shown that often startling predictions made from theories of this nature can be validated and tested with experimental data (e.g., Cosmides 1989).

So what? What difference does it make to us in how we conduct our lives or structure our institutions; if our TV viewing habits are somehow subject to genetic influence? What significance should we ascribe to the evolutionary psychological finding that we are particularly good at solving logic puzzles when they are posed as problems in detecting cheating in ancient social exchange problems? A great deal of heat has been generated around discussions of nature vs. nurture, but when we critically scrutinize this debate, it is not clear what we should be concerned about.

In this chapter, we want to accomplish three things. First, we will argue that most of the reasons why people have believed the nature/nurture controversy to be important are wrong. Given the current understanding of evolution, saying a behavior is genetically influenced is dramatically far from an ethical justification of such behavior. Further, the notion that if a behavior is genetically influenced, it is unchangeable is also wrong—even if the basis for saying so is a very high heritability. We believe that it is confusion about this last point that leads people to think that whether or not group differences have a genetic source is relevant to discussions of whether or not they are just. Second, we want to develop a framework for thinking about the influence of genes on behavior that is consistent with our perception of ourselves as rational decision makers. We submit that the economist's model of human behavior as the result of rational choice is a good point of departure for such a framework.[4] Third, another advantage of the rational choice model of behavior is that it can be used as the basis for an elaborate normative theory of institutions—it can serve not only as a guide to how people will behave but also how they should behave and how they should structure their institutions to improve their well-being. Thus, this model of behavior is also a vehicle for under-

---

[3]See for example Barkow, Cosmides, & Tooby (1992).
[4]For a description of the economic method see Frank (1997, pp. 63–92).

standing what the real implications of genetic influences on behavior for social policy and well-being might be.

Here we explain why we think that people have been drawing the wrong conclusions from what some have interpreted as the triumph of nature over nurture in the long war between their advocates. From there we move on to describe the economist's model of behavior in which people are seen as making optimal choices given their preferences and constraints. In the third section, we discuss the relevance of genetic research for public policy when genetic influences are imbedded in the rational choice model. A far more important application of the study of how genes influence behavior may be in providing better theoretical foundations for the emerging field of behavioral economics. Later in this chapter, we argue for developing such a research program.

WHAT GENETIC INFLUENCES ON BEHAVIOR DO *NOT* IMPLY

In this section, we consider the mistaken policy inferences that people have drawn from evidence of genetic influences on behavior. Many of the arguments we present here have been made before, but we feel obliged to restate them because the errors we are highlighting persist in popular and scientific writing. We begin by pointing out that showing that a trait is genetically influenced is a far cry from showing that it can't be changed or even that it is difficult to change. Then we contend that if arguments that natural equals good or right ever had any appeal, they shouldn't in light of evolutionary theory. Finally, some believe that whether or not group differences have genetic origins bears on the justice of their existence. We suspect this view exists because it confuses genetic origins with inevitability. We present a few examples that we believe illustrate that the source of group differences (environmental or genetic) has little to do with whether differences are just.

Genetic Does Not Mean Unchangeable

Most people assume that if something is genetically influenced it is inevitable, or at least very difficult to change. The message that many people took from Herrnstein and Murray's *The Bell Curve* (1994) was that there is a strong and unbreakable link from genes to IQ to poverty and social deviance, and because nothing can be done to break this link, nothing should be done. In particular, Herrnstein and Murray railed against affirmative action and antidiscrimination efforts as having pushed the drive for equality too far. In the 1970s, critics of sociobiology were concerned that if people didn't conclude that genetically dictated sex roles were good or right, they might nevertheless conclude that they were unavoidable.[5] Why pass the Equal Rights Amendment if sexual inequality is in our genes?

---

[5]See *The Economist*, January 1, 1977, p. 44, for a description of the controversy around sociobiology.

People's tendency to view genetic as synonymous with unchangeable probably arises from two mistaken impressions about how genes shape behavior. People may assume that if something like IQ is "substantially genetically determined," that must mean that it has a proximate biological cause and that one's IQ is the inevitable result of possessing a particular combination of genes—as inevitable as having two arms and two legs. However, no such link has ever been demonstrated. Further, geneticists can provide many examples of even physical traits that are clearly coded in the genetic structure but that are only expressed in particular environments.[6]

Of course, at *some* level genes must have *some* physical manifestation if they affect behavior, but how remote the physical manifestation of those genes is from a particular behavior is an empirical question. A circuitous route from biological cause to social effect seems necessary to any explanation of at least some behaviors that have been shown to have genetic influences. But just because a cause is circuitous or contingent does not mean that in any practical sense it is less important. We want to look further into why people may falsely equate genetic influence with inevitability, but first we need to clarify what we mean when we say that a behavior is genetically influenced.

Does it make any sense to distinguish between genetically influenced behavior and socially influenced behavior? At least at one level the answer has to be "no." We are biological organisms, and all our behavior is conditioned by our physical make-up. The fact that speech is nearly universal and sign language rarely used is in part a consequence of how our bodies are constructed. The nature of the shelters we build for ourselves is affected by how we are built. Doors would be wider if we were wider, or we might be more concerned with keeping our shelters cool if we had heavy fur. There are an infinite number of ways we can imagine how our behavior would be different if our genes were different. On the other hand, as the examples just given illustrate, genes aren't destiny. If we need wider doors to accommodate cars instead of bodies, we build them. If we live in a warm climate, our houses don't have big heaters if any at all. If people like wide doors or a cold house, they can build them to suit their tastes. So what is all the fuss about?

Controversy seems to arise concerning the two most common types of evidence cited to show that a particular behavior is subject to genetic influence. The nature of the evidence suggests to some that the gene-outcome link is inescapable. The first is a trait's heritability. Heritability is defined as the fraction of the variance of a trait within a population that is due to genetic differences. A common mistake is to conclude that if a trait is highly heritable, then there is little role left for environment. Examples of this mistaken reasoning are Jensen (1998, pp. 445–458) and Herrnstein and Murray (1994, pp. 298–299) who present formal arguments that

---

[6]For a summary, see Gottlieb (1998). Recently Rowe, Jacobson, & Van den Oord (1999) and Turkheimer, Haley, Waldron, D'Onofrio, & Gottesman (2002) have demonstrated some interaction between genes and environment in the formation of IQ. Additional interaction effects could be very hard to detect (Turkheimer and Gottesman [1996] and Turkheimer [1997]).

the high heritability of IQ virtually precludes environmental explanations for Black-White IQ differences. A second approach to discerning genetic influences on behavior has been to find a behavior that is nearly universal, to look for explanations as to why the behavior would be evolutionarily advantageous, and then to look for other implications of the hypothesized evolutionary cause and check to see if they can be confirmed. The facts that the behavior is universal (or nearly so) and that it can be explained as being a product of biological evolution may give it the sense of inevitability. But in neither case is inevitability inevitable.

Consider first traits that are highly heritable. Recall the definition of heritability—the fraction of population variance explained by genetic differences. Heritability is not a characteristic of a trait, it is a characteristic of a trait in a particular population facing a particular environment. Take a group of genetically diverse organisms and put them all in an identical environment and in theory heritability will be 100%.[7] Put a group of genetically identical organisms into a wide range of different environments and heritability will be zero. This has enormous practical importance. There are genetic diseases such as phenylketonuria (or PKU—a metabolic disorder that can produce mental retardation), the symptoms of which in another era would have been 100% heritable. But because we have learned how to treat PKU with diet, those with the gene for the disease need never develop the advanced symptoms so that today the heritability of those symptoms is virtually zero in populations screened for the disease. Heritable does not mean inevitable.

But this observation is small solace if we want to influence a trait that is highly heritable in a population despite considerable variance in the environments of the members of the population. This is the case that Jensen, and Herrnstein and Murray, consider. To make their formal arguments simple, they argue that if all the environmental variance we observe in our society explains so little of the variance of a trait such as IQ, how can we expect to find environmental interventions that could change IQ?

It has been clear for a while that there must be something wrong with this argument. It implies that large environmental effects on any highly heritable trait are impossible without huge differences in environment, yet there has long been evidence that large environmental effects on IQ are possible. This point was driven home with the discovery of huge IQ gains over time. Evidence now demonstrates gains in more than 20 different countries, with data going back in some cases to the earliest IQ tests.[8] Until recently, the juxtaposition of this evidence with high heritability seemed paradoxical. But Dickens and Flynn (2001) presented a formal model of the process generating IQ that explains why high heritability not only does not preclude large environmental effects but may be an indicator of the presence of strong reciprocal effects between environment and phenotype that produce both high heritability and the possibility of large environmental effects.

---

[7] In fact, measured heritability would probably be less than 100%, because there may be aspects of an organism's development that are essentially random even with a tightly controlled environment.

[8] See Flynn (1998) for a summary.

Briefly, the Dickens-Flynn argument is that those whose genes give them a slight edge in those aspects of intellectual performance measured by IQ tests will tend to find themselves in a better environment for the development of those talents. For example, those who do well on tests are more likely to get into more intellectually stimulating schools or get more challenging jobs. This in turn will lead them to develop greater ability that may lead to further improvements in their environments. An initial environmental advantage could seize control of the process of reciprocal causation with similar effects, but though our genes are always with us, those aspects of our environments that are not a response to our genes are relatively fickle. Thus, most variance appears to be due to genes when looking at a cross section of the population—even though variance in the trait would be considerably smaller if good genes weren't being matched with good environments. But if something comes along and makes a consistent change in the average environment, the process of reciprocal causation can magnify the effects of the initial change several times over. Therefore, relatively small initial differences in the circumstances of different generations (or different ethnic groups) can be magnified into large induced environmental differences in a behavioral trait. Any change that produced the same sort of small consistent change in the circumstances of a large group of interacting individuals could realistically produce similarly large changes in the most heritable trait.

But what about the claim that there are evolved human universals? Suppose that sex roles are in some important sense programmed in our genes. Does this mean that Bill can't cook and Jessica can't do math? Hardly. Doors have pretty much the same shape around the world, and as we described earlier, that is in some sense a genetically influenced behavioral trait of the human population. Our height and width may well have evolved to make us efficient hunter-gatherers in the environments in which our ancestors lived long ago, so how we build doors can be described as resulting from evolutionary adaptation. But that doesn't mean we can't or shouldn't bother trying to build larger doors if we need them. This example illustrates yet another point we will expand upon in the following sections. Unless we know how genes influence a behavioral trait, we know nothing about how easy or hard the trait is to change. Simply knowing that it is genetically influenced tells us nothing about how responsive it might be to changes in the environment.

Natural Does Not Mean Good or Right

One fear often mentioned by opponents of genetic approaches to behavior is that saying something is evolved or natural in some sense justifies or rationalizes it. This was a common criticism of the writing by sociobiologists on sex roles in the mid 1970s. Many saw sociobiology as an attack on the progress women had made toward equality in the job market and in personal relations that aimed to make the traditional sex roles seem natural and right and thus change seem unnatural and wrong.[9] We think such concerns are misplaced. Taking this perspective may have

---

[9]See footnote 5.

done more harm than good by making the misinterpretation seem more reasonable than it is. Critics might have done better to point out that the sociobiologists' views of how sex roles arose completely undermine the claim that those roles have any moral authority today. Civilization is too new to have had much impact on our evolution. To the extent that our behavior has evolutionary roots, they can be found in the survival demands put on Pleistocenian hunter-gatherer tribes. If that is the source of the modern sexual division of labor: (a) why would anyone think that "natural" meant "right," and (b) given the rather substantial change in our circumstances since then, shouldn't this be an appropriate time to be consciously considering some changes?

This last point anticipates one of the arguments we will be making later. As beings who can make conscious choices about our behavior, evidence that a particular behavior is genetically influenced may in some cases indicate that we are not fully aware of why we do what we do. That means we may not have thought carefully through the individual or social costs and benefits of the behavior. Thus knowing that a behavior is genetically influenced may provide a motivation for critically reconsidering it. Knowing how it is influenced could not only provide motivation for reconsidering the behavior but also for thinking about what sorts of alternatives might be preferable. For example, some have suggested that xenophobia or ethnocentrism may have an evolved basis (Reynolds, Falger, & Vine, 1986). If true, we certainly would not conclude that xenophobia was natural and therefore good. To the contrary, it might help people understand their feelings as anachronistic and inappropriate in modern society. Further, it might help us anticipate the nature, causes, and consequences of unconscious racism, and the circumstances in which it is likely to arise. Such information might help us design social systems to mitigate the undesirable effects of such behavior.

Genes and Justice

The most pernicious application of arguments for genetic influences on behavior has been the rationalization of unequal treatment of different groups—sometimes as horrific as slavery or extermination. The use of genetic theories of group differences to support legal discrimination against ethnic groups and for restricting women to traditional roles has been justifiably condemned. We do not expect much of value to come from studies of group differences in genetic influences on behavior. Knowledge about the extent and malleability of developed differences in ability among groups can inform us about the costs of pursuing equality in economic and social outcomes. Knowledge of whether group differences have genetic origins is not informative on either point.[10] Direct measures are more salient on the extent of differences, and the existence of a genetic role in determining group differences tells us almost nothing about the malleability of those differences, as we have already argued. Understanding how genes influence individual behavior

---

[10]Though knowledge of a trait's etiology, genetic or environmental, could be, as explained earlier.

could help us design solutions for social problems, but we do not see how information on group differences could be used for this purpose.

Some have suggested to us that knowledge of how group differences arise could influence reasonable judgments about social justice—particularly if the differences are genetic in origin. For example, some argue that a just society need only give everyone equal opportunity to use whatever talents they are born with and need not endeavor to equalize outcomes (Nozick, 1974). Thus, group differences that arise from differences in talents would be acceptable, whereas those that result from unequal treatment by others would be unjust. In fact, most Americans do not seem to consider it unjust that a few exceptionally talented sports stars get a far larger share of society's rewards than everyone else, nor do they consider it unjust that mentally retarded adults typically don't have the resources to afford $300,000 homes. We accept that knowledge of the origins of group differences could be informative about their justice, but we do not believe that genetically induced differences would necessarily be judged just while environmentally induced differences would be judged unjust. Two examples should suffice to make this point.

Consider the children of a religious group that eschews machinery that is neither human nor animal powered. The group might very well live in conditions that would be considered extreme poverty and their children would have no choice but to accept their circumstances, but few if any would see the children's deprivation as unjust even though their circumstances resulted from environmental deprivation that was imposed upon them.

Alternatively, suppose that we were to discover that many people's low IQs were caused by a genetic disorder that could be treated with a single very expensive dose of some drug during a child's first month. Suppose that this drug was so expensive as to be effectively out of the reach of families with incomes in the bottom third of the distribution of incomes. Even though this form of low IQ was genetic in origin, we suspect that few, if any, people would consider it just to allow children with this disorder to go untreated. This example suggests that if we knew how to raise the IQs of low IQ groups or individuals, and doing so was easily within our means, it wouldn't matter at all what the source of the differences was, their continued existence and consequences would be viewed as unjust. We suspect that people who think that group differences in economic and social outcomes that are due to genetic differences are just are implicitly assuming that initial genetic differences could never be overcome. But, as the previous discussion has shown, this need not be the case.

The social implications of genetic influences on behavior can't hinge on mistaken notions that natural equals good or that genetic means inevitable or just. But it is still possible that research on the role genes play in shaping behavior could help us improve society. But as the discussion of this section indicates, we need a framework for understanding the complicated ways in which genes may influence behavior to realize this potential. We turn now to a model of behavior that we feel is a good starting place for such a framework.

THE MODEL OF RATIONAL CHOICE

Over the last 50 years, the boundaries of economics have come to be defined more by the methodology of the discipline than by its subject matter. At the core of that methodology is the rational actor model of behavior.[11] That model is unique among models of human behavior in providing both a positive description of behavior that is quite analytically powerful and a normative standard by which to evaluate social choices. If we want to be able to evaluate the implications of genetic influences on behavior in the context of a model of behavior that fits our understanding of ourselves as making conscious choices, this seems like a good place to start.

Constrained Optimization (the Positive Model of Behavior)

Central to the economist's analysis of behavior is the theory of constrained optimization. That model of behavior takes as given peoples' preferences for different states of the world and the constraints they face and assumes that they will act to achieve the most preferred state of the world given those constraints. For example, a person might prefer consuming one orange to consuming only one apple, and consuming two oranges to consuming two apples or only one of either. A complete statement of the person's preferences with respect to apples and oranges would involve a rank ordering of all possible combinations of apples and oranges. The constraints a person faces in satisfying these preferences could be the money available to purchase apples and oranges together with the prices of apples and oranges. The behavioral assumptions are that such a preference ordering exists and that individuals will choose the most preferred combination of apples and oranges they can afford. The model assumes that individuals are (typically) fully informed and perfectly strategically rational in this decision and can thus choose the optimal behavior out of all possible strategies.[12]

Sometimes it is assumed that peoples' preferences can be summarized by a utility function—a mapping from all possible states of the world into the real number line where states of the world that correspond to higher values for the utility function are preferred to states corresponding to lower values.[13] In such a framework, we can view tastes as the parameters of such a function. That is, a taste is the relative weight we put on apples versus oranges, being comfortable versus being cold, or being with people we like versus those we don't like, in deciding whether one state of the world is preferred to another. But, more generally, preferences are the result of a process of evaluating different states of the world. We will use the term "tastes" (in a nonstan-

---

[11]See Frank (1997, pp. 63–92) for a description of this methodology.

[12]We discuss criticisms of these assumptions later.

[13]Utility functions are also assumed to be such that if the utility of one state of the world is twice that of another, there is a meaningful sense in which the first is twice as good as the second. Specifically, a person will be indifferent between the certainty of one outcome and a 50% possibility of each of two outcomes with utility values equally above and below that value.

dard way) to represent only one input into that process—the relative extent to which a particular mental or physical state produces pain or pleasure.

In our previous example, constraints were the limits imposed by budget and prices, but the concept can be expanded to include everything from the laws of a society to physical limits on movement. Most generally, the constraints facing individuals are the limitations on the resources that they can deploy to adjust the state of the world.

Note at this point that neither tastes nor constraints determine behavior alone. A person may prefer one apple to one orange, and two apples and one orange to two oranges and one apple, but that doesn't mean that that person will necessarily consume more apples than oranges. If an apple costs five times as much as an orange, and a person has enough money to buy two apples, then that person's preferences might very well lead this person to buy and consume five oranges and one apple even though, in some sense, this person prefers apples to oranges. In fact, if the price of apples was high enough, someone who prefers one apple to three oranges might still end up consuming only oranges. This discussion reinforces what we said above about how genetic influence doesn't mean that a behavior is inevitable. In the rational actor model, no one factor always (i.e., under all circumstances) determines behavior. Change one of the other inputs to the choice process and you can get a different choice.

Explicit or implicit in the optimizing model of behavior are a number of assumptions about the information available to people and their ability and desire to process that information to make the best possible choice. Specifically, individuals have complete knowledge of all possible opportunities available to them and how they would feel in each possible state. If the outcomes of their actions cannot be predicted with certainty, they know the probabilities of all possible outcomes. They are able to consider the entire range of possible actions and decide which of these maximizes their welfare. Not only are individuals fully informed and able to apply rationality universally, but it is also often assumed that it is costless for them to do so (e.g., people don't need to pay to acquire information necessary to make a decision either in terms of time or money).

These behavioral assumptions are unrealistic. After all, we don't always make carefully, thoroughly weighed, and fully rational decisions in which we have considered all possible options. Decisions that approach this standard are the exception rather than the rule, and most behavior seems habitual. The rational actor model has not gone unchallenged in economics. In fact, behavioral economics—a subdiscipline that focuses on the contributions that psychology, sociology, and other social sciences can make to the economic model of behavior—has become a much more active and accepted area of research in the past decade (Rabin, 1998). Still, the rational actor model, even in its strongest and unrealistic form, has a number of important uses.

The most famous defense of the model was made by Milton Friedman (1953) who argued that models, by their very nature as abstractions, are necessarily unrealistic and that they should be judged not by their assumptions but by the accuracy of their predictions. Friedman has been criticized for the argument that models should never be judged by their assumptions, but he made an important point in his essay; even if people don't behave exactly the way economists assume they do, the model could still provide a good description of their behavior. He gave the example of how an expert billiards player's shots could be modeled using spherical trigonometry whether or not the person taking the shots understood the model. Similarly, people may not be the omniscient calculators that economists assume they are, but if they generally try to do things to improve their well being, if they experiment and learn from their mistakes, and if they have plenty of opportunities to learn, then much behavior may be well described by a model that assumed perfectly informed hyperrationality. Such a model might also be an analytic convenience and that consideration may be decisive in those cases where the deviations from the model are minor.

Normative Analysis

It's not a big step from the assumption that people are always choosing to make themselves as well off as they possibly can to what is called the fundamental welfare theorem of economics. Without going into details,[14] under a set of assumptions about what people know, how trades are made, and the nature of peoples' preferences, it is possible to show that if actors behaving according to the rules of constrained optimization engage in trade so as to exhaust all possibilities for individual welfare improvement, the resulting distribution of goods is Pareto efficient—that is, no one can be made better off without making someone else worse off.

Given this result, a particular global outcome can be criticized on two grounds: One may argue that the conditions necessary for Pareto efficiency don't exist and that some institutional changes are necessary to improve efficiency. Alternatively, one can criticize the distribution on grounds of equity even if the allocation is Pareto efficient.[15] Ethical arguments can be made for preferring more equal distributions over less equal distributions, particularly if more equal distributions are achievable without an efficiency cost. But social policy aimed at reducing inequality will frequently involve some loss of efficiency. Economics can describe this trade-off but has little to say about how to compromise between these competing interests. This is why normative economics generally focuses on the question of

---

[14]For the proof of the fundamental welfare theorem, see Arrow and Debreu (1954); for a more accessible treatment, see Varian (1987). Frank (1997, pp. 564–565) provides a yet more accessible treatment.

[15]This is because there is not necessarily a unique Pareto efficient allocation of goods. Suppose that person 1 starts off with four left shoes and no right shoes, and person 2 starts out with four right shoes and no left shoes. That is not a Pareto efficient allocation if they both wear the same size shoe and neither likes to wear the wrong shoe on one foot. If the two trade two left shoes for two right shoes, both now have two pairs of shoes and that could be a Pareto efficient allocation. But suppose that person 1 is a very hard bargainer and holds out for three right shoes in exchange for one left shoe. Person 2 tires of haggling and agrees. Person 1 now has three pairs of shoes, and person 2 has only one. That too is a Pareto efficient allocation. No trade would make one of either better off without making the other worse off. See Frank (1997, pp. 564–565) for a discussion of the concepts of equity and efficiency.

the efficiency of a set of institutions and how changes to them will either increase or decrease efficiency.

Economists have identified a number of categories of reasons why ideal efficiency might not be obtained by the free interaction of agents, each corresponding to either a violation of the assumptions of the behavioral model described earlier or a failure of one of the other assumptions of the fundamental welfare theorem. For example, lack of perfect information can lead to failures in insurance markets.[16] The inability to exclude some people from being affected by your consumption can lead to a number of problems with the allocation of goods that can be cured by changing institutions.[17] For example, if people don't take into account the environmental damage done by the exhaust from their cars, a tax on cars based on the amount of pollution they produce can make everyone better off by leading each individual to choose a car that produces the socially optimal level of pollution (the level at which the cost of additional abatement exactly equals the total gain in social welfare from the abatement, and additional abatement would cost more than the welfare gain that would result).

The pollution example is a special case of a general problem for the fundamental welfare theorem called external economies or externalities. In most examples in economic textbooks, externalities are due to the nature of the technology of production or consumption (e.g., sparks from train wheels setting fires, loud music that is audible beyond the site of an outdoor concert, a well-maintained house or yard that can be enjoyed by all those in the neighborhood). However, external economies can also result from the nature of people's tastes. If one person's welfare is directly affected by that person's perception of the welfare of others, then an externality exists and the fundamental welfare theorem may not apply. Empathy, jealousy, and hatred are all examples of emotions that people feel that seem to make their welfare depend on the perceived welfare of others—sometimes positively and sometimes negatively. Such emotions are thought to be very important in explaining collective action which otherwise appears irrational from the perspective of individual welfare maximization (Bowles, 1998; Fehr & Gachter, 2000).

If the assumption of complete rationality is not satisfied—for example, if people do not understand probability theory and must make decisions about very low probability events with little opportunity to learn from mistakes—the outcome can be suboptimal as well. Dickens (1986) used observations from psychological decision theory to argue for regulation of occupational and product safety on these grounds.

What does all this have to do with the importance of genetic influences on behavior for social welfare? We intend to argue that a good first step toward incorporating genetic influences into a reasonable model of behavior is to view them as influencing people's tastes or constraints and to analyze their consequences using rational choice theory. We further argue that unless genetic influences on

[16]See Frank (1997, pp. 189–190, 207–208) for a discussion of how information problems cause adverse selection and moral hazard and the effect on insurance markets.

[17]The original article making this point is Samuelson (1954). See Frank (1997, pp. 576–577) for a simple presentation of the concepts.

behavior create other-regarding tastes or cause the decision-making process to be less than fully rational the importance of genetic influences on behavior for policy analysis is limited. This is because whether tastes are genetically determined or not and whether or not genes impose limits on the types of behavior that can be undertaken doesn't matter for the assumptions of welfare analysis in the model we have just described. If however, genetic influences give people other-regarding tastes or affect the decision-making process itself—that is, they affect the ability to choose the optimal behavior—then the implications for the analysis of policy could be quite profound.

GENES AS A POTENTIAL SOURCE OF TASTES
AND CONSTRAINTS THAT AFFECT BEHAVIOR

In the model of behavior just described, people choose to do what maximizes their well-being given their tastes and their constraints. If we want to understand genetic influences on behavior in the context of such a model, a natural place to start is with tastes.

Where Do Tastes Come From?

We all experience hunger pangs (which are sometimes quite specific), desires to be warm when we are cold, and sexual desire, and it's not hard to imagine that these feelings and impulses arise in part because of some genetic programming. On the other hand, certainly not all of our preferences are rooted in our genes. Though some aspects of aesthetic judgment are conceivably inherited, what art we find appealing evolves far more rapidly than our biology. Many of our preferences are developed or learned in some significant sense. Nonetheless, if we are looking for ways in which our behavior as self-conscious organisms might be shaped by genes, tastes seem a promising place to start.

There is another reason to think that genetic influences on behavior may come largely through this channel. Selection has pushed our genetic programming toward fitness—an important component of which is the efficiency with which traits are coded in our genes. In giving instructions there is a clear trade-off between giving detailed step-by-step contingent plans and giving more general information and the goals to be attained. Humans have extremely highly developed general-purpose problem-solving ability.[18] It makes sense that it would be more efficient for fitness-improving behaviors to be encoded in our genes by giving us

---

[18]In the next section, we consider the implications of arguments that in addition to a general purpose problem-solving ability, we have genetically programmed highly specific problem-solving abilities as well. However, we see no contradiction in believing that our conscious mind has access to both powerful specialized modules as well as a general purpose cognitive mechanism. The demonstrated ability of humans to design solutions to an enormous range of problems virtually on demand is evidence for what must certainly be seen as a general purpose cognitive ability. Evidence discussed later provides strong support for the view that we have relatively specialized abilities as well.

general goals and letting us figure out the specifics of how to implement those goals in these different environments.[19] By making certain things pleasurable and others unpleasant in a state contingent manner, our biology can influence our minds in a way that takes greatest advantage of our most developed capabilities.

Can Genetic Influence on Tastes Account for Differences in Behavior?

We have already discussed the long list of behaviors that seem to vary to some degree due to variation in genetic make-up. It is also often the case that genetic differences explain more variance in traits than family background (Turkheimer, 2000). Here is a real challenge to our images of ourselves as conscious actors with similar biological make-up. How could genes be so important for describing such a wide range of behaviors? How could evolution have anything to do with how much television we watch?

Suppose there is some variance between us in how much discomfort we feel when engaging in rigorous physical activity in the cold outdoors. Someone who had the gene or genes for a rather extreme lack of discomfort might choose to spend more time playing outdoors from an early age—even in extreme weather. Such a person might develop abilities in winter sports to a greater extent than the typical person in a self-reinforcing cycle of more practice meaning better performance meaning more enjoyment and more opportunity for improvement leading to still more time spent in the pursuit of such activities. As a result, such a person might not spend much time watching television. Such a person also might not spend as much time reading or in the company of people whose conversations typically involve a high degree of cognitive sophistication. Thus, the person might underdevelop certain cognitive skills. Through a roundabout path, a gene for how much pain one feels from muscle ache in the cold could also be contributing to TV watching and perhaps be even one of many for IQ.

We are not claiming that this is the mechanism that explains why genetic differences account for so much variation in TV viewing, but the story is illustrative of what might be the nature of many genetic effects on behavior. As such, it is not hard to imagine that there could be a genetic component to the type of cars we drive though the path from tastes for such things as tolerance for cold to make and model could be quite circuitous. The cascading effects of multiple adjustments of choice of lifestyle to accommodate even one difference could lead to genetic influence on an enormously wide range of behaviors.

Implications of Genetic Influences on Tastes

Economists give considerable deference to individuals' preferences (as reflected in those individuals' actions) in judging costs and benefits. Whatever assumptions of the fundamental welfare theorem may be called into question in a particular

---

[19]See Robson (2001).

analysis, it is almost never the case that well-informed people are assumed to make choices that are not in their best interest.[20] Thus, the ultimate touchstone of what is to be socially preferred in economic analysis is what well-informed individuals would choose in a world free of the limitations imposed by failures of the assumptions of the fundamental welfare theorem. But why give such deference to genetically imposed tastes in determining what is good or right? Isn't this just a repetition, once removed, of the fallacy that natural is good? We don't think so. A host of arguments can be advanced for respecting individual choice, none of which involve appeals to the natural origin of those preferences.

Therefore, if we choose to respect individual preferences, if the effects of genes on behavior come by affecting our tastes (but not by giving us interdependent preferences), and if people make the best use of the resources available to them to satisfy those tastes, then the analysis of a particular policy is completely unaffected by the knowledge that a relevant behavior is highly heritable or the result of some evolutionary imperative. The question of how much a behavior can be affected by incentives remains an empirical one that may be informed by knowledge of a genetic source but is not prejudiced by such knowledge. From the perspective of welfare economics, the question of whether we want to change a behavior still depends on the presence of market failures that prevent society from achieving an optimal allocation of time and resources or a desire to change the distribution of resources to make it fairer. But our first cut is not our last. We can think of three ways in which the knowledge that a particular behavior was the result of a genetically induced taste might affect how one would think about public policy.

Despite the need to respect individual preferences, knowing the etiology of a particular taste, knowing that the behavior can be altered, and knowing that it is in some sense an evolutionary anachronism might help both individuals and policymakers make better choices. Respecting individual preferences can be rationalized on the grounds that they are the product of a critical, self-conscious process. More precise knowledge about the source of preferences could help inform that critical process. It might also inform public dialogue about public values. For example, suppose that we were to identify an anachronistic genetically programmed fear of heights as the reason for an excessive concern about airplane safety relative to other forms of travel. Doing so might allow individuals to appreciate and tame their own impulses in such a way as to make them better able to identify and attain important goals. As a matter of public policy, we may decide to put less weight on air safety than we would if we took consumers' willingness to pay for it as the sole indicator of its true value.

Second, someday it may be possible for people to manipulate their children's (or even their own) tastes through genetic engineering. This possibility raises many seri-

---

[20]This does not need to be only selfish interest: the rational actor model can accommodate altruistic as well as fully-selfish preferences, and says only that people seek to maximize their own welfare, defined in terms of their own preferences. Thus those who feel very strongly about charity, for example, may be maximizing their welfare through altruistic behavior and this is well within the bounds of the rational actor model.

ous ethical questions—particularly if parents are making choices about things like the personality of their children. Because we can imagine many potentially beneficial uses of such technology (eliminating phobias for example), identification of how genes influence behavior for the purpose of genetic manipulation impresses us as a good motivation for research on the links between genes and behavior.

For discrete behaviors caused by a single gene, the manipulation of behavior may be close at hand. Linkage techniques can reliably identify genes associated with traits when the association is simple and the degree of association is very high. However, we suspect that many, if not most, genetic effects on behavior are complex and polygenic (involving many genes), because very few seem to follow Mendelian laws (Plomin et. al., 2001). The identification of specific genetic causes of specific behaviors then becomes extremely difficult. Reliably identifying genetic causes becomes an enormous problem if one cannot narrow the search to specific areas of the genome using prior knowledge of the physical structures involved. Huge samples are required to allow sufficiently high threshold p values to preclude false positives.[21]

Third, knowledge that a certain behavior results from one or more genetically programmed tastes could only come along with some understanding of the route by which that taste affected behavior. Knowing that route might suggest several different ways to modify the behavior besides changing the incentives for the target behavior directly. This is the third way in which we can imagine that knowledge about the genetic origins of a behavioral trait could be important for policy. It is possible that research on genetic influences on behavior could help us identify important causal paths given the importance of genetic differences for explaining behavioral variance. It could be particularly important if the behavior we were trying to affect was hard to monitor or otherwise difficult to shape with incentives. It is possible that an antecedent to the target behavior could be more susceptible to manipulation. It is also possible that this type of knowledge could save us from folly. Genetic influences on behavior may sometimes account for the correlation of behaviors and their antecedents, and knowledge of this can prevent mistaken imputations that the antecedents are manipulatable causes.

The second and third motivations for interest in understanding the genetic basis for behaviors beg the question of how we would know the path by which a particular behavior and its biological source were related. We have already described why we expect this could be very difficult, but we have one suggestion as to a methodology that might help in identifying chains of causation. The genetic contribution to covariance of traits can be analyzed using similar techniques to those used to analyze the genetic contribution to variance. With more study of the patterns of correlation in the genetic components of behavior, we might be able to get a better understanding of how causation works. For example, if we found that nearly all of the genetic influence on marital status could be explained by its correlation with

---

[21]See chapter 6 of Plomin et al. (2001) for a discussion of the methods available and an optimistic assessment of what might be possible in the near future.

genetic influence on alcoholism that would be a very different picture of the chain of causation than if we found that IQ, marital status, and income were tied up in a web of correlation. The latter might also make us want to consider the possibility that not all genetic influences on behavior come through their influences on the tastes that motivate our choices. There is also the possibility that genes influence our behavior by affecting the constraints we face.

Genetic Effects on Constraints

If genes influence behavior not through our tastes but rather through the constraints we face, would that change any of the conclusions we have drawn? We argue that insofar as genetic influence on behavior comes through shaping constraints of the type economists typically analyze—such as budget (income) constraints—their presence is basically insignificant for the analysis of efficiency.[22] However, if genetic influence on behavior comes through effects on our cognitive structures, which shape the way we solve problems, constraints and tastes may not be the best way to think about genetic influence. Instead, we may want to consider alternative formulations of the choice process by which tastes and constraints get transformed into behavior. We consider that possibility in the next section. Here we ask whether modeling genetic influences as constraints has different implications from modeling them as tastes.

In the past, health, size, strength, and agility mattered quite a bit in determining how much physical labor one could do and thus how many goods one could obtain by hunting, gathering, farming, and so forth. Still today, genetic influence on characteristics such as strength and health influence how many apples and oranges one will buy, though perhaps a bit more indirectly, for example, through the type of job one selects and, hence, income. Similarly, one's cognitive abilities may influence what work one can do and that also affects what one acquires and consumes.

However, as long as people are doing the best with what they have, most of the analysis of the previous section applies here as well. It is arguably of less consequence for the analysis of economic efficiency where constraints come from than where tastes come from. Evolutionary origins don't raise the question of the relevance of constraints for welfare analysis as they do with tastes, because the legitimacy of a constraint is not an issue for welfare analysis while the legitimacy of a particular taste might be. For this reason, the first motive for identifying the origins of genetic influences on behavior that come through tastes is irrelevant for constraints. Though we may learn about ourselves and better serve our own interests by critically considering the role of our genetic programming in determining our preferences, knowing that a constraint has a genetic origin tells us nothing useful about it as we have argued before. But, both the second and third motives

---

[22]If we were to tax people on the basis of their genetic potential, there could be an improvement in the efficiency of the tax system, but we doubt that many people would viewing taxing people on the basis of their potential, as opposed to their actual, incomes fair even if it was practical.

are at least as important here as with tastes. Understanding the genetic origins of constraints on our behavior may allow us to modify those constraints either by intervening in the causal path from gene to behavior or by direct manipulation of the genes in question.

There is one very important sense in which genetically influenced constraints on behavior might change how we think about social problems. If our genes limit or shape the way we make decisions in such a way as to make the rational optimizing model of our behavior inappropriate, then we may have a much more important reason for understanding genetic effects on behavior than any we have discussed so far. This will also be true if genes give us interdependent preferences.

A FOUNDATION FOR BEHAVIORAL ECONOMICS

Given the extreme assumptions of the rational actor model (e.g., full information, universally strategically rational behavior), it is easy to imagine how people could fail to make decisions in the way it predicts. As we noted previously, it doesn't necessarily matter if people are truly making decisions in the way economists assume, as long as the predictions of the model closely approximate actual behavior. If people are not always exactly right in their choice of optimal behavior because of cognitive limitations, it may not be a serious problem for the model. However, the nature of cognitive structures become significant for the analysis of social institutions when they cause people to systematically make decisions that the behavioral model would not predict (i.e., those which are, from the standpoint of strategic rationality, not in their best interest). Further, economic analysis of many types of problems is greatly complicated if people care not only about their own welfare but that of others as well.

For at least a decade before mainstream economists became interested in failures of the model of rational choice, researchers in the field of behavioral decision theory were carefully demonstrating consistent failures in judgment—particularly judgments involving probabilistic outcomes.[23] For the past two decades, behavioral economics—a branch of economics that focuses on forms of behavior that deviate from the standard model—has been expanding in scope and influence. Building on behavioral decision theory, behavioral economists employ traditional economic methods, along with new (to economics) experimental methods, to test the behavioral predictions of the rational actor model. Many of the discoveries within this subdiscipline have been extremely important for economic theory, but behavioral economics has not yet been very influential in policy formation. This is in part because the field is still largely underdeveloped, with the many deviations from rationality that have been identified lacking a framework for explaining or predicting them. We propose that evolutionary psychology could provide a framework for understanding behavior that violates the predictions of the rational actor

---

[23]For reviews of this early literature see Nisbett & Ross (1980) or Slovic, Fischoff, & Lichtenstein (1977).

model, and organizing the work of behavioral economists to help extend the influence of this research into the realm of policy analysis.[24] Further, we believe that the tools of behavioral genetics could be used to aid this endeavor as well as providing techniques that could be used more generally in economics to solve problems of sorting out causality in complex systems.

Systematic Deviations From Individual Rationality

Behavioral decision theory researchers and behavioral economists have generated good evidence for some forms of behavior that imply violations of the assumptions and predictions of the rational actor model. We describe some of these phenomena below and suggest how we might be able to understand the foundations of such behavior using an evolutionary psychology approach.

A behavioral phenomenon that has received considerable attention from economists is time preference anomalies. Because I can invest money today, receive interest on it, and have more money next year, I should prefer money today to the same amount of money next year. Because compound interest means that the value of my investments grow geometrically, the normative economic model implies constraints on how I should be willing to trade-off money today versus money a year from now versus money 5 years from now. It can be shown that people's behavior regularly violates these constraints (Laibson, 1997). People seem to value money today far too much based on projections from their willingness to trade money a year from now for money 5 years from now. Alternatively, they value money a year from now far less than they should based on how much they are willing to trade-off money today for money five years from now. People discount the future heavily, but are not very discriminating between different times in the future. Such behavior can have important implications for many aspects of social policy. For instance, people who behave this way may not save enough, or may display other problems with self-control (Laibson, Repetto, & Tobacman, 1998). If we knew with certainty that the decision problems that can be demonstrated in a laboratory setting were behind anomalous behavior in the economy, we might be inclined to adopt policies to protect people from decision errors. A wide range of social policies including the structure of the Social Security system could be affected. But without a theory of why people behave this way, or any theory for predicting when they will or won't behave this way, economists are reluctant to suggest such policies.

Like us, David Friedman (2001) argues that evolutionary psychology has much to contribute to the growing field of behavioral economics. In his paper, he provided a compelling account of why people may have evolved a tendency to evaluate present and future opportunities in the way that experimental economics suggests they do. He argued that in making decisions about the present versus the future, we may confound uncertainty about future events with judgments about the

---

[24]Cohen & Dickens (2002) presents a discussion of these issues written for economists.

time value of resources. For a Pleistocenian hunter-gatherer, a promise of some consideration next month in exchange for some action today may not have been very reliable and may not have been much less reliable than the promise of the same consideration a year from now. Thus, something I can get today is valued a lot more than what I can get at any time in the future, but how far in the future doesn't matter very much. In the same article, Freidman provided evolutionary explanations for several other phenomena that have puzzled economists. His suggestions represent good first steps toward the development and verification of evolutionary theories for these behaviors using the methods that have been demonstrated by evolutionary psychologists.

Another cognitive constraint on decision making that people often encounter is the tendency to either underweight or overweight low-probability events. Economists typically assume that people make decisions on the basis of expected utility—they consider the utility they would gain from two different states of the world, weighted by the probability of each event occurring. There is evidence, however, that people sometimes ignore very low-probability events when making complex decisions. This is understood as the result of a decision heuristic of editing. People with unlimited time and resources might take all information into account in making a decision, but in most complex decisions that is infeasible. It is hypothesized that people have rules of thumb for deciding what to consider and what not to consider, and a frequently used rule of thumb is to ignore very low-probability events. When people don't ignore low-probability events, they often behave as if the event was much more likely than it actually is.[25]

Editing could have serious consequences when people purchase insurance and could lead some people to be overly likely to choose some hazardous occupations. If people indeed tend to weigh outcomes in this manner, the normal economic incentives employers would face to improve work safety (having to pay higher wages to attract workers to more dangerous jobs) may be ineffective. The workers who overweight the likelihood of an accident would find employment elsewhere, leaving only those who treat the probability as essentially zero. Again there could be implications for policy. Workers who view their jobs as essentially safe are not likely to be willing to pay as much to make them safer as someone who correctly perceives the danger, therefore, employers won't be able to fund safer jobs by offering lower wages. Thus, there could be an under provision of safety that would not occur if people were omniscient and rational and that could provide a rationale for safety intervention. But economists are reticent to develop these implications, because no theory can predict when people will or won't appropriately weight low-probability events.

A third example of behavioral anomalies is cooperation and people's willing participation in activities that benefit a group with little benefit to the individual participant. People regularly behave in cooperative ways when their individual

---

[25]See the discussion of biases with respect to low probability events in Kahneman, Slovic, and Tversky (1982) and in Kahneman and Tversky (1974).

self-interest is clearly not being served (e.g., stopping to give directions to strangers who they are never likely to see again). The voting paradox is one example of "irrational" social participation. The chance that your vote will influence the outcome of an election is infinitesimal, but that doesn't stop most people from voting. But while people often exhibit irrational cooperation or social participation, at other times they behave selfishly or even with hostility toward others. If we could understand why and when people will cooperate as opposed to behave selfishly, it could have enormous implications for how we design institutions and conduct social policy. Recently, economists taking an evolutionary perspective have made important progress in analyzing such problems.[26]

Evolutionary Psychology as a Theoretical Framework for Behavioral Economics

Evolutionary psychologists argue that adaptive pressures have shaped the functions of the mind through natural selection, just as our bodies have evolved in response to environmental pressures. They provide evidence that the mind is composed of a number of domain-specific, content-dependent information processing mechanisms that were well suited to solve problems faced by our ancestors living in the Pleistocene. For example, evidence shows that the human brain has complex algorithms designed to facilitate social exchange (Cosmides, 1989; Cosmides & Tooby, 1992), mate selection (Buss, 1992), emotional recognition between mother and child (Fernald, 1992), and incest avoidance (Wolf, 1966).

The methodology that evolutionary psychologists have adopted is to first develop a theoretical model of what an evolutionary explanation for a class of behaviors might be. This step often involves induction from observed behavior and has been the source of accusations that what practitioners are doing is nothing more than post-hoc story telling. But the next step in exploring the possible evolutionary origins of a behavior is deducing and testing implications of the theory for other behaviors. It is the sometimes startling nature of the predictions and findings that suggest that this method has considerable scientific merit. They also suggest that such an approach to behavioral economics could be fruitful.

We can imagine such a program proceeding in two ways. Where evolutionary psychologists have already worked on problems of interest to economists, behavioral economists might proceed by trying to identify implications of existing research on evolutionary psychology for economic theory. Where evolutionary psychologists have not worked on a problem, behavioral economists might wish to emulate their methodology in trying to formulate evolutionary theories to explain some of the anomalous behaviors that have been identified. If they are lucky, doing so will yield theories with excess empirical content that can be tested in the labora-

---

[26]For example, Sethi & Somanathan (2001) show that a class of utility functions with conditional interdependence of individual utility that have been shown capable of rationalizing behavior in a wide range of cooperation experiments is evolutionarily stable.

tory and/or by observing people's real world economic behavior. Some of that excess empirical content might include additional implications for behavior and policy beyond those of the behavioral observations motivating the theory. Confirmation of those implications would give us confidence in the predictions of the evolutionary theory that hopefully would include guidance as to when the anomalous behavior may arise and what other behaviors we might expect to observe concomitantly. This approach would be most useful for dealing with behavioral anomalies such as time preference and judgment about probabilistic outcomes that have not yet been studied by evolutionary psychologists.

Some evolutionary psychologists have gone to great lengths to distance themselves from behavioral genetics. Tooby and Cosmides (1990) argued that the demands of sexual reproduction tend to make evolved traits universal. But this argument doesn't stand up to the wide range of evidence that behavioral geneticists can offer that important behavior does differ across individuals in part due to genetic differences. We suspect that some of the very behaviors that evolutionary psychologists have been concerned with, such as cooperation, show important variation across individuals, which is due in some sense to genetic differences. Behavioral economists would do well to take note of this and think of ways to use this essentially exogenous source of variation in behavior to identify causality in statistical analysis. A greater use of data sets with information on degrees of relatedness in economic research, along with more careful thought about how to use that information, may be in order.

As optimistic as we are about the prospects for an evolutionary basis for behavioral economics, we have one important concern about that promise. It is relatively easy to develop theories of the product of evolution when the product is viewed as the optimal equilibrium solution to a reproductive fitness problem. In our view it is possible, but not likely, that the decision heuristics that sometimes lead to errors in judgment represent optimal solutions to problems our ancestors faced in the Pleistocene. Humans, however, haven't had much time to evolve. In particular, they haven't had that much time to evolve optimal structures for using our unique computing machinery. We think it is more likely that if decision heuristics have an evolutionary basis, they are a biological rough first or second attempt at an optimal decision algorithm, which is still in the process of improvement. It is much more difficult to develop useful theories of dynamic evolution or transitions between equilibria—which is what would be required for a theory of fitness-enhancing cognitive adaptations to changing environments—than to model optimal equilibrium solutions.

CONCLUSION

We set out to accomplish three tasks: 1) to show that the social implications of research on the genetic influences on behavior are not what many people have thought, 2) to develop a framework in which we can understand how genes might influence behavior that is consistent with our perceptions of ourselves as making choices about our behavior, and 3) to present a framework in which the social implications of genetic influences on behavior might be understood.

As such, we have argued that concerns that genetic influences on behavior either justify those behaviors or imply their inevitability are misguided as is the view that group differences due to genetic differences will necessarily be viewed as just. We have described the rational actor model and suggested that the role of genes in shaping behavior can be understood in that framework as shaping people's tastes, the constraints they face in satisfying those tastes, and the decision-making process itself. This way of viewing the role of genes in shaping behavior suggested a number of things about the relevance of behavioral genetics and evolutionary psychology to social policy.

We began by noting that the initial reaction to the findings of high heritability of many behaviors and the possible existence of specialized evolved cognitive mechanisms should be "so what?" At least in the context of the normative model we describe, the origins of behavior can be completely irrelevant for social policy. However, we can imagine several ways in which the study of behavioral genetics and evolutionary psychology could inform social choice.

We noted that understanding the origins of behaviors could be useful in a number of ways: It could help us understand how to more effectively intervene to change undesirable behaviors, it could allow us to better understand our own motivation and thus to act in ways that are more productive of our well being, it could inform discourse about social values, it might aid in the development of gene therapy for behavior, and might help us understand and even anticipate areas where our cognitive structures lead us to systematically do less well than we might. Finally, we considered how evolutionary psychology might inform the work of behavioral economics and lead to a more useful theory that would be more widely applied.

Looking at this list, it is clear that the potential benefit of research on genes and behavior is largely unrealized. We hope that the framework we have presented will inspire economists to think more about how to incorporate insights from biology, psychology, and cognitive sciences into their work. We also hope that our framework will help behavioral geneticists and evolutionary psychologists focus their work on questions that are most important if we are to derive social benefit from that work.

ACKNOWLEDGMENT

We would like to thank Daniel Puskin and Hayden Smith for research assistance and Henry Aaron, Bryan Caplan, James Flynn, and Judith Harris for many very helpful comments on an earlier draft.

REFERENCES

Arrow, K., & Debreu, G. (1954). The existence of an equilibrium for a competitive economy. *Econometrica, 22,* 265–290.

Barkow, J., Cosmides, L., & Tooby, J. (1992). *The adapted mind: Evolutionary psychology and the generation of culture.* New York/Oxford, UK: Oxford University Press.

Bell, G., & Maynard S. J. (1987). Short-term selection for recombination among mutually antagonistic species. *Nature, 328,* 66–68.

Bowles, S. (1998, March). Endogenous preferences: The cultural consequences of markets and other economic institutions. *Journal of Economic Literature, 36,* 75–111.

Buss, D. (1992). Mate preference mechanisms: Consequences for partner choice and intrasexual competition. In J. Barkow, L. Cosmides, & J. Tooby (Eds.), *The adapted mind: Evolutionary psychology and the generation of culture* (pp. 249–266). New York/Oxford, UK: Oxford University Press.

Cohen J. L., & Dickens, W. T. (2002, May). A foundation for behavioral economics. *American Economic Review, 92*(2), 335–338..

Cosmides, L. (1989). The logic of social exchange: Has natural selection shaped how humans reason? Studies with the Wason Selection Task. *Cognition, 31,* 187–276.

Cosmides, L., & Tooby, J. (1992). Cognitive adaptations for social exchange. In J. Barkow, L. Cosmides, & J. Tooby (Eds.), *The adapted mind: Evolutionary psychology and the generation of culture* (pp. 163–228). New York/Oxford, UK: Oxford University Press.

Dickens, W. T. (1986). Safety regulation and "irrational" behavior. In B. Gilad & S. Kaish (Eds.), *Handbook of behavioral economics* (pp. 325–348). JAI Press.

Dickens, W. T., & Flynn, J. R. (2001). Heritability estimates versus large environmental effects: The IQ paradox resolved. *Psychological Review, 108*(2), 346–369.

Eaves, L., Martin, N., Heath, A., Schieken, R., Meyer, J., Silberg, J., Neale, M. and Corey, L. (1997). Age changes in the causes of individual differences in conservatism. *Behavioral Genetics, 27,* 121–124.

Ellis, B. J. (1992) The evolution of sexual attraction: Evaluative mechanisms in women. In J. Barkow, L. Cosmides, & J. Tooby (Eds.), *The adapted mind: Evolutionary psychology and the generation of culture* (pp. 267–288). New York/Oxford, UK: Oxford University Press.

Fehr, E., & Gachter, S. (2000). Fairness and retaliation: The economics of reciprocity. *Journal of Economic Perspectives, 14,* 159–181.

Fernald, A. (1992). Human maternal vocalizations to infants as biologically relevant signals: An evolutionary perspective. In J. Barkow, L. Cosmides, & J. Tooby (Eds.), *The adapted mind: Evolutionary psychology and the generation of culture* (pp. 391–428). New York/Oxford, UK: Oxford University Press.

Flynn, J. R. (1998). IQ gains over time: Toward finding the cause. In U. Neisser (Ed.), *The rising curve: Long-term gains in IQ and related measures* (pp. 25–66). Washington, DC: American Psychological Association.

Frank, R. H. (1997) *Micro economics and behavior* (3rd ed.). New York: McGraw-Hill.

Friedman, D. D. (2001). Economics and evolutionary psychology. *InDret.* Retrieved November 16, 2001, from http://www.indret.com/eng/artdet.php?Idioma=eng&IdArticulo=167#uno; see also later version at http://www.daviddfriedman.com/Academic/ econ_and_evol_ psych/economics_and_evol_psych.html

Friedman, M. F. (1953). The methodology of positive economics. In M. Friedman (Ed.), *Essays in positive economics.* Chicago: University of Chicago Press.

Gottlieb, G. (1998). Normally occurring environmental and behavioral influences on gene activity: From central dogma to probabilistic epigenesis. *Psychological Review, 105*(4), 792–802.

Herrnstein, R. J., & Murray, C. (1994). *The bell curve: Intelligence and class structure in American life.* New York: Free Press.

Jensen, A. R. (1998) *The g factor: The science of mental ability.* Westport, CT: Praeger.

Kahneman, D., Slovic, P., & Tversky, A. (1982). *Judgment under uncertainty: Heuristics and biases.* Cambridge, UK: Cambridge University Press.

Kahneman, D., & Tversky, A. (1974). Judgment under uncertainty: Heuristics and biases. *Science, 185,* 1124–1131.

Laibson, D. (1997). Golden eggs and hyperbolic discounting. *Quarterly Journal of Economics, 112*(2), 443–477.

Laibson, D., Repetto, A., & Tobacman, J. (1998). Self control and saving for retirement. *Brookings Papers on Economic Activity, 1,* 91–196.

Loehlin, J. C. (1992). *Genes and environment in personality development.* Newbury Park, CA: Sage Publications, Inc.

Lykken, D. T., Bouchard, T. J., McGue, M., & Tellegen, A. (1993). Heritability of interests: A twin study, *Journal of Applied Psychology, 78,* 649–661.

Martin, N. G., Eaves, L. J., Heath, A. C., Jardine, R., Feingold, L. M., & Eysenck, H. J. (1986). Transmission of social attitudes. *Proceedings of the National Academy of Science, 83,* 4364–4368.

Mann, J. (1992) Nurturance or negligence: Maternal psychology and behavioral preference among preterm twins. In J. Barkow, L. Cosmides, & J. Tooby (Eds.), *The adapted mind: Evolutionary psychology and the generation of culture.* New York/Oxford, UK: Oxford University Press.

Nisbett, R. E., & Ross, L. (1980). *Human inference: Strategies and shortcomings of social judgements.* Englewood Cliffs, NJ: Prentice-Hall.

Nozick, R. (1974). *Anarchy, state, and utopia.* New York: Basic Books.

Orians, G., & Heerwagen, J. (1992). Evolved responses to landscapes. In J. Barkow, L. Cosmides, & J. Tooby (Eds.), *The adapted mind: Evolutionary psychology and the generation of culture.* New York/Oxford, UK: Oxford University Press.

Plomin, R., Corley, R., DeFries, J. C., & Fulker, D. W. (1990). Individual differences in television viewing in early childhood: Nature as well as nurture. *Psychological Science, 1,* 371–377.

Plomin, R., DeFries, J. C., McClearn, G. E., & McGuffin, P. (2001). *Behavioral genetics* (4th ed.). New York: Worth.

Rabin, M. (1998). Psychology and economics. *Journal of Economic Literature, 36*(1), 11–46.

Reynolds, V., Falger, V., Vine, I. (1986). *The sociobiology of ethnocentrism: Evolutionary dimensions of xenophobia, discrimination, racism and nationalism.* Athens: University of Georgia Press.

Robson, A. (2001). The biological basis of economic behavior. *Journal of Economic Literature, 39*(1), 11–33.

Rowe, D. C., Jacobson, K. C., & Van den Oord, E. J. C. G. (1999). Genetic and environmental influences on vocabulary IQ: Parental education level as moderator, *Child Development, 70,* 1151–1162.

Samuelson, P. A. (1954). The pure theory of public expenditure. *Review of Economics and Statistics, 36*(4), 387–389.

Sethi, R., & Somanathan, E. (2001). Preference evolution and reciprocity. *Journal of Economic Theory, 97,* 273–297.

Slovic, P., Fischoff, B., & Lichtenstein, S. (1977). "Behavioral decision theory." *Annual Review of Psychology, 28,* 1–39.

Tooby, J., & Cosmides, L. (1990). On the universality of human nature and the uniqueness of the individual: The role of genetics and adaptation. *Journal of Personality, 58*(1), 17–67.

Tooby, J., & Cosmides, L. (1992). The psychological foundations of culture. In J. Barkow, L. Cosmides, & J. Tooby (Eds.), *The adapted mind: Evolutionary psychology and the generation of culture.* New York/Oxford, UK: Oxford University Press.

Trumbetta, S. L., Gottesman, I. I., & Turkheimer, E. N. (c. 1999). *Genetic influences on heterosexual pair-bonding: Psychopathology and patterns of never marrying, marriage, and divorce.* Reported by the NAS-NRC World War II Veteran Twin Registry, Charlottesville, University of Virginia, mimeograph.

Turkheimer, E. (1997). *Spinach and ice cream: Why environmentalist social science is so difficult.* Charlottesville, University of Virginia, mimeograph.

Turkheimer, E. (2000). Three laws of behavior genetics and what they mean. *Current Directions in Psychological Science, 9*(5), 160–164.

Turkheimer, E., Haley, A., Waldron, M., D'Onofrio, B., & Gottesman, I. I. (2002). *Socioeconomic status modifies heritability of IQ in young children.* University of Virginia Working Paper.

Turkheimer, E., & Gottesman, I. I. (1996). Simulating the dynamics of genes and environment in development. *Development and Psychopathology, 8,* 667–677.

Varian, H. R. (1987). *Intermediate microeconomics.* New York: Norton.

Waller, N. G., Kojetin, B. A., Bouchard, T. J., Lykken, D. T., & Tellegen, A. (1990). Genetic and environmental influences on religious interests, attitudes, and values: A study of twins reared apart and together. *Psychological Science, 1,* 138–142.

Wolf, A. (1966). Childhood association, sexual attraction and the incest taboo. *American Anthropologist, 68,* 883–898.

10

Behavior as Influence and Result of the Genetic Program: Non-kin Rejection, Ethnic Conflict, and Issues in Global Health Care

Elaine L. Bearer
Brown University Medical School

Interplay between the genetic program and the experiential and physical environment is extremely complex. The genetic program is enacted biologically through a system of complex interacting biochemical reactions. The environment of the organism, both social and physical, influences the expression of genes which in turn can affect the biological and social environment. A rigorous understanding of this interacting network is required if we are to define the relative contribution of any of its parts.

The premise of this chapter is that behavior drives genetic change over generations. This idea was prompted by a parallel hypothesis presented by Newman and Muller (Muller & Newman, 1999; Newman & Muller, 2000) that proposes that morphology of an animal drives genetic programming. As an example of a human behavioral ability that has the potential to influence the genetic program, I have selected discrimination. I define discrimination as the ability—the propensity—to distinguish between those people who are similar, "us," and those who are different, "them." This ability underlies kin selection and can thereby influence genes over evolutionary time (Wilson, 2000). The ability to identify kin in humans may be accomplished by phenotypic matching (Pfennig & Sherman,

1995). Recent advances in digital imaging have provided improved means to measure this ability quantitatively (DeBruine, 2002). This ability to distinguish phenotypic differences has been used to excuse prejudices that result in ugly acts of violence and repression.

Misuse of the ability to identify kin may be at the root of inequities in health care access. While this is a more passive expression of discrimination, it could impact survival of whole populations in similar or even greater proportions than the Holocaust. Those identified as being members of the kin group of those who own patented medications, or those who dispense them, receive a disproportionate share. There are many examples of disparities in health care. Those occurring in the United States have been debated over many years. Recently, more debate has erupted over disparities in access to anti-HIV drug therapies between industrial and developing countries and between colonial and indigenous societies, such as the Ladino and Maya of Guatemala (Glei & Goldman, 2000; Gonzalez Block, Ruiz, & Rovira, 2001; Sud, Starbuck, Dalal, Page, & Bearer, 2003; Wheeler et al., 2001). Perhaps because our discriminatory abilities can lead to negative outcomes, we often fail to recognize this ability as a normal part of the human social/behavioral repertory. My hope is that by acknowledging it as part of our biological endowment, its power to do harm may be diminished and its negative impact on the human gene pool reduced.

In this chapter, it is first necessary to provide definitions for inherited abilities and disorders that distinguish them from actions (complex behaviors) that are under the influence of conscious thought. I then describe some of the many steps in the enactment of the genetic program that are flexible and potentially influenced both by the physical and emotional environment and by conscious intention. In support of the thesis that behavior influences genetic inheritance, I use an example from the Cichlid fish in which evolution of the genome was influenced by behavior. It is hoped that as a by-product of this discussion, the reader will acquire a new perspective on this issue that will prompt further ideas of strategies for prevention of inequities and violence based on prejudice and discrimination.

THE ABILITY TO DISCRIMINATE—DISCERNMENT

There is a large literature on how humans perceive others and classify them. Rather than cite the many examples, let me rather propose a thought experiment for the reader to test this ability in herself. Pose the following questions to yourself: What categories of characteristics in another person do you evaluate to detect differences? How different does another person have to be in any of these categories for a difference to be detected? How different can the other person be and still be recognized as similar to you? Are there differences that lead you to reject another person as different or foreign? How do you feel and behave toward those whom you identify as similar, how to those identified as different?

By observing others and answering these questions, the reader may come up with the following list:

Categories of characteristics that are easily noticed include:

Gender, age;

Appearance—skin color, clothing, facial features and expression, size (height and weight), hair color and texture;

Body language—movements, style, tempo, stance;

Speech—language, accent, choice of words; and

Content of speech—Religion, political opinions, educational background, temperament, priorities, intelligence, competence and efficiency.

This is by no means an exhaustive list. Many additional characteristics could be added. From sensory perceptions, we draw clues of expected performance, and we predict the type and quality of interactions we will have with another person. This has been studied recently in experiments that test response to faces (DeBruine, 2002). For each of us, there are limits to what we perceive as acceptably similar and what we reject as foreign. Through experience, appearance becomes linked with expectations of behavior. It may also be that certain facial structures are interpreted "intuitively" as being expressions of a mood or emotion, and these moods are responded to even when the individual displaying the particular facial structure is not experiencing the predicted mood. An example of the optical illusions in facial structure is Mona Lisa's famous smile (Adour, 1989; Borkowski, 1992; Stoller, 1984).

This ability to detect individual differences, and to use these differences to predict who belongs to our group, "us" and who does not, "them" is not culturally restricted—humans from around the world share this ability (Pfennig & Sherman, 1995). Thus, this ability appears to be "innate"—in other words, likely to be inherited along with all the other genes that make us human.

Culture impacts which characteristics receive attention. In addition, once a difference is detected, many other variables affect consequent behavior. These variables include cultural indoctrination, personal history, and the immediate circumstances of the initial encounter and the ensuing relationship.

This ability can lead to specific behaviors that benefit related individuals or disadvantage those identified as non-kin. Thus, if the ability were an inherited trait, in other words, genetically encoded, then it could be selected over evolutionary time (Wilson, 2000). Next, I will discuss evidence in support of this hypothesis.

A GENERAL DEFINITION OF "ABILITY" AND "BEHAVIOR"

There is a large literature on the definitions of behavior and ability. Rather than reiterating this literature, I will use a simple definition from the common language dictionary for the purposes of this discussion. According to *Webster's College Dictionary*,

"Behavior *n.* **1.** The manner of conducting oneself. **2.** Observable activity of a human or animal … the aggregate of responses to internal and external stimuli."

In practice, the word "behavior" is often used to describe actions over which the individual is presumed to have choice. Such action is therefore assumed to be "volitional." Later, I will discuss whether such an assumption is appropriate if an action is the consequence of a genetic disorder. For some types of metabolic, anatomic, and genetic disorders, resultant behavior is not under the control of the afflicted person. In contrast, "Ability is the general term for a natural or acquired capacity to do things."

THE INHERITANCE OF "BEHAVIOR" AND "ABILITIES"

Evolutionary theory as long ago as Darwin has hypothesized a link between behavior and genetic inheritance in humans . But a direct association between a specific gene and a behavior has been difficult. The challenges to finding such links are two-fold—(a) "behavior" is difficult to define precisely; (b) the genetic program is variable in its expression and particularly responsive to the environment.

Recently, in the genomic era, more concrete data has established specific links between human activities and particular genes by focusing on well-defined pathologic behaviors (McGuffin, Riley, & Plomin, 2001). Pathologic behaviors can be subdivided into four categories:

1. A set of physical activities that (a) can be well-defined, such as abnormal bodily movements, and (b) occur in similar versions in all afflicted persons. An example of this is Huntington's chorea (Narding & Zitman, 2001; Thompson, Craufurd, & Neary, 2002);
2. A set of different activities that occur in varying constellations and degrees and at varying time intervals in any given individual, but are still recognizable as a similar disease process. An example of this is schizophrenia (Goff et al., 2001);
3. A disability in a single mental activity. Examples of this include inability to read or compose words (dyslexia), attention deficit disorder, or mental retardation (McGuffin, Riley, & Plomin, 2001); and
4. Complex behaviors that result from the interaction between learning and memory and the genetic program. This category includes all those syndromes for which no clear definition has yet emerged. There are many considerations involved in assigning even candidate genes to roles in complex behaviors (Tabor, Risch, & Myers, 2002).

IDENTIFICATION OF GENES FOR SPECIFIC
BEHAVIORAL DISORDERS

Evidence for a link between behavior and genes has been accomplished by studying psychiatric disorders. Those disorders that produce a single, well-defined activity have been the most amenable to genetic dissection. For such disorders, traditional genetic techniques have been applied. These techniques begin with a family tree in which affected individuals are identified by their symptoms. Chromosomal markers, such as restriction fragment polymorphisms or micro-satellite markers, are used to determine which chromosomal region is inherited only by affected symptomatic family members. An example from our work is shown in Fig. 10.1 (Bearer, Chen, Li, Marks, Smith, et al., 2000). In this example, a family in which deafness occurs was tested for markers along chromosome 19. People who inherit a small portion of chromosome 19 become deaf in the fourth decade of life.

The size of the chromosomal region that is coinherited with the disorder is defined as much as possible by a variety of techniques, and then the genes in that region are identified and sequenced. In this example, naturally occurring recombination during gametogenesis resulted in different family members inheriting different parts of chromosome 19, and narrowing the region of interest to 4 cM of DNA length.

Differences in the DNA sequence in the coding region of a particular gene in affected but not unaffected family members were originally thought to be responsible for inherited disorders. Such sequence alterations must then be found in an affected person who is not a member of the index family to confirm the correlation between the sequence alterations and the disease. Sometimes the same gene is mutated but at different points in various families. Sometimes the same symptoms arise from a mutation in another gene. In the case of the deafness gene described above, two genes are thought to be involved in similar biological pathways; defects in either one affects the same pathway which gives rise to deafness. In some rare cases, different mutations in the same gene can produce different diseases. Examples for all of these correlations between gene and outcome can be found in studies on the *ret* proto-oncogene. At least two different mutations in the ret coding sequence give rise to Multiple Endrocine Neoplasias (Mulligan, Eng, Healey, Clayton, Kwok, et al., 1994), while mutations in another domain of the coding region of the same *ret* gene cause a different disease, Hirschprung's megacolon, a developmental lack of sympathetic neurons in the colon (Edery, Lyonnet, Mulligan, Pelet, Dow, et al., 1994; Romeo, Ronchetto, Luo, Barone, Seri, et al., 1994).

To determine whether one mutation or several different mutations could each cause a particular disorder, data from different families is compared. Such comparison of genetic sequences for the mutated gene from different unrelated families identifies whether most people with the disorder have the same mutation, or if more than one mutation can produce the same disorder.

Disorders that display dramatic symptoms allow definitive identification of affected family members. Such identification allows the pattern of inheritance within families and between families to be determined. Three "behavioral" disorders for which identification of responsible gene(s) has been possible are: Huntington's chorea, early onset (familial) Alzheimer's disease, and Fragile X mental retardation (Table 10.1; McGuffin et al., 2001).

For Huntington's chorea, a single gene is mutated in all families in which the disorder occurs (Harding, 1993). This mutation is dominant, and thus when inher-

Family 1030

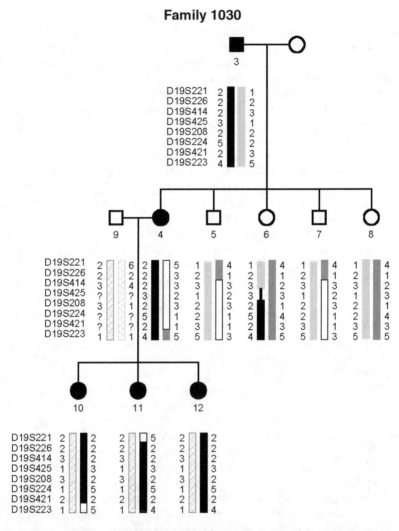

FIG. 10.1. Inheritance pattern for a chromosomal region co-inherited with deafness. Square (male) and circles (female) of family members with affect (filled) and non-affected (open) individuals. Microsatellite markers indicated numerically as D19Sxxx, and the number of repeats at each position in the chromosome given. Different alleles of each chromosomal region have different numbers of repeats. The gene causing the disorder is co-inherited with the chromosome indicated in black. Recombination events during mieosis in gametes result in re-distribution of alleles along the chromosome in subsequent generations. Individuals 6 and 11 demonstrate that the gene must lie below the D19S221 and above the D19S425 markers, since D19S221 is not required for deafness and from D19S425 on, no deafness occurs. Reproduced with permission from Bearer, Chen, Li, Marks, Smith, and Jackson.

TABLE 10.1
Genetic Disorders That Produce Behavioral Phenotypes

Name of disorder	Behavioral effects	Genetic locus
Huntington's Chorea	Emotional disturbance Choreic movements Progressive dementia	Gene Huntington Chromosome 14q16.3 CAG repeat expansion
Fragile X	Mental retardation at birth	Two different loci (FMR1 and 2) X chromosome Trinucleotide repeat s
Familial Alzheimer's Disease (Early onset)	Progressive dementia Memory loss Emotional instability	Any one of three distinct loci: Amyloid precursor protein Presenilin 1, chromosome 14 Presenilin 2, chromosome 1

ited always causes disease. For Fragile X Syndrome, a mutation in either of two different genes can cause the disorder (Connor, 1991). For the third disease, Early Onset Alzheimer's, three distinct genes have been implicated, any one of which will cause the syndrome (St George-Hyslop, Tanzi, Haines, Polinsky, Farrer, et al., 1989; Tanzi, 1989; Roses & Saunders, 1994; Selkoe, 2001). These three diseases were amenable to genetic sleuthing because they are relatively frequent, have a well-defined phenotype, and result from a mutation in a single gene.

Each of these three disorders manifests as what might be termed a "behavior" or "behavioral syndrome" when more than one behavior occurs. Huntington's chorea is manifested by a trio of symptoms: emotional disturbance, choreic movements, and progressive dementia (Naarding & Zitman, 2001). It is now known to be due to degeneration of specific regions of the brain, predominantly the basal ganglia and the cerebral cortex. On autopsy, the brain is atrophied with striking decrease in size of the caudate nucleus and to a lesser degree of the putamen. Striatal neurons are also affected, with both large and small neuronal loss. Neurologic symptoms may precede detectable morphological changes. The genetic locus for Huntington's is on chromosome 14p16.3, a gene that encodes a predicted 348 kDa protein, named "huntingtin," which is not processed normally because of changes in the protein caused by the mutation (Walter, Grunberg, Capell, Pesold, Schindzielorz, et al., 1997; Gafni & Ellerby, 2002). The coding sequence contains a trinucleotide repeat (CAG). In normal people, this repeat occurs from 11 to 34 times. In affected individuals, the repeat occurs more than 34 times. The age of onset of symptoms decreases with increasing numbers of repeats. The reason for delayed onset (in midlife) and progression is unknown, and the normal function of the protein in the brain remains a mystery.

At this point, we might ask whether Huntington's chorea is really a "behavior?" The choreic movements and mental disturbances could be viewed as symptoms of neuro-degeneration. Once a disorder that influences "the manner of conducting oneself," that is, a physical activity, is linked directly to a genetic mutation, does the manifestation of the disorder still qualify as a "behavior," since the element of choice, and therefore responsibility, might be lacking?

That some disorders previously thought to be behavioral have genetic linkages raises the question of how many other behaviors might also be linked to genes. As discussed later with reference to specific examples, this question is difficult to answer for two reasons: (a) behavioral phenotypes are very difficult to describe accurately; and (b) for complex behaviors, more than one gene is likely to be involved. In addition to these impediments, the combined influences of experience, of the physical environment as well as of allelic variation in noncoding genetic sequences on the expression of the genetic program and the structure of the brain adds many more variables.

INHERITANCE PATTERNS FOR COMPLEX
DISORDERS, BEHAVIORS, AND ABILITIES

Studies of monozygotic twins provide further evidence that some behaviors and abilities can be genetically inherited. Such twins are nearly identical in genetic inheritance. Thus for behaviors that are uniquely dependent on genetic expression, both twins should be equally affected. Indeed, abilities (intelligence, perfect pitch) and behaviors (hyperactivity, personality) are more concordant between genetically identical twins even when raised apart than between the twin and his nonrelated adoptive siblings (Plomin, DeFries, McClearn, McGuffin, 2001).

But even identical twins are not always completely alike, indicating that expression of the behavior is not an inevitable consequence of inheritance, nor solely determined by genetic inheritance. For schizophrenic twins raised apart, concordance between twins for schizophrenia is only from 30 to 50%, not 100% as would be expected if this disorder were entirely based on genetic encryption (Russo, 2002). However, for a range of complex behavioral traits, twins adopted and raised apart were more like each other and their natural parents than like the nongenetically identical adoptive family they grew up in, but they are never identical. Hence, twin studies provide evidence that genetic inheritance increases susceptibility for complex behavioral outcomes, but additional, unidentified, environmental or experiential factors are also important.

Identification of specific genes involved in complex pyschological states will not be straightforward for two main reasons: (a) for schizophrenia, manic depressive syndrome, intelligence, and attention deficit disorder, the expression of the disease is variable, and thus difficult to define precisely and follow through a family tree; and (b) genetic interactions may involve several different genes, with additional variables including expression levels, posttranslational modifications, and biochemical environmental effects. Because the enactment of the genetic program depends upon the activity of the proteins encoded in the genome, any variation in the amount, activity, chemical composition or stability of these proteins can effect the expression of the program.

Furthermore, some of these psychological states may have a specific genetic locus but vary due to experiential influences, whereas others may actually be the result of a combination of interactions between any number of different genetic backgrounds. Indeed, the impact of experience on the expression patterns of genes in the brain is only now being examined with high resolution techniques, albeit for only a small set of genes as yet (see later in this chapter).

As an example of the challenge to the identification of a correlation between inheritance and a psychological disorder, consider schizophrenia. The constellation of symptoms labeled schizophrenia actually presents with a wide range of signs and symptoms, including variations in: age of onset, degree of normal mental functioning, rate of progression, fluctuations in mental ability, and severity of specific symptoms, such as auditory hallucinations and delusions. Indeed, the disorder now termed "schizophrenia" is likely to arise from many different distinct etiologies, all of which lead to schizophrenic symptoms in the final stage. Distinguishing characteristics for each of these underlying etiologies must be determined before genetic linkage can be performed.

The complexity of this problem does not stop with establishing criteria to identify the phenotype. For phenotypes whose manifestation depends on the expression of several genes, each of which is responsive both to the physical and psychological environment, the complexity of the task of linking the phenotype to the set of genes involved increases exponentially. In addition, the very structure of the brain upon which its circuitry depends, as well as how this structure changes in response to neuronal activity, is dependent on both the genetic background and experiential history. After writing this, I found some of these ideas echoed and given in more detail in a recent review by Steve Hyman, former Director of the National Institute of Mental Health (Hyman, 2002) who also contributed the Foreword to this volume.

In summary, establishing links between complex behavioral traits and the genetic program will require precise definitions of the behavior, large families or sets of twins in which the behavior is manifest and easily detected, an experimentally controlled environment providing uniform life experiences, and molecular analysis of the genetic sequences among family members.

EXPRESSION OF THE GENETIC PROGRAM IS VARIABLE AT MANY LEVELS

Further complicating the process of linking sets of genes to particular behaviors is the flexibility of the genome and its responsiveness to the environment. Two draft sequences of the entire human genome were published in February 2001, one in *Nature* and the other in *Science Magazine*. This is a millennial achievement. For the purposes of this essay, I want to focus on three significant facts that emerge from this sequence:

1. The human genome may encode only 30,000 genes (+/– another 10-20,000). If there are only 30,000, there would be only 1/3 more than the 20,000 genes of the lowly worm, *c. elegans*. This means that it is not our genes that determine our immense complexity, but something else.
2. An enormous amount of DNA between genes does not encode for proteins. The function of this "junk" DNA is still being ellucidated, but it appears to contain information that regulates packaging of the chromosome and activation of expression of genes, as well as the age of the cell (telomeres) and machinery for nuclear division (centromere).
3. Proteins synthesized from genes do the work of the gene, but are themselves subject to variable modifications at all levels of synthesis and even during activity. During synthesis, mRNA encoding a protein can be spliced into various forms, producing proteins with alterations in different segments of peptide sequence (see later in this chapter). In addition, cells sense their environment through receptors on the surface that transmit information into the interior using a series of protein modifications, the best studied of which is phosphorylation—the covalent attachment of phosphate to specific amino acids within the peptide sequence that comprises the protein. Phosphorylations are reversible. The enzymatic activity of the protein is changed according to its phosphorylation state. In the brain, interactions in the postsynaptic neuron as it receives the neurotransmitter signal involve these protein modifications. For example, the postsynaptic receptor for the neurotransmitter, glutamate, is phosphorylated as is a calcium-signaling protein, CAM kinase II, upon synaptic activity (Lisman, 2001).

These variables provide enormous support for the idea that our genome is not hard wired. In fact, if human beings were hard wired, we could lose our environmental adaptability, which is thought to be based on the intellectual capacity which allows us to control our habitat and provides us with the ability to learn, remember, and be conscious. Consciousness permits some degree of choice in our actions. At least some of this noncoding DNA and of these protein modifications specifies environmentally responsive elements at all levels of the expression of our genetic program.

At this point, I want to stop and provide those who are not biologists with some definitions. I hope that this will not bore those already versed in genomic lingo. Hopefully, these definitions will prove useful not only for this essay, but for subsequent chapters in this book. Additional genetic terminology can be found on the web at: http://www.genomicglossaries.com

WHAT IS A "GENE"?

A gene is a stretch of DNA that contains the coding region that specifies the amino acid sequence of a protein flanked by non-coding DNA sequences that regulate its expression (Fig. 10.2A). Proteins perform the functions of the cell, which in turn determine the morphological structure and function/behavior of the organism. In

A. Gene structure

B. mRNA Splicing

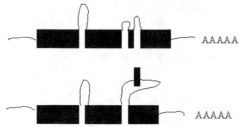

FIG. 10.2. Genes and mRNA.

A. Genes, a length of chromosomal DNA, includes the coding sequence for a protein as well as a number of structural units that play roles in regulating the timing and level of production of that protein. Exons contain the coding sequence. For a single sequence there are multiple interruptions in the continuity along the DNA of coding sequences. These interruptions, introns, are spliced out of the final mRNA that traffics to the cytoplasm and directs actual protein synthesis. Regulatory regions include silencing domains, found at either end of the gene, and the promoter region where transcription factors bind and regulate the activity of RNA polymerases. The promoter region is often but not always found at one end of the gene.

B. Alternative splicing can produce more than one product from the same coding region. Ligation between different splice sites can excise exons encoding regions in the middle of the protein. Other alternatives for producing different products from the same gene, not shown, are alternative stop and start sites, which can produce smaller proteins by omitting the ends. The polyA tail contains sequences that regulate the amount of protein produced from any particular mRNA, as do other regions in both 5' and 3' end of the mRNA. The timing and location of protein synthesis, which affects its activity in the cell, is also regulated partly by non-coding sequences at the beginning and ends of the mRNA.

many organisms, the coding sequence is interrupted by introns, stretches of DNA that are not used for protein synthesis. Messenger RNA (mRNA) is synthesized (transcribed) based on the DNA sequence. During and after transcription, mRNA is processed by splicing, which removes introns. Many mRNAs have more than one way that they can be spliced, which adds to the number of protein isoforms that can be produced by translation from a single gene (Fig. 10.3B). Once spliced to its

A. Gel shift of Xrel transcription factors and DNA sequences.

In vitro synthesized X-rel and v-rel
shift degenerate oligos

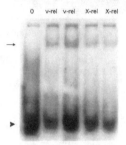

B. Sequences of DNA bound to Xrel

IN VITRO TRANSLATED XREL
1   GGGAATCCCC
2   GGGAATCCCC
3   GGGGAAACCC
4   GGGAATCCCC
5   GGGAATCCCC
6   GGGGATCCCC
7   GGGAAGCCCC
8   GGGGAGCCCC
9   GGGAATCCCC

EMBRYO EXTRACT
LOWER (SMALLER) BAND
10   GGGGAACCCC
11   GGGGAATTCCC
12   GGGAAACCCC
13   GGGAAACTCC
14   GGGAAATCCC
15   GGGGAATCCC
16   GGGGAGCCCC

FIG. 10.3. Transcription factor wobble.
A. Gel shift of Xrel transcription factor and DNA sequences.
The transcription factor Xrel was synthesized in vitro and incubated with a mixture
of DNA sequences. After incubation, the DNA-Xrel was separated by electrophoretic
passage through a flat non-denaturing gel. The DNA bound to Xrel was retarded
(shifted) in its electrophoretic mobility through an acrylamide gel (arrow), while the
unbound DNA migrated to the bottom of the gel (arrowhead).
B. Sequences of DNA bound to Xrel.
Sequencing of the DNA bound to Xrel demonstrated that position 4, 6, and 7 were
variable.

final form, mRNA is then trafficked out of the nucleus to the cytoplasm where complex ribosomal machinery translate its nucleotide sequence into an amino acid sequence, which when folded properly becomes the protein. Once synthesized, most proteins undergo various biochemical alterations that change their activity. These posttranslational modifications are often in direct response to an external stimulus to the cell.

It is now hypothesized that one way species complexity is generated is through the process by which genes are transcribed, translated, and posttranslationally modified. Some recent strong evidence for this comes from analysis of gene expression profiles in chimpanzee brains compared to humans. While humans and chimpanzees share 98.7% of their DNA sequences, expression patterns of genes in the brain exhibit pronounced differences between the two species (Enard, Przeworski, Fisher, Lai, Wiebe, et al., 2002b).

Genetic differences between individuals and across species occur in both coding and noncoding regions. Coding regions are more constant than the sequences between them. Differences in DNA sequence can affect the amino acid sequence of the protein when they occur in the coding regions. The effect of DNA sequence differences in noncoding regions is less well understood but could affect splicing of introns, regulation of expression levels, and silencing of alleles. These differences would result in variations in the amount of a particular protein in a cell and, thus, affect the function of that protein and thereby the behavior of the cell. Evidence that sequence variation in noncoding DNA affects the expression level of genes has just recently been reported (Yan, Yuan, Velculescu, Vogelstein, & Kinzler, 2002).

Not all nucleotide differences in a DNA sequence have functional significance. For coding regions of genes, each amino acid is encoded by a triplet of nucleotides. For many amino acids, what the third nucleotide is does not matter (Crick, 1966). Thus, differences in the third nucleotide have no affect on the amino acid sequence of the protein. Differences in length and sequence of noncoding regions are more common than those in coding regions, and these differences are used to determine inheritance patterns of genes, such as that shown in Fig. 10.1. Humans are diploid, having two copies of each chromosome. Each of these copies is slightly different. Differences that do not give rise to recognizable disease are called alleles. For any single gene, there can be dozens of naturally occurring alleles, all of which have no definable symptomatic (phenotypic) effect. Allelic variation without consequence must always be considered when any new variation in a DNA sequence is identified. The distinction between an allelic variation and a mutation is still fuzzy.

WHAT ARE THE KNOWN FLEXIBILITIES IN OUR GENOME?

Alternative Splicing

Alternative splicing of the coding region occurs when the introns are spliced out from different points along the protein. This can create different proteins from the same gene. Often these proteins perform functions so similar that the purpose of splicing has been hard to identify, as in the case of the molecular motor, myosin II (Pato, Sellers, Preston, Harvey, & Adelstein, 1996). This myosin is involved in axoplasmic transport (DeGiorgis, Reese, & Bearer, 2002) and required for hearing (Heath, Campos-Barros, Toren, Rozenfeld-Granot, Carlsson, et al., 2001). However, in some instances, splice forms are expressed only under unique circumstances and have enough functional differences as to make their expression significant for the life of the cell.

Recent evidence suggests that one familial type of schizophrenia might be a result of mutations in an intron in the gene encoding dysbindin (Straub, Jiang, MacLean, Ma, Webb, et al., 2002). Such a mutation could alter the levels of dysbindin or produce a more or less active isoform of the protein. Because splicing affects the size of the mRNA and consequently of the protein, if the intron mutations affect splicing, inappropriately sized mRNA and the protein it encodes should result. Such proteins will have altered function. How this alteration affects the cell will depend upon how often it happens, whether it happens in a domain needed for the protein's function, and whether one or both of the alleles in the individual are affected by the mutation, either genetically (as in homozygotes) or through interactions between the protein products (as in dominant negatives).

The sequence in the intron of a gene specifies splice sites. However, whether these sites are used depends on splicing machinery in the nucleus, which is activated by stimuli external to the cell. In other words, the expression of particular, functionally different, isoforms from a single gene is environmentally responsive. How splice sites are chosen is an active area of current biological research.

J. Craig Venter, one of the leaders in the Human Genome Project, estimated that 40% of our genes encode proteins with different spliced variants (Cravchik, Subramanian, Broder, & Venter, 2001; Myers, Sutton, Smith, Adams, & Venter, 2002; Venter, 2000; Venter, Adams, Myers, Li, Mural, et al., 2001). Thus, opportunities for multiple effects via minor alterations in splice sites exist within the genome. While some alterations can produce dramatic effects, it is likely that most allelic variations and single nucleotide polymorphisms produce effects on function that are extremely subtle.

Regulation of Expression

Another mechanism by which our genome responds to the environment is regulation of the amount of each protein that is expressed. This regulation is achieved at two levels: (a) by the state (packaging) of the chromosome and biochemical modification of the DNA itself (Bird, 2002; Emerson, 2002), and (b) by the activity of transcription factors (Pabo & Sauer, 1992), and by the coordinated action between packaging and transcriptional activation (Wollfe, 2001). The signals that determine chromosome packaging and gene silencing are a vigorous area of research now, and the process is as yet poorly understood.

Transcription factors are known to activate the expression of cassettes of genes, each cassette encoding proteins whose activity combines to produce a biological outcome, a cellular behavior. A single transcription factor can activate or repress the expression of many different genes. Mutations encoding a transcription factor could alter expression patterns of a whole set of other genes. Thus, if a transcription factor, encoded by a single gene but regulating the expression of many genes, were mutated, then this would produce global effects on expression patterns. Thus, alterations in the activity of a single gene encoding a transcription factor could underlie a complex trait. Just as this chapter goes to press, a single gene has been proposed to be responsible for the human ability for speech (Enard et al., 2002; Lai et al., 2001). This gene encodes a transcription factor.

Transcription factors interact with the regulatory regions of genes to turn them on or off. Transcription factors are therefore DNA-binding proteins that would be expected to recognize a specific DNA sequence, bind to it and activate a single downstream gene. If our genome were hard wired, lacking in flexibility, this would be the case. Indeed, the competition between scientists to identify the exact sequence that each individual transcription factor binds was intense. To win this race, the code—the specific unique DNA sequence that each transcription factor recognized—was sought (Pabo & Sauer, 1992).

Surprisingly, it was found that one of the transcription factors we studied, Xrel, did not bind to a unique DNA sequence—Xrel was promiscuous there was wobble in the system. While Xrel required specific nucleotides at some positions in its DNA recognition sequence, nucleotides at other positions were interchangeable. Xrel could bind to DNA sequences with any nucleotide in those positions (Fig. 10.3). The DNA sequence that Xrel binds is 10 bases long. Three of these bases are interchangeable. Kirthi Reddy, who did an undergraduate honor's thesis in my lab, discovered this for Xrel (Bearer, 1994; Bearer, Kantorowitz-Gordon, & Reddy (1995), but it seems to be a general principle—that the same transcription factor can bind to different DNA sequences, and different amino acid sequences can bind the same DNA sequence (Pabo & Nekludova, 2000).

Indeed, there is no general code for transcription factor-DNA recognition. Through elegant Xray crystallography of many different transcription factors followed by protein engineering, the Pabo lab has demonstrated that there is no simple code that restricts a given zinc-finger-type of transcription factor to a unique and specific DNA binding sequence (Pabo & Nekludova, 2000). What can be seen in superimposed atomic images of many different transcription factors is that different amino acid sequences can bind different DNA sequences, and vice versa (Fig. 10.4).

The lack of a code for transcription factor-DNA interactions adds both flexibility and stability to the machinery regulating protein expression. Single amino acid substitutions or nucleotide changes could either be immaterial or make a dramatic difference. In the absence of a code, the effect of mutations is unpredictable, and genetic engineering cannot indulge in targeted design (Pabo, Peisach, & Grant, 2001). It is tempting to speculate that evolution may be served by such unpredictable consequences to minor variations, such that major changes might arise from some

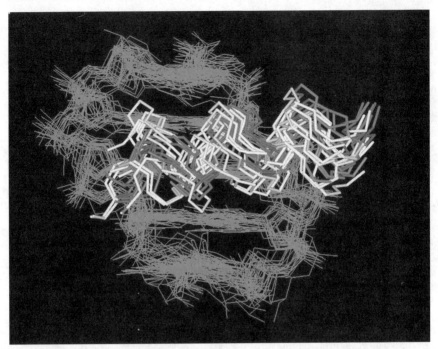

FIG. 10.4. DNA-transcription factor interactions with atomic resolution. By superimposing information from Xray crystallography of multiple zinc-finger DNA binding transcription factors, Pabo and Nekludova (2001) showed that many different amino acid sequences can interact with different DNA sequences. While some residues in each partner are constant, others are interchangeable. DNA is shown in blue, and the different amino acid structures in colors (by permission, Pabo and Nekludova, 2001).

minor alterations, while for other variations, protein expression would remain unchanged. The implication of this is that a single base pair change could profoundly affect protein expression if it occurred at one position in the site on the DNA where the transcription factor binds, whereas a single base pair change at an adjacent position could have no effect. Thus, the precise location of single nucleotide changes and the correlation with transcriptional activation will have to be examined before deductions can be made about the impact on the cell of nucleotide change.

To summarize:

1. Transcription factors regulate the expression of proteins from genes;
2. Single transcription factors regulate more than one gene, either in tandem along the DNA or at different sites on the same or different chromosomes;
3. Transcription factor activity is influenced by signals that come from outside the cell;

4. Single base pair mutations in the DNA at the binding site can affect transcription factor binding and therefore the expression of specific proteins inside cells.

Most transcription factors are activated by signaling pathways within the cell. In the absence of activation, these factors do not increase protein expression. Some signaling pathways involve a chemical event occurring at the cell surface that is propagated across the membrane by a receptor transducer. Receptor activation results in a cascade of events inside the cell that culminate in a biochemical modification of the transcription factor. This signaling network is so complex that even in the haploid yeast cell, its precise mechanics are not know. It will require extensive biochemical, genetic, and computational efforts to create a predictive model of even one such pathway, for the yeast pheromone receptor signaling (Dohlman, 2002; Dohlman & Thorner, 2001; Elion, 2000; Endy & Brent, 2001; Withe & Rose, 2001). This is only one of many pathways in a simple organism whose genome is known. Yeast are easily manipulated genetically. If delineating this single signaling pathway is so difficult in yeast, what can we expect from the vastly more complex human repertoire of environmental signaling responses?

High Density DNA Arrays Detect Expression Levels of Different Genes

Expression profiles using the coding sequences as probes show that there is great variability in the expression of genes across different human cell lines (Ross, Scherf, Eisen, Perou, Rees, et al., 2000). The genome project has made comprehensive analysis of expression patterns of all 30,000+ genes and many of their isoforms possible by DNA microarray (DNA chip) analysis. This computer experiment from my lab (Fig. 10.5) shows the expression pattern of the same gene, KPTN, across 61 different human cancer cell lines. In the figure, black represents no change over baseline, and grey increasing to white indicates increasing diffence in expression levels, with white representing the highest difference measurable, > 8 fold. Note that expression of KPTN over the 60 human cells varies significantly by these criteria. (On the web, these differences are represented in color, with red indicating more of the gene product is made compared with the standard pooled mRNA, and green indicating less is made (see http://genome-www5.stanford.edu/cgi-bin/SMD/publication/viewPublication.pl?pub_no=81). These differences in expression levels could be either a result of differing activity of transcription factors in individual cell lines or because of differences in the sequence of the gene's regulatory region.

Regulatory regions are also inherited and can confer phenotypic variation. In addition to differences in their DNA sequence, noncoding DNA also contains microsatellites, which are short (6–12 base pair) stretches of DNA that repeat variable numbers of times in different individuals (Weissenbach, 1993). The impact of these repeats on protein expression is still being assessed, but what we do know is that these repeats can be used to determine inheritance patterns. Most of the family

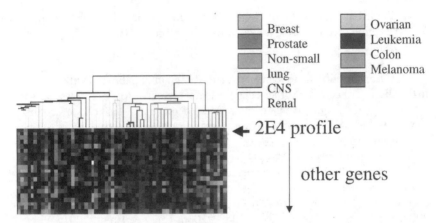

FIG. 10.5. Expression profiling. DNA high density array to detect mRNA levels across 60 different human cancer cell lines demonstrates that each cell expresses a different amount of the deafness gene, 2E4/kaptin (Bearer, Chen, Li, Marks, Smith, & Jackson, 2001). Interestingly, the expression pattern of 2E4/kaptin and the other genes whose pattern is similar, segregates the cell lines into tissue types, with most renal carcinomas, melanomas, and colon cancers clustering together.

trees now being generated use "GeneBridge 4," a set of DNA primers that identify common microsatellites that are used as markers for particular common alleles with differing lengths of sequence between each marker.

The family tree shown in Figure 10.1 was generated using microsatellite polymorphism to investigate a family in which deafness was an inherited trait. We found that the disorder was inherited along with the gene for KPTN. But upon sequencing the gene, we found no mutation in the coding region (Bearer, Chen, Li, Marks, Smith, et al., 2000). This suggests that a difference in the DNA sequence in the regulatory region, or in the intronic sequence spliced out during mRNA processing, for this gene could be responsible for the inherited deafness.

Single Nucleotide Polymorphisms

Allelic variation, microsatellite poymorphisms and single nucleotide changes all contribute to heritable differences in DNA sequences (Table 10.2). These differences are likely to underlie individual variation in morphologic phenotype as well as in susceptibility to environmental events and to various pyschological and behavioral traits.

Single nucleotide changes (polymorphisms, or SNPs) are being used to determine human population genetics and understand our evolutionary history (Sachidanandam, Weissman, Schmidt, Kakol, Stein, et al., 2001; Lewis, 2002). These single base-pairs that differ in at least 1% of the population account for 1 position every ~ 1,250 bases

TABLE 10.2

Degrees of Freedom in the Genome

1) Transcription from DNA to mRNA
    Chromatin packing and accessibility
        DNA chemical modification (Ex. Methylation)
        Histone chemical modification (Ex. Acetylation)
        Silencing
    Transcription factor activation
        Abundance of transcription factors
        Transcription factor cofactors
        Abundance and activity of enzymes and cofactors
    DNA sequence effects
        Sequence of the promoter, relative affinity for the transcription factor
        Microsatellites in the promoter region, distance between promoter and coding region

2) mRNA splicing
    Sequence in the splice site of the mRNA
    Abundance and activity of splicing machinery
    Recognition of the splice site by splicing machinery

3) Nuclear to cytoplasmic transport rates
    Sequence in the mRNA noncoding region
    Abundance and activity of transport machinery

4) mRNA stability
    Sequences that protect or target for degradation
    Abundance and activity of degradation machinery

5) mRNA transcription
    Rates of synthesis from mRNA to protein
    Abundance of ribosomal machinery and of amino acid substrates and cofactors
    Regulation of transcription rates by mRNA binding proteins (Ex. TOR)
    Location of synthesis in the cell
    Folding of the protein during or after synthesis

6) Protein enactment: Enzymatic activity
    Chemical modifications, abundunce and activity of modifying enzymes
    Abundance of cofactors or protein binding partners
    Rate of degradation, turnover, of the protein
    Proteolytic processing

along a DNA strand (Kwok, 2001). These can occur either in coding or noncoding regions of DNA. Those that occur in coding regions either cause an amino acid change that affects protein function or have no effect. Those occurring in noncoding regions could influence transcription factor binding, govern whether a gene is open to transcription or silenced, or have no effect. Most SNPs are in noncoding regions.

The ALFRED consortium is exploring those genes that do account for obvious morphological differences between a Swede and a Nigerian, a Native American and an Asian (Cheung, Miller, J. R. Kidd, K. K. Kidd, Osier, et al., 2000; Osier, Cheung, Kidd, Pakstis, Miller, et al., 2000). This consortium considers 180 sites in the genome that present in two alternate forms that display different frequencies in at least six populations. This work is being used retrospectively to study prehistoric human migrations out of Africa (Cann, de Toma, Cuzes, Legrand, Morel, et al., 2002; Lewis, 2002).

From a study of 724 genes, which included 11,209 SNPs, from 82 people and a chimp, it was conluded that 56% of SNPs located in coding domains are population-specific. In contrast, only 21% are cosmopolitan—that is, both variants are present in equal distribution in four American populations (ethnic groups): African-Americans, European-Americans, Asian Americans, and Hispanic-Latino-Americans (Judson & Stephens, 2001; Judson, Salisbury, Schneider, Windemuth, & Stephens, 2002; Stephens, Schneider, Tanguay, Choi, & Acharya, et al., 2001). This means that there are heritable differences between these populations in specific genes that correlate with morphological differences. Recent data also supports the idea that similar genetic differences confer inherited disease susceptibility traits in different populations (Romualdi, Nasidze, Risch, Robichaux, Sherry, et al., 2002). It seems logical to suppose that similar SNPs might influence the expression of structural genes involved in specifying and creating brain anatomy upon which circuitry, and thereby function, depends.

SUMMARY

The genetic program is flexible in response to the environment, both chemical and experiential. In addition, small individual variations in single nucleotides in either coding or noncoding regions of the DNA can affect protein expression. Protein expression is also under the influence of the physical/chemical and experiential/emotional environment. A Biological Systems Analysis with computational modeling will no doubt be necessary before the many variables in the interactions between the cellular environment and the expression of its genetic program can be understood at a level where precise relationships and predictions can be made.

HOW CAN BEHAVIOR AFFECT THE GENOME?

Evolutionary theory proposes that the only significant behavior is that which influences the number of surviving offspring. Behavior can be defined as a series of events that produce viable reproductively healthy offspring. The series of events leading to an action are diagrammed in the cartoon (Fig. 10.6).

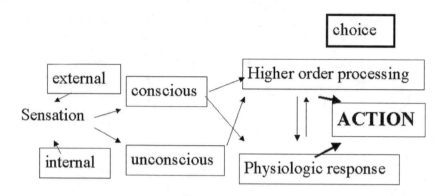

FIG. 10.6. A simplistic diagram of behavior.

If a particular ability is encoded in a genetically inheritable form and if this behavior leads to an action that increases the number of offspring, then individuals
with the same genes can be selected, that is, their allelic frequency increased in the
population. Two such behaviors that, if genetically encoded, could influence their
own selection are mate selection and kin selection. A corollary to this is that any
action that leads to selection (preferential propagation) of a set of genes will ultimately become genetically encoded.

Environmental Influences on Mate Selection

One example from nature of how behavior influences mate selection comes from
studies of the Cichlid fish in Lake Victoria, Lake Malawi, and Lake Tanganyika in
Africa (Fig. 10.7; Meyer, Kocher, Basasibwaki, & Wilson, 1990; Newman, 1994;
Newman & Muller, 2000). Briefly, Lake Victoria is one of the remnants of a larger
lake that recently (1.4 million years ago) partially dried, leaving behind three separate bodies of water that had once been confluent. This separation isolated a single
population of fish into different groups. These groups took on different morphological features, including coloration, partly as a consequence of differing levels of
metal ions in the waters of each of the three lakes. These differences also occurred
within the bounds of one lake, where fish would presumably have had the opportunity to interbreed. This would have appeared to be a very rapid evolutionary process, but when genetic analysis was performed, no significant DNA differences
were identified (Meyer, Kocher, Basasibwaki, & Wilson, 1990; Nagl, Tichy,
Mayer, Samonte, McAndrew, et al., 1998). Indeed, the morphological variations
appear to be caused by events occurring during development, events that were subject to local water conditions and not due to changes in the genome. These physical

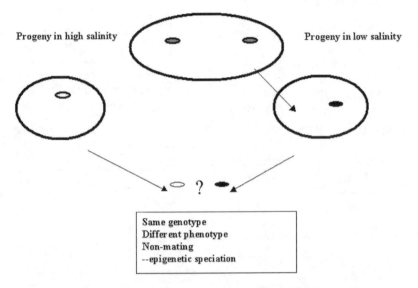

FIG. 10.7. Cichlid fish in Lake Victoria. Original population of fish become separated into different local environments with differing metal ions and salinity in water
during embryogenesis. This results in differing coloration and other morphological
characteristics. Resultant progeny do not recognize each other as mates. This produces a type of genetic isolation that will ultimately promote the inheritance of a different set of alleles in each population.

effects of the environment influenced morphological features of the fish such that
they did not recognize each other as mating partners. One of the features, differences in coloration, affects female mate selection. Darkly colored females do not
recognize lighter males (Lande, Sechausen, & van Alphen, 2001; van der Meer,
1995). This failure to select males of a different coloration may also be related to
the physical conditions of the water during or after development, as the female fish
have alterations in the photoreceptors of the eye. A simplistic cartoon showing
how this might work is shown in Fig. 10.7.

Thus, the physical conditions of the environment during development resulted
in groups of morphologically different fish who share the same genotype but do
not recognize each other as prospective mates. A genome flexible enough to respond to the environment to the extent of mate selection can permit an effective *environmental speciation*. In the case of these fish, they might also be defined as
behaviorally speciated. These observations suggest that epigenetic events that influence mate selection will ultimately influence the genotype. Although they are
genetically almost identical now, continued failure to breed between groups of
morphologically distinct fish will ultimately result in genetic differences between

the two groups. This is an example of environmental effects influencing behavior and thereby driving genetics, as Newman and Muller (2000) proposed.

Kin Selection, an Environmentally Influenced Behavior?

If a genetic program is environmentally responsive during development, then exposure of the embryo to different environments would produce adults with different characteristics. Thus, adults raised in different environments might not recognize each other as potential mates, producing *pseudo-speciation* wherein individuals with similar genomes do not mate. One hypothesis is that such restricted mating produces a genetic isolation in which mutations that mimic the environmental effect are positively selected. In this scenario, environmentally influenced phenotype produces an evolutionary pressure that eventually programs the genome to produce the same phenotype independent of the environment. In the next section, I describe some observations that support this idea.

E. O. Wilson's (2002) sociobiology proposes that behaviors that enhance the survival of the gene, even at the expense of the individual, can be selected. This theory is based on a logic that predicts that behavior is genetically encoded.

Even minor advantages for the propagation of a particular gene in subsequent generations are magnified over generations. In Fig. 10.8 is shown a schematic of how this works, using as an example a hypothetical allele or set of alleles encoding cooperative behavior. The frequency (p) of the allele of a gene encoding cooperative behavior that enhances the survival of genetically related individuals is shown as

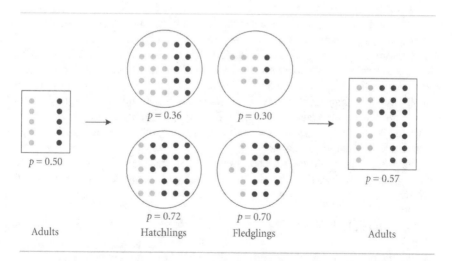

FIG. 10.8. Kin selection: A cooperativity allele? (adapted from Futuyama, 1997).

black dots. In this theoretical example for birds, initially there are equal numbers of individuals with and without the cooperativity allele(s) (Futuyama, 1997; Wilson, 2000). Random pairing results in asymmetric distribution of the allele in consequent families. Although individuals who carry this allele may be less fit and thus not survive, if their behavior benefits the overall survival of the family unit, more family members will survive. Thus, when resultant fledglings leave the nest and regroup, there are more individuals with the cooperativity allele in the total population.

Kin selection depends upon the ability to recognize kin (Pfennig & Sherman, 1995). Kin are defined as those individuals who share genetic material, such as a large set of similar alleles for genes in which the population at large may have much allelic variation. In many species of animals, recognition of kin often comes in by way of physical proximity. For the cichlid fish, mate recognition is related to coloration and visual perception. Similarly, I have previously proposed that human culture creates recognition devices that prompt humans to distinguish who is related and who is not (Bearer, 1999).

Kin recognition when proximity is not sufficient depends on the ability to discriminate between those individuals who share traits from those who do not. Kin recognition possibly influences mate selection as well as affecting cooperative actions that result in benefit to the family gene pool, even if such cooperativity reduces the fitness of a particular individual.

A direct corollary of kin recognition is *non-kin rejection*. The same ability that leads to the recognition of kin also detects those who are not kin (Bearer, 1999). Detection of differences, if it enhances gene survival, can therefore be a driving force leading to further evolutionary (genetic) changes.

It is likely that the same ability to detect differences and recognize kin influences both mate selection and kin selection, although one does not mate with siblings, so the consequent behavior differs. This ability also leads to the exclusion and/or rejection of non-kin from the circle of beneficiaries, as well as from the pool of potential reproductive partners. How do we recognize an "appropriate" mate? And whom do we recognize as kin and worthy of altruistic efforts? Whom do we help, whom do we not help, whom do we hinder? What characteristics do we recognize when making these choices? How do we learn to recognize those differences? What human abilities are involved in detecting individual differences and in recognizing mates and kin? Which are mostly inherited and which mostly learned? How much choice do humans have over how these abilities are translated into actions? Must we attack any whom we recognize as "other," as non-kin, for whom we have no evolutionarily programmed cooperation imperative? And, if we have choice, how does the exercise of such "free will" influence our societies, our governance, and our cooperation in global economies?

Impact on Global Health Care

While the following comment is outside the logic of the argument presented here, a conclusion that can be drawn from these ideas is that the "will" to provide life-saving health care to those who are not recognized as sharing our gene pool is lacking. To understand how we recognize our kin, and select our mates, it will be necessary to confront the ability to discriminate directly, understand it, and work with it.

As an example, the provision of health care for those afflicted with HIV in the developing world has recently come to the attention of the popular press in wealthier countries. The HIV epidemic is affecting populations worldwide. Mate recognition and selection will play a role in how the disease is passed, who is exposed and infected, who survives, as will kin selection behaviors, not only among the communities afflicted, but across the global community. One question is whether wealthier nations can recognize their distant relatives, their "kin," in the developing world and be more likely to adopt an altruistic stance.

Even more important, HIV transmission is dependent on lifestyles and behaviors. And HIV is a lethal disease, with almost 100% mortality. Maternal-child transmission propagates the infection into the subsequent generation, decimating populations. Thus, behaviors that decrease risk of infection with HIV will increase survival and be preferentially propagated into the next generation, possibly on a massive scale. The impact of the HIV epidemic on the genome of the survivors will be enormous, possibly greater than that of the Black Death in Europe.

All of the theories of human behavior discussed in this brief chapter are likely to be operative in the future unfolding of this epidemic and its subsequent effects on the genetics of the surviving human species. Transmission of HIV involves sexual selection and mate recognition. Therapeutic intervention will require altruistic behavior on the level of kin selection if the challenge of preserving our genetic diversity is met. In addition, if these activities are genetically encoded at any, even remote, level, which behavioral traits will survive this epidemic, which will not?

But if we intervene by promoting behavioral modification, how will this influence culture and its role in the many complex issues of human reproduction? The National Institutes of Health has called for proposals to study and implement strategies for behavioral modification worldwide, to affect peoples of widely divergent cultures. Such interventions must be carefully considered for their potential impact in directing and influencing human genetic traits in subsequent generations.

Kin selection and non-kin rejection are likely to influence the role of the international community in supplying aid and advice to HIV-affected populations. Can these behavioral effects of our evolutionarily encoded biological abilities be consciously assessed and critically evaluated? Can the human species perceive itself as one global family and respond appropriately? Perhaps only future historians will be able to answer these questions.

This chapter is offered in the hope that awareness leads to deliberate and ethically considered actions.

REFERENCES

Adour, K. K. (1989). Mona Lisa syndrome: solving the enigma of the Gioconda smile. *Ann Otol Rhinol Laryngol, 98*(3), 196–199.

Bearer, E. L. (1994). "Distribution of Xrel in the early Xenopus embryo: A cytoplasmic and nuclear gradient. *Eur J Cell Biol, 63*(2), 255–268.

Bearer, E. L. (1999). Altruism, evolution, and ethnic cleansing. Editorial, *Providence Journal.*

Bearer, E. L. (2001). "Microsequencing of myosins for PCR primer design. *Methods Mol Biol, 161,* 9–15.

Bearer, E. L., Chen, A. F., Li, Z., Marks, H.-F., Smith, R. J., & Jackson, C. L. (2000). "2E4/Kaptin (KPTN)—a candidate gene for the hearing loss locus, DFNA4. *Ann Hum Genet, 64* (Pt 3), 189–196.

Bearer, E., Kantorowitz-Gordon, I., & Reddy, K. (1995). *Xrel recognizes different DNA sequences.* NE meeting, Society for Developmental Biology, Woods Hole, MA.

Bird, A. (2002). DNA methylation patterns and epigenetic memory. *Genes Dev, 16*(1), 6–21.

Borkowski, J. E. (1992). Mona Lisa: the enigma of the smile. *J Forensic Sci, 37*(6), 1706–1711.

Cann, H. M., de Toma, C., Cuzes, L., Legrand, M. F., Morel, V., et al. (2002). A human genome diversity cell line panel. *Science, 296*(5566), 261–262.

Cheung, K. H., Miller, P. L., Kidd, J. R., Kidd, K. K., Osier, M. V., & Pakstis, A. J. (2000). ALFRED: A Web-accessible allele frequency database. *Pac Symp Biocomput,* 639–650.

Claverie, J. M. (2001). Gene number. What if there are only 30,000 human genes? *Science, 291*(5507), 1255–1257.

Connor, J. M. (1991). Cloning of the gene for the fragile X syndrome: Implications for the clinical geneticist. *J Med Genet, 28*(12), 811–813.

Cravchik, A., Subramanian, G., Broder, S., & Venter, J. C. (2001). Sequence analysis of the human genome: implications for the understanding of nervous system function and disease. *Arch Neurol, 58*(11), 1772–1778.

Crick, F. (1966). Codon—anticodon pairing: the wobble hypothesis. *J Mol Biol, 19,* 548–,555.

DeBruine, L. (2002). Facial resemblance enhances trust. *Proc R Soc Lond B Biol Sci, 269,* 1307–1312.

DeGiorgis, J. A., Reese, T. S., & Bearer, E. L. (2002). Association of a Nonmuscle Myosin II with Axoplasmic Organelles. *Mol Biol Cell, 13*(3), 1046–1057.

Dohlman, H. G., & Thorner, J. W. (2001). Regulation of G protein-initiated signal transduction in yeast: Pparadigms and principles. *Annu Rev Biochem, 70,* 703–754.

Dohlman, H. G. (2002). G proteins and pheromone signaling. *Annu Rev Physiol, 64,* 129–152.

Edery, P., Lyonnet, S., Mulligan, L. M., Pelet, A., Dow, E., Abel, L., Molder, S., Nihod-Fekele, C., Ponder, B. A., & Muinich, A. (1994). Mutations of the RET proto-oncogene in Hirschsprung's disease. *Nature, 367*(6461), 378–380.

Elion, E. A. (2000). Pheromone response, mating and cell biology. *Curr Opin Microbiol, 3*(6), 573–581.

Emerson, B. (2002). Specificity of gene regulation. *Cell, 109,* 267–270.

Enard, W., Khaitovich, P., et al. (2002a). Intra- and interspecific variation in primate gene expression patterns. *Science, 296*(5566), 340–343.

Enard, W., Przeworski, M., Fisher, S. E., Lai, C. S., Wiebe, V., Kitano, T., Monaco, A. P., Paabo, S. (2002b). Molecular evolution of FOXP2, a gene involved in speech and language. *Nature, 418,* 869–872.

Endy, D., & Brent R. (2001). Modelling cellular behaviour. *Nature, 409*(Suppl), 391–395.

Futuyama, D. J. (1997). *Evolutionary biology.* Sunderland, MA: Sinauer.

Gafni, J., & Ellerby, L. M. (2002). Calpain activation in Huntington's disease. *J Neurosci, 22*(12), 4842–4849.

Glei, D. A., & Goldman, N. (2000). Understanding ethnic variation in pregnancy-related care in rural Guatemala. *Ethn Health, 5,* 5–22.

Goff, D. C., Heckers, S., et al. (2001). Schizophrenia. *Med Clin North Am, 85*(3), 663–689.

Gonzalez Block, M. A., Ruiz, J. A., & Rovira, J. (2001). Beyond health gain: The range of health system benefits expressed by social groups in Mexico and Central America. *Soc Sci Med, 42,* 1537–1550.

Harding, A. E. (1993). The gene for Huntington's disease. *BMJ, 307*(6901), 396–397.

Hearne, C. M., Ghosh, S., et al. (1992). Microsatellites for linkage analysis of genetic traits. *Trends Genet, 8*(8), 288–294.

Heath, K. E., Campos-Barros, A., Toren, A., Rozenfeld-Granot, G., Carlsson, L. E., Savige, J., et al. (2001). Non-muscle in yosin heavy chain IIA mutations define a spectrum of autosomal dominant macrothrombocytopenias: May-Hegglin anomaly and Fechtner, Sebastian, Epstein, and Alport-like syndromes. *Am J Hum Genet, 69,* 103–1045.

Hyman, S. E. (2002). Neuroscience, genetics, and the future of psychiatric diagnosis. *Psychopathology, 35*(2–3), 139–144.

Judson, R., & Stephens, J. C. (2001). Notes from the SNP vs. haplotype front. *Pharmacogenomics, 2*(1), 7–10.

Judson, R., Salisbury, B., Schneider, J., Windemuth, A., & Stephens, J. C. (2002). How many SNPs does a genome-wide haplotype map require? *Pharmacogenomics, 3*(3), 379.

Kwok, P. Y. (2001). Genomics. Genetic association by whole-genome analysis? *Science, 294*(5547), 1669–70.

Lai, C. S., Fisher, S. E., Hurst, J. A., Vargha-Khadem, F., Monaco, A. P. (2001). A forkhead-domain gene is mutated in a severe speech and language disorder. *Nature, 413,* 519–23.

Lande, R., Sechausen, S. O., & van Alphen, J. J. (2001). Mechanisms of rapid sympatric speciation by sex reversal and sexual selection in cichlid fish. *Genetica, 112,* 435–443.

Lewis, R. (2002). SNPs as windows on evolution. *The Scientist, 16*(1), 16–18.

Lisman, J. E. (2001). Synaptic plasticity: A molecular memory switch. *Curr Biol, 11,* R788–R791.

McGuffin, P., Riley, B., & Plomin, R. (2001). Genomics and behavior: Toward behavioral genomics. *Science, 291*(5507), 1232–1249.

Meyer, A., Kocher, T. D., Basasibwaki, P., & Wilson, A. C. (1990). Monophyletic origin of lake Victoria cichlid fishes suggested by mitochondrial DNA sequences. *Nature, 347,* 550–554.

Muller, G. B., & Newman, S. A. (1999). Generation, integration, autonomy: three steps in the evolution of homology. *Novartis Found Symp, 222,* 65–79.

Mulligan, L. M., Eng, C., Healey, C. S., Clayton, D., Kwok, J. B., Gardner, E., Ponder, M. A., Frilling, A., Jackson, C. E., Lehert, H., et al. (1994). Specific mutations of the RET proto-oncogene are related to disease phenotype in MEN 2A and FMTC. *Nat Genet, 6*(1), 70–74.

Myers, E. W., Sutton, G. G., Smith, H. O., Adams, M. D., & Venter, J. C. (2002). On the sequencing and assembly of the human genome. *Proc Natl Acad Sci U S A, 99*(7), 4145–4146.

Naarding, P. K. H., Zitman, F. G. (2001). Huntington's disease: a review of the literature on prevalence and treatment of neuropsychiatric phenomena. *Eur Psychiatry 16*(8), 439–445.

Nagl, S., Tichy, H., Mayer, W. E., Samonte, I. Z., McAndrew, B. J., & Klein, J. (1998). Persistence of neutral polymorphisms in Lake Victoria cichlid fish. *PNAS, 95,* 14238–14243.

Newman, S. A. (1994). Generic physical mechanisms of tissue morphogenesis; A common basis for development and evolution. *J Evol Biol, 7,* 467–488.

Newman, S. A., & Muller, G. B. (2000). Epigenetic mechanisms of character origination. *J Exp Zool, 288*(4), 304–317.

Osier, M. V., Cheung, K. H., Kidd, J. R., Pakstis, A. J., Miller, P. L., Kidd, K. K., et al. (2000). ALFRED: an allele frequency database for diverse populations and DNA polymorphisms. *Nucleic Acids Res, 28*(1), 361–363.

Pabo, C. O., & Sauer, R. T. (1992). Transcription factors: Structural families and principles of DNA recognition. *Annu Rev Biochem, 61,* 1053–1095.

Pabo, C. O., & Nekludova, L. (2000). Geometric analysis and comparison of protein-DNA interfaces: Why is there no simple code for recognition? *J Mol Biol, 301*(3): 597–624.

Pabo, C. O., Peisach, E., & Grant, R. A. (2001). Design and selection of novel Cys2His2 zinc finger proteins. *Annu Rev Biochem, 70,* 313–340.

Pato, M. D., Sellers, J. R., Preston, Y. A., Harvey, E. V., & Adelstein, R.S. (1996). Baculovirus expression of chicken nonmuscle heavy meromyosin II-B: Characterization of alternatively spliced isoforms. *J Biol Chem, 271*(5), 2689–2695.

Pfennig, D. W., & Sherman, P. W. (1995). Kin recognition. *Sci Amer, 272,* 98–103.

Plomin, R., DeFries, J., McClearn, G., & McGuffin, P. (2001). *Behavioral genetics.* NewYork: Freeman.

Romeo, G., Ronchetto, P., Luo, Y., Barone, V., Seri, M., Cecherini, I., Pasani, B., Bocciardi, R., Lerone, M., Koariainon, H., et al. (1994). Point mutations affecting the tyrosine kinase domain of the RET proto-oncogene in Hirschsprung's disease. *Nature, 367*(6461), 377–378.

Romualdi, C. B. D., Nasidze, I. S., Risch, G., Robichaux, M., Sherry, S. T., Stoneking, M., Batzer, M. A., & Barbujani, G. (2002). Patterns of human diversity, within and among continents, inferred from biallelic DNA polymorphisms. *Genome Res, 12*(4),: 602–612.

Roses, A. D., & Saunders, A. M. (1994). APOE is a major susceptibility gene for Alzheimer's disease. *Curr Opin Biotechnol, 5*(6), 663–667.

Ross, D. T., Scherf, U., Eisen, M. B., Perou, C. M., Rees, C., & Spellman, P. (2000). Systematic variation in gene expression patterns in human cancer cell lines. *Nat Genet, 24(3),* 227–235.

Russo, E. (2002). Researchers find no clear paths on road to unraveling schizophrenia. *The Scientist, 16*(2), 30–31.

Sachidanandam, R., Weissman, D., Schmidt, S. C., Kakol, J. M., Stein, L. D., et al. (2001). A map of human genome sequence variation containing 1.42 million single nucleotide polymorphisms. *Nature, 409*(6822), 928–933.

Selkoe, D. J. (2001). Presenilin, Notch, and the genesis and treatment of Alzheimer's disease. *Proc Natl Acad Sci U S A, 98*(20), 11039–41.

St George-Hyslop, P. H., Tanzi, R. E., Haines, J. L., Polinsky, R. J., Farrer, L., Myers, R. H., & Gusella, J. F. (1989). Molecular genetics of familial Alzheimer's disease. *Eur Neurol, 29*(Suppl 3), 25–27.

Stephens, J. C., Schneider, J. A., Tanguay, D. A., Choi, J., Acharya, T., et al. (2001). Haplotype variation and linkage disequilibrium in 313 human genes. *Science, 293*(5529), 489–493.

Stoller, R. J. (1984). Psychiatrys mind-brain dialectic, or the Mona Lisa has no eyebrows. *Am J Psychiatry, 141*(4), 554–558.

Straub, R. E., Jiang, Y., MacLean, C. J., Ma, Y., Webb, B. T., Myskisher, M. V., Harris-Kerr, C., Wormley, B., Sadek, H., Kadamloi, B., Cesaro, A. J., Gibberman, A., Wang, X., O'Neill, F. A., Walsh, D., & Kendler, K. S. (2002). Genetic variation in the 6p22.3 Gene DTNBP1: The human ortholog of the mouse dysbindin gene is associated with schizophrenia. *Am J Hum Genet, 71*(2), 337–348.

Sud, S., Starbuck, K., Dalal, M., Page, T., & Bearer, E. L. (2003). *HIV among the Maya: Studies in risk factors and women's reproductive health.* Senior honor's thesis, Brown University..

Tabor, H. K., Risch, R. N., & Myers, R. M. (2002). Opinion: Candidate-gene approaches for studying complex genetic traits: practical considerations. *Nat Rev Genet, 3*(5), 391–397.

Tanzi, R. E. (1989). Molecular genetics of Alzheimer's disease and the amyloid beta peptide precursor gene. *Ann Med, 21*(2), 91–94.

Thompson, J. C., Craufurd, D., & Neary, D. (2002). Behavior in Huntington's disease: dissociating cognition-based and mood-based changes. *J Neuropsychiatry Clin Neurosci, 14*(1), 37–43.

van der Meer, H. J. (1995) Visual resolution during growth in a cichlid fish: A morphological and behavioural case study. *Brain Behav Evol, 45*, 25–33.

Venter, J. C. (2000). Remarks at the human genome announcement. *Funct Integr Genomics, 1*(3), 154–155.

Venter, J. C., Adams, M. D., Myers, E. W., Li, P. W., Mural, R. J., et al. (2001). The sequence of the human genome. *Science, 291*(5507), 1304–1351.

Walter, J., Grunberg, J., Capell, A., Pesold, B., Schindzielorz, A., Citron, M., Mendla, K., St George-Hyslop, P., Multaup, G., Selkoe, D. J., & Haas, C. (1997). Proteolytic processing of the Alzheimer disease-associated presenilin-1 generates an in vivo substrate for protein kinase C. *Proc Natl Acad Sci U S A, 94*(10), 5349–5354.

Webster's College Dictionary. (1990). New York: Random House.

Weissenbach, J. (1993). Microsatellite polymorphisms and the genetic linkage map of the human genome. *Curr Opin Genet Dev, 3*(3), 414–417.

Wheeler, D. A., Arathoon, A. E., Pitts, M., Cedillos, R. A., Bu, T. E., Porras, G, D., Herrera, G., & Sosa, N. R. (2001). Availability of HIV care in Central America. *JAMA, 286*(7), 854–860.

White, J. M., & Rose, M. D. (2001). Yeast mating: Getting close to membrane merger. *Curr Biol, 11*(1), R16–R20.

Wilson, E. O. (2000). *Sociobiology.* New Haven, CT: Yale University Press.

Wollfe, A. (2001). Transcriptional regulation in the context of chromatin structure. *Essays Biochem, 37*, 45–57.

Yan, H., Yuan, W., Velculescu, V. E., Vogelstein, B., & Kinzler, K. W. (2002). Allelic variation in human gene expression. *Science, 297*, 1143.

11

Embodied Development: Ending the Nativism-Empiricism Debate

Willis F. Overton
Temple University

In this chapter, I discuss the importance of the concept of embodiment in the understanding of human behavior and development. My general argument is that embodiment is central to any discussion of the relation of biological systems and psychological systems or cultural systems and psychological systems. I also argue that seriously embracing the concept of embodiment represents a move away from unproductive questions entailed in the nativism-empiricism or nature-nurture debate and toward a more productive arena of inquiry and research—the examination of questions of the nature of the relations that operate among biological systems, psychological systems, and cultural systems. In developing this argument, I first discuss the role metatheory—especially relational metatheory—plays in contexualizing the concept of embodiment. I then discuss embodiment as a concept that bridges biological, cultural, and person-centered approaches to psychological inquiry. And finally, I focus on a brief elaboration of the place and nature of the embodied person-centered approach.

Most simply stated, embodiment is the affirmation that the lived body counts in our psychology. It is not a split-off disengaged agent that simply moves around peeking at a preformed world and drawing meaning directly from that world. It is not a set of genes that causes behavior, nor a brain, nor a culture. Behavior emerges from the embodied person actively engaged in the world. The concept of embodiment was first fully articulated in psychology by Maurice Merleau-Ponty (1962, 1963), and it represents a movement away from any dichotomous understanding of behavior as an additive product of environmental and genetic determinants. Embodiment has a double meaning, referring both to the body as physical structure, and the body as a form of lived experience, actively engaged with a world of sociocultural and physical objects.

Embodiment is the claim that perception, thinking, feelings, desires—that is, the way we behave, experience, and live the world—is contextualized by our being active agents with this particular kind of body (Taylor, 1995). In other words, the kind of body we have is a precondition for our having the kind of behaviors, experiences, and meanings that we have. As Mark Johnson (1999) stated, "Human beings are creatures of the flesh. What we can experience and how we make sense of what we experience depend on the kinds of bodies we have and the on the ways we interact with the various environments we inhabit" (p. 81). And as Esther Thelen (2001) continued:

> To say that cognition is embodied means that it arises from bodily interactions with the world. From this point of view, cognition depends on the kinds of experiences that come from having a body with particular perceptual and motor capabilities that are inseparably linked and that together form the matrix within which reasoning, memory, emotion, language and all other aspects of mental life are meshed. (p. 1)

From the perspective of an approach that includes this concept of embodiment, any suggestion that genes operate as independent units or have a linear causal impact on psychological functioning represents a conceptual confusion. Genes are the expression of biological-environmental interpenetrating relations, they are not split-off causal entities. Genes themselves enter into other interpenetrating environmental relations and are synthesized as proteins; proteins enter into interpenetrating environmental relations and are synthesized as cells; cells become synthesized as organs; and this process continues until body enters into a final environmental relation (i.e., the relation with culture) and is synthesized as the psychological person. Any human act is, thus, 100% genetically determined, as it is also 100% environmentally determined, and as—it is most important to note—it is also 100% determined by the intentionality of the psychological subject (i.e., the person; see Lerner, 1978, 2000; Overton 1973, 1998).

All concepts and methods are contextualized by some specific metatheoretical framework. A metatheory provides basic constructs that articulate the meaning of concepts and methods in a domain of inquiry. A metatheoretical frame offers advice, guidelines, and criteria for decisions concerning the nature, and the adequacy or inadequacy of a theoretical and methodological approach to the domain under investigation. A metatheory is prescriptive in the sense that it defines what is meaningful and what is meaningless, what is acceptable and unacceptable, what is central and what is peripheral to inquiry. Thus, to understand an argument regarding embodiment it is necessary to understand the relational metatheory from which embodiment derives its meaning. And it is necessary to understand that this relational metatheory stands in contrast to split metatheory with respect to meanings, guidelines, and criteria. Relational and split metatheories compose the world in different ways; relational metatheory paints the world as systems of dynamic changing part-whole relations, split metatheory paints the world as aggregates of dichotomous elements.

SPLIT METATHEORY

Split metatheory entails several basic defining principles, including splitting, foundationalism, and atomism. Splitting is the separation of components of a whole into mutually exclusive pure forms or elements. But, in order to split, one must accept the twin principles of foundationalism and atomism. These are the metatheoretical axioms that there is ultimately a rock bottom unchanging nature to reality (the foundation of foundationalism) and that this rock bottom is composed of elements—pure forms—(the atoms of atomism) that preserve their identity regardless of context. A corollary principle here is the belief that all complexity is simple complexity in the sense that any whole is taken to be a purely additive combination of its elements.

Splitting, foundationalism, and atomism are all principles of decomposition; breaking the aggregate down to its smallest pieces, to its bedrock (Overton, 2002). This process also goes by other names including reductionism and the analytic attitude (Overton, 2002). Split metatheory requires another principle to reassemble or recompose the whole. This is the principle of unidirectional and linear (additive) associative or causal sequences. The elements must be related either according to their contiguous cooccurrence in space and time or according to simple efficient cause-effect sequences that proceed in a single direction (Bunge, 1963; Overton & Reese, 1973). In fact, split metatheory admits no determination other than individual efficient causes or these individual causes operating in a conjunctive (i.e., additive) plurality. That is, no truly reciprocal causality is admitted (Bunge, 1962; Overton & Reese, 1973).

The field of behavior genetics illustrates an approach to inquiry that is defined within a split metatheory. The broad goal of behavior genetics, using the methods of family, twin, and adoption studies, is to partition (split) the variation in any behavioral score (e.g., a measure of personality, psychopathology, intelligence, language, cognition, etc.) into the proportion of the variation caused by foundational genes (pure form) and the proportion caused by the foundational environment (pure form; Plomin, 1986, 1994). "Behavior genetic models use quantitiative genetic theory and quasiexperimental methods to decompose phenotypic (measured) variance into genetic and environmental components of variance" (McGuire et al., 1999, p. 1286). The primary tool employed to effect this splitting is the quantitative formula, called the heritability index or heritability coefficient. This index itself entails a commitment to the additive components-of-variance statistical model (including analysis of variance and all correlation based statistics) whose basic assumption is that each score is a linear function of independent elements, (i.e., the score is the sum of component ef-

fects, Winer, 1962, p. 151; see also Overton & Reese, 1973). Further, it is generally assumed that the correlational patterns produced through the application of
this formula are reflections of an underlying causal reality in which genes and environment primarily contribute additively to the behavior under investigation
(Vreeke, 2000). Within the behavior genetic frame, the ultimate goal is to discover the specific genetic causal pathways. The idea here is to unravel and parse
conjunctive pluralities of efficient causes believed—within the context of a split
metatheory—to explain any behavior and, thereby, arrive at an ultimate genetic
bedrock of explanation. As Plomin and Rutter (1998) said with respect to the an-
ticipated discovery of genes associated with specific behaviors:

> The finding of genes will provide the opportunity to unravel the complicated causal
> processes .... No longer will we have to focus on how much variation in the general
> population is genetically influenced; instead we can make the crucial transition from
> "black box" inferences regarding genetic influences to the observation of specific
> genes (p. 1238).

RELATIONAL METATHEORY

Holism

The basic principle that guides a relational metatheory is holism, the assertion that
the identities of objects and events derive from the relational context in which they
are embedded. Here, the whole is not an aggregate of discrete elements but an organized and self-organizing system of parts, each part being defined by its relations to other parts and to the whole. Complexity in this context is organized
complexity (Luhmann, 1995; von Bertalanffy, 1968a, 1968b), in that the whole or
system is not decomposable into elements arranged in additive linear sequences of
cause-effect relations (Overton & Reese, 1973). Nonlinear dynamics are a defining characteristic of this type of complexity. In the context of holism, principles of
splitting, foundationalism, and atomism are rejected as meaningless approaches to
analysis, and fundamental antimonies such as nature–nurture are similarly rejected as false dichotomies.

With holism as the starting point, relational metheory moves to specific
principles that define the relations among parts and the relations of parts to wholes.
In other words, relational metatheory articulates principles of analysis and synthesis necessary for any scientific inquiry. These are the principles of (a) the identity
of opposites, (b) the opposites of identity, (c) the synthesis of wholes (see Overton
2003 for a full discussion).

The Identity of Opposites

The principle of the identity of opposites establishes the identity among fundamental parts by casting them not as exclusive contradictions as in the split method-

ology but as differentiated polarities of a unified inclusive matrix; as a relation. As differentiations, each pole is defined recursively; each pole defines and is defined by its opposite. There are a number of ways of articulating this principle, but perhaps the clearest articulation is found in considering the famous ink sketch by M.C. Escher titled "Drawing Hands." In this sketch, a left and a right hand assume a relational posture according to which each is simultaneously drawing and being drawn by the other. In this relational matrix each hand is identical with the other in the sense of each drawing and each being drawn. This a moment of analysis in which the law of contradiction (i.e., Not the case that A = notA) is relaxed and identity (i.e., A = notA) reigns. In this identity moment of analysis pure forms collapse and categories flow into each other. Here each category contains and, in fact, is its opposite, and as a consequence, there is a broad inclusivity established among categories. If we think of inclusion and exclusion as different moments that occur when we observe a reversible figure (e.g., a necker cube or the vase-women illusion), then in this identity moment we observe only inclusion. In the next (opposite) moment of analysis the figures reverse, and there we will again see exclusivity as the hands appear as opposites and contradictions.

Within the identity moment of analysis, it is a useful exercise to write on each hand one of the bipolar terms of a traditionally split concept (e.g., biology and culture; see Table 11.1 for further examples) and to explore the resulting effect. This exercise is more than merely an illustration of a familiar bidirectionality of effects suggested by many scientific investigators. The exercise makes tangible the central feature of the relational metatheory; seemingly dichotomous ideas that are often thought of as competing alternatives can, in fact, enter into inquiry as complementary supportive partners. It also concretizes the meaning of any truly nonadditive reciprocal determination (Overton & Reese, 1973)

If inquiry concerning biology, culture, and behavior is undertaken according to the principle of the identity of opposites various constraints are imposed as constraints are imposed by any methatheory. An important example of such a constraint is that behavior, traits, styles, and so forth cannot be thought of being decomposable into independent and additive pure forms of genes and environment. Thus, from the perspective of relational metatheory the goals of behavior genetics simply represent a meaningless approach to inquiry. The percentages derived from the application of heritability indicies, whatever their value, can never be taken as a reflection of the separate contributions of genes and environment to individual differences, because the relation of genes and environment (a left Escherian hand and a right Escherian hand) is not independent and additive. Further, moving beyond behavior genetics to the broader issue of biology and culture, conclusions such as "contemporary evidence confirms that the expression of heritable traits depends, often strongly, on experience" (Collins, Maccoby, Steinberg, Hetherington, & Bornstein, 2000, p. 228) also fail, and for the same reason. That is, within a relational metatheory, they fail because they begin from the premise that there are, in fact, pure forms of genetic inheritance termed "heritable traits."

TABLE 11.1
Fundamental Categories Expressible as Exclusive Either/or Dichotomies
or Inclusive Bipolar Unities.

Subject	Object
Mind	Body
Biology	Person
Culture	Biology
Person	Culture
Person	Situation
Intrapsychic	Interpersonal
Nature	Nurture
Stability	Change
Expressive	Instrumental
Variation	Transformation
Reason	Emotion
Form	Matter
Universal	Particular
Transcendent	Immanent
Analysis	Synthesis
Unity	Diversity

The principle of the identity of opposites introduces constraints and also opens possibilities. The most important possibility is the recognition that, to paraphrase the philosopher John Searle (1992), the fact that a behavior is biologically determined does not imply that it is not culturally determined and the fact that it is culturally determined does not imply that it is not biologically determined. In other words, the identity of opposites establishes the metatheoretical position that genes and culture, like culture and person, and brain and person and so forth, operate in a truly interpenetrating manner, and further, that any concept of interaction (e.g., interaction, coaction, transaction) must be interpreted not as the cooperation or competition among elements but as the interpenetration among parts. With this recognition the whole nativism-empiricism debate ceases to have merit. That is, given the explicit denial of pure forms implied by the identity of opposites it is impossible to cast questions of development as having a nativistic or empiricist origin as has often been done within split metatheories (see Spelke & Newport, 1998).

The Opposites of Identity

While the identity of opposites sets constraints and opens possibilities, it does not in itself set a positive agenda for empirical inquiry. The limitation of the identity moment of analysis is that, in establishing a flow of categories of one into the other, a stable base for inquiry that was provided by bedrock elements of the split metatheory is eliminated. Reestablishing a stable base within relational metatheory requires moving to a second moment of inquiry. This is the oppositional moment, where the figure reverses and the moment is dominated by exclusivity. Thus, in this opposite moment of analysis, it becomes clear that despite the earlier identity, Escher's sketch shows a *right* hand and a *left* hand. In this moment the law of contradiction (i.e., Not the case that A = notA) is reasserted and categories again exclude each other. As a consequence of this exclusion, parts exhibit unique identities that differentiate each from the other. These unique differential qualities are stable within any general dynamic system and, thus, may form a relatively stable platform for empirical inquiry. The platforms created according to the principle of the opposites of identity become standpoints, points-of-view, or lines-of-sight, in recognition that they do not reflect absolute foundations (Harding, 1986). Again considering Escher's sketch, when left hand as left hand and right as right are the focus of attention, it then becomes quite clear that—were they large enough—one could stand on either hand and examine the structures and functions of that hand. Thus, to return to the biology and culture example, while explicitly recognizing that any behavior is 100% biology and 100% culture, alternative points of view permit the scientist to analyze the behavior from a biological, or, from a cultural standpoint. Biology and culture no longer constitute competing alternative explanations; rather they are two points-of-view on an object of inquiry that has been both created by, and will only be fully understood through multiple viewpoints. To state this more generally, the unity that constitutes human identity and human development becomes discovered only in the diversity of multiple interrelated lines of sight.

The Synthesis of Wholes

Engaging fundamental bipolar concepts as relatively stable standpoints opens the way, and takes an important first step, toward establishing a broad stable base for empirical inquiry within a relational metatheory. This solution is incomplete, however, as it omits a key relational component, the relation of parts to the whole. The oppositional quality of the bipolar pairs reminds us that their contradictory nature still remains and still requires a resolution. Further, the resolution of this tension cannot be found in the split approach of reduction to a bedrock reality. Rather, the relational approach to a resolution is to move away from the extremes to the center and above the conflict and to here discover a novel system that will coordinate the two conflicting systems. This is the principle of the synthesis of wholes, and this synthesis itself will constitute another standpoint.

At this point the Escher sketch fails as a graphic representation. Though "Drawing Hands" illustrates the identities and the opposites, and though it shows a middle space between the two, it does not present a coordination. In fact, the synthesis for this sketch is the unseen hand that has drawn the drawing hands. The synthesis of interest for the general metatheory would be a system that is a coordination of the most universal bipolarity we can imagine. Undoubtedly there are several candidates for this level of generality, but the polarity between matter or nature and society seems sufficient for present purposes (Latour, 1993). Matter and society represent systems that stand in an identity of opposites. To say that an object is a social object in no way denies that it is matter, to say that an object is matter in no way denies that it is social. And further, the object can be analyzed from either a social or a physical standpoint. The question for synthesis becomes what system will coordinate these two systems. Arguably the answer is that it is life or living systems that coordinate matter and society. Because our specific focus of inquiry is the psychological, we can reframe this matter-society polarity as the polarity of biology and culture. In the context of psychology then, as an illustration, write "biology" on one and "culture" on the other Escher hand, and what system coordinates these systems?—the human organism, the person (see Fig. 11.1A). Persons—as an integrated self-organizing dynamic system of cognitive, emotional, and motivational processes and the behaviors this systems expresses—represents a novel level or stage of structure and functioning that emerges from, and constitutes a coordination of, biology and culture (see Magnusson & Stattin, 1998).

At the synthesis then, there is a standpoint that coordinates and resolves the tension between the other two members of the relation. This provides a particularly broad and stable base for launching empirical inquiry. A person standpoint opens the way for the empirical investigation of universal dimensions of psychological

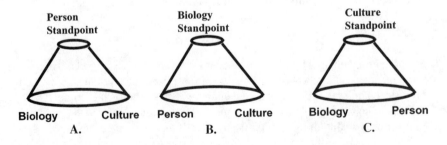

FIG. 11.1. Relational standpoints in psychological inquiry: Person, biology, and culture.

structure-function relations (e.g., processes of perception, thought, emotions, values), their individual differences, and their development across the lifespan. Because universal and particular are themselves relational concepts, no question can arise here about whether the focus on universal processes excludes the particular, it clearly doesn't as we already know from the earlier discussion of polarities. The fact that a process is viewed from a universal standpoint in no way suggests that it is not contextualized. The general theories of Jean Piaget (1952), Heinz Werner (1957, 1958), James Mark Baldwin (1985), William Stern (1938), attachment theory and object relations theories of John Bowlby (1958), Harry Stack Sullivan (1953), Donald Winnocott (1965, 1971), all are exemplars of developmentally oriented relational person standpoints.

It is important to recognize that one standpoint of synthesis is relative to other synthesis standpoints. Life and Society are coordinated by Matter, and thus, within psychological inquiry, biology represents a standpoint as the synthesis of person and culture (Fig. 11.1B). The implication of this is that a relational biological approach to psychological processes investigates the biological conditions and settings of psychological structure-function relations and the behaviors they express. This exploration is quite different from split foundationalist approaches to biological inquiry that assume an atomistic and reductionistic stance toward the object of study. The neurobiologist Antonio Damasio's (1994, 1999) work on the brain-body basis of a psychological self and emotions is an excellent illustration of this biological relational standpoint. And in the context of his biological investigations Damasio (1994) pointed out that "a task that faces neuroscientists today is to consider the neurobiology supporting adaptive supraregulations [e.g., the psychological subjective experience of self] ... I am not attempting to reduce social phenomena to biological phenomena, but rather to discuss the powerful connection between them" (p. 124). And further that "realizing that there are biological mechanisms behind the most sublime human behavior does not imply a simplistic reduction to the nuts and bolts of neurobiology" (p. 125).

A similar illustration comes from the Nobel laureate neurobiologist Gerald Edelman's (1992; Edelman & Tononi, 2000) work on the brain-body base of consciousness:

> I hope to show that the kind of reductionism that doomed the thinkers of the Enlightenment is confuted by evidence that has emerged both from modern neuroscience and from modern physics .... To reduce a theory of an individual's behavior to a theory of molecular interactions is simply silly, a point made clear when one considers how many different levels of physical, biological, and social interactions must be put into place before higher order consciousness emerges. (Edelman 1992, p. 166)

A third synthesis standpoint recognizes that Life and Matter are coordinated by Society, and again granting that the inquiry is about psychological processes, culture represents a standpoint as the synthesis of person and biology (Fig. 11.1C).

Thus, a relational cultural approach to psychological processes explores the cultural conditions and settings of psychological structure-function relations. From this cultural standpoint, the focus is upon cultural differences in the context of psychological functions as complementary to the person standpoint's focus on psychological functions in the context of cultural differences.

This standpoint is illustrated by cultural psychology, or developmentally oriented cultural psychology. Not all cultural psychologies, however, emerge from relational metatheory. When, for example, a cultural psychology makes the social constructivist assertion that social discourse is " prior to and constitutive of the world" (Miller, 1996, p. 99), it becomes clear that this form of cultural psychology has been framed by split foundationalist background ideas. Similarly, when sociocultural claims are made about the primacy of social forces, or claims arise suggesting that mediational means (i.e., instrumental-communicative acts) constitute the necessary focus of psychological interest (see, e.g., Wertsch, 1991), the shadow of split foundationalist metatheoretical principles are clearly in evidence.

A recent example of a relational developmentally oriented cultural standpoint emerges in the work of Valsiner (1998), which examined the social nature of human psychology. Focusing on the social nature of the person, Valsiner stressed the importance of avoiding the temptation of trying to reduce person processes to social processes. To this end, he explicitly distinguishes between the dualisms of split foundationalist metatheory and dualities of the relational stance he advocates. Ernst Boesch (1991) and Lutz Eckensberger (1990) have also presented an elaboration of the cultural standpoint. Boesch's cultural psychology and Eckensberger's theoretical and empirical extensions of this draw from Piaget's cognitive theory, from Janet's dynamic theory, and from Kurt Lewin's social field-theory and argues that cultural psychology aims at an integration of individual and cultural change, an integration of individual and collective meanings, a bridging of the gap between subject and object (see, e.g., Boesch, 1991, p. 183).

As a final point, concerning syntheses and the view from the center, it needs to be recognized that a relational metatheory is not limited to three syntheses. For example, discourse or semiotics may also be taken as a synthesis of person and culture (Latour, 1993). In this case, biology and person are conflated and the biological/person and culture represents the opposites of identity that are coordinated by discourse.

As a general summary to this point, the argument has been made that metatheoretical principles form the ground out of which grow the concepts and methods of any domain of empirical inquiry. Split metatheory produces dichotomous understandings of the world and methods that rely exclusively on the analytic ideal of the reduction of psychological process and behaviors to elements, followed by the additive linear causal recomposition of elements. Split metatheory, in fact, creates all varieties of the nativist-empiricist debates from the debate about relative merits of genes and culture to the debate about innate versus learned modules of mind to the debate about the proper understanding of the nature of evolution as it applies to human development (see Gottlieb, 2002; Overton,

1998). Relational metatheory produces inclusive holistic understandings of the world and methods that operate within an analytic (identity and opposites)—synthetic relational frame that examines psychological processes and behaviors as dynamic self-organizing systems that can be approached empirically from several noncompeting standpoints of inquiry.

Like any concept, embodiment can be contextualized by split or by relational metatheory. Within a split approach, embodiment refers exclusively to physical structures, and as such it constitutes one variable among others. Within a relational system, however, embodiment includes, as mentioned earlier, not only the physical structures but the body as a form of lived experience, actively engaged with the world of sociocultural and physical objects. The body as form references the biological, the body as lived experience references the psychological person, the body actively engaged with the world represents the cultural. Within a relational system, embodiment is a concept that bridges and joins in a unified whole these several research standpoints without any appeal to splits, foundationalism, elements, atomism, reductionism (see Fig. 11.2). In the following sections, I very briefly point to some work being conducted within the biological and cultural embodiment standpoints. I then focus some additional attention on the embodied person-centered standpoint as an approach to inquiry.

EMBODIMENT FROM THE BIOLOGICAL, THE CULTURAL, AND THE PERSON-CENTERED STANDPOINTS

Biological Embodiment

I have already mentioned the work of the neurobiologists Antonio Damasio—exploring the neurological dimension of emotions—and Gerald Edelman—exploring the neurological dimensions of consciousness—with respect to their re-

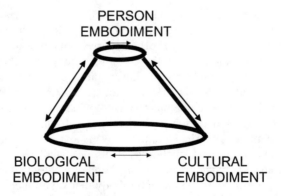

FIG. 11.2. Embodiment as synthesis.

lational stance and opposition to reductionism. These scientists along with Joseph LeDoux (1996)—exploring the neurological dimension of emotions—all support an embodied approach to biological-psychological inquiry and all argue that the cognitive, affective, and motivational meanings that constitute mind can no longer be thought of as the direct expression of genetic modularities (as nativists such as Steven Pinker [1997] would claim), nor can they be thought of as a functionalist piece of software, nor even as merely a function of brain processes. Rather, they argue, these meanings must be considered in a fully embodied context. Damasio (1994) said that "mind is probably not conceivable without some sort of embodiment" (p. 234). He further commented on contemporary perspectives on mind:

> This is Descartes' error: the abyssal separation between body and mind .... The Cartesian idea of a disembodied mind may well have been the source, by the middle of the twentieth century, for the metaphor of mind as software program .... [And] there may be some Cartesian disembodiment also behind the thinking of neuroscientists who insist that the mind can be fully explained in terms of brain events [i.e., connectionism], leaving by the wayside the rest of the organism and the surrounding physical and social environment—and also leaving out the fact that part of the environment is itself a product of the organism's preceding actions. (pp. 249–250)

Similarly, Edelman (1992) argued:

> The mind is embodied. It is necessarily the case that certain dictates of the body must be followed by the mind .... Symbols do not get assigned meanings by formal means; instead it is assumed that symbolic structures are meaningful *to begin with*. This is so because categories are determined by bodily structure and by adaptive use as a result of evolution and behavior (p. 239).

Cultural Embodiment

From the cultural standpoint, social constructivists such as Harre (1995) and Sampson (1996) have increasingly embraced embodied action as a relational anchoring to the relativism of split-off discourse analysis. Sampson, for example, argues for "embodied discourses" as these "refer to the inherently embodied nature of all human endeavor, including talk, conversation and discourse itself" (p. 609; see also, Csordas, 1999; Ingold, 2000; Overton 1997b). Perhaps the most fully articulated contemporary employment of embodiment in a developmentally oriented cultural psychology is found in Boesch (1991). Boesch's presentation of "The I and the body" is a discussion of the centrality of embodiment for a cultural psychology. Thus, he states "The body, obviously, is more than just an object with anatomical and physiological properties: *it is the medium of our actions*, it is with our body that we both conceive and perform actions" (p. 312, emphasis added).

Person-Centered Embodiment

A person-centered standpoint represents the third synthesis of the biology-culture-person triangle of psychological inquiry, and it is as necessary to understanding human action and human development as is the biological synthesis and the cultural synthesis. By an embodied person-centered approach, I mean a theoretical and empirical focus of inquiry on the psychological processes and patterns of psychological processes as these explain the individual's actions and behaviors in the world. This orientation to psychological inquiry generally and developmental inquiry specifically is perhaps best defined by contrast with what has been termed a variable approach in which the focus is not on the action systems that characterize the person's acts and behaviors but on biological, cultural, and individual variables as these are understood to operate as predictors, correlates, or antecedent causes of behavior. Magnusson (1998) noted that from a variable approach, various individual and contextual variables are understood as the explanatory actors in the processes being studied, while from a person-centered approach, action systems operate as the main vehicles of explanation.

Including a person-centered synthesis to inquiry offers several novel benefits: One of these is that it rescues *psychology* as *a psychology* from becoming a mere adjunct to biology, or to culture, or to discourse, or to computer science. That is, it rescues psychological processes from being understood and explained as mere reflections of biology, culture, discourse, and so forth. Another benefit is that a person-centered approach highlights the fact any act or behavior can be profitably understood—again in a complementary bipolar fashion—as both expressive/constitutive and as instrumental/adaptive. Split or dichotomous approaches, and especially split variable approaches, lead to the conceptual confusion that the only possible function of any act or behavior is an adaptive or instrumental function. A person-centered approach argues that any act or behavior may also be understood as an expression of underlying dynamic self-organizing cognitive, affective, and motivational systems and meanings, and this expression operates to constitute the world as known, felt, and desired. Here, Lois Bloom's (2001) work on the development of language provides an excellent example of the power of conceptualizing language acquisition in the context of the expression of person-centered cognitive, affective, motivational meanings, rather than exclusively as an instrumental tool operating solely for communicative ends.

Given these and other benefits (see Overton, 2003) of a person-centered approach to inquiry, the next question concerns the specific nature of this approach. Fundamentally, a detailed specification of a person-centered approach requires the description of four critical interwoven concepts: Person, Agent, Action, Embodiment.

Person-Agent. Person and Agent are complementary Escherian levels of analysis of the same whole. The person level is constituted by genuine psychological concepts (e.g., thoughts, feelings, desires, wishes) that have intentional qualities, are open to interpretation, and are available to consciousness (Shanon, 1993).

In other words, at the person level, these concepts have psychological meaning for the person. The Agent level—called the subpersonal level by some (Dennett, 1987; Russell, 1996)—here refers to action systems or dynamic self-organizing systems. Schemes, operations, ego, attachment behavioral system, and executive function, are some of the concepts that describe these action systems.

Taken as a whole, the person-agent forms the nucleus of a psychological theory of mind. And in this context, mind is defined as a self-organizing dynamic system of cognitive (knowings, beliefs), emotional (feelings), and conative or motivational (wishes, desires) meanings or understandings, along with procedures for maintaining, implementing, and changing these meanings. Importantly, it must be noted and underlined that a person-centered theory of mind is not an encapsulated cognition but rather a theory that includes emotions, wishes, and desires as well as cognition. Further, there is no question about where mind is located. Mind emerges from a relational biocultural activity matrix. In the present context mind is a person-centered concept because the approach being described takes the person standpoint. As a person-centered concept, mind bridges naturally to both the biological and the cultural.

Action, Intention, Behavior, & Experience.   Person-agency is the source of action and a person-centered approach constitutes what has traditionally been termed an action theory (Brandstädter, 1998; Brandstädter & Lerner, 1999; Mueller & Overton, 1998b). At the agent level, action is defined as the characteristic functioning of any dynamic self-organizing system. For example, a plant orients toward the sun. Weather systems form high and low pressure areas and move from west to east. Human systems organize and adapt to their biological and sociocultural worlds. At the Person level, action is defined as intentional activity (i.e., meaning giving activity). Action is often distinguishable from behavior, as the action of the Person-Agent implies a transformation in the intended object of action, while behavior often simply implies movement and states (von Wright, 1971, p. 199). Thus, when the infant chews (action)—something that from a sociocultural environmental standpoint is called a basket—the infant, from a person-centered standpoint, is transforming this part of her actual known world into a practical action—chewable.

Action serves at least three major functions in the development of mind. First, action expresses cognitive/affective/conative meaning. Here it is important to recognize that 'meaning' itself has a bi-polar relational status (Overton, 1994b). "I mean" (what the subject intends) and "it means" (the object referent) operate in a relational matrix. The former is concerned with person-centered meanings, the latter with sociocultural meanings and reference. From a person-centered standpoint the focus of analysis is on "I mean" and secondarily on how "I mean" comes to hook up with "it means." Considered in its expressive moment, action entails the projection of person-centered meanings, thus transforming the objective environmental world (i.e., an object point-of-view) into an actual world as known, felt, desired. "World," here, is another bipolar concept. The actual world is the world of meanings constructed by the person—the known world; the environmental or objective world is the world examined from a sociocultural standpoint.

The second function that action serves is the instrumental function of communicating and adjusting person-centered meanings. Communication, dialogue, discourse, and problem solving, all call attention to the relational to and fro movement between the expression of the self-organizing system, and instrumental adaptive changes. Completely adapted action (i.e., successful) entails only projection. Partially adapted (i.e., partially successful) action results in exploratory action, or variations. Exploratory action that is adaptive leads to reorganization of the system (transformational change) and, hence, new meanings.

This general cycle of expressive transformational action projected as meanings, and exploratory variational action as the accommodation (transformation) of these meanings to resistances encounter in the objective world constitutes the third and most general function of action: Action defines the general mechanism of all psychological development. From a person-centered developmental action standpoint all development is explained by action. However, action is also identified with experience and, thus, it is possible to say that all development is explained by experience. But caution is necessary here because experience, like meaning and world, is itself a bipolar relational concept. From a person-centered perspective experience is the person-agent action of observing, manipulating, exploring. From a sociocultural and objective environmental point-of-view, experience is often identified as an event or stimulus that is independent of the person and imposes on or is imposed on the person. For purposes of clarity, it would better to retain the former action definition as experience and redefine the latter as opportunity for experience. Similarly, it should be pointed out that when experience is described as a feeling, the reference here is the person-centered felt meaning of the observational, manipulative, and explorational action.

In defining experience as the developmental action cycle of projection-transformation (of the known world) exploration-transformation (of the system), experience also becomes the psychological bridge between biological and cultural systems. There is no sense here of an isolated, cut off, solitary human psyche. Person-centered experience emerges from a biosociocultural relational activity matrix (see, e.g., Gallese 2000a, 2000b; Suomi, 1999, 2000) and this experience both transforms the matrix and is transformed by the matrix. Person development is neither a split-off nativism, nor a split-off environmentalism, nor a split-off additive combination of the two. The neonate is a dynamic system of practical action meanings. These meanings represent the outcome of nine months of the interpenetrating action (Tobach & Greenberg, 1984) of biology-environment, and this interpenetration stretches all the way down to DNA (Gottlieb, 1997, 2002; Lewontin, 1991, 2000). Finally, it should be explicitly understood that to say that development is explained by experience is not to deny that development is explained by biology and that development is explained by culture. What is denied is the absolute exclusivity of any of these standpoint explanations.

Person Development.   Psychological development of the person-agent entails the epigenetic stance that novel forms emerge through the interpenetrating actions of the dynamic system of interest, and the resistances that system encounters in its environmental world (see Overton, 1994a, 1997a). It is through interpenetrating actions that the dynamic self-organizing system changes and, hence, becomes internally differentiated. But the differentiation of parts implies a novel coordination of parts and this coordination itself identifies the emergence of novelty. Thus, for example, the neurological action system becomes differentiated through the interpenetrating actions of neurological-environmental functioning. This differentiation leads to a novel coordination or reorganization that constitutes the adapted level of conscious practical action found in the neonate. Consciousness is a systemic property of this emergent action system. The initial adapted practical consciousness entails a minimum awareness of the meaning entailed by an act (Zelazo, 1996). Consciousness cannot be reduced to or squeezed out of lower stages as split metatheories would propose; rather, it is the result of a transformation. Similarly, further developmental differentiations and coordinations of actions—described as higher levels of consciousness—emerge as transformations through the interpenetrations of conscious practical action and the sociocultural and physical worlds it encounters. Symbolic meaning and the symbolic representational level of meanings (Mueller & Overton, 1998a, 1998b) describe forms of consciousness that arise from the coordination of practical action meanings; reflective and transreflective (reflective symbolic understandings of reflective symbolic understandings) meanings describe further developmental advances in the coordination of symbolic action systems.

To summarize, to this point I have described the nucleus of a relationally informed person-centered developmental theory of mind, where mind is defined as a dynamic self-organizing system of meanings that—through projected acts—transforms the world as known, and—through exploration—transforms itself (i.e., develops). This remains, however, a nucleus and only a nucleus, because it lacks the critical necessary feature of embodiment.

Embodiment.   As discussed earlier, embodiment is the claim that our perception, thinking, feelings, desires—that is, the way we experience or live the world—is contextualized by our being active agents with this particular kind of body (Taylor, 1995). At the agent level, embodiment specifies the characteristic nature of the activity of any living system (e.g., the actual world of the fly is necessarily shaped by the nature of the fly's embodied acts). At the person level embodiment affirms that—from the beginning—bodily acts constrain and inform the nature of intentionality (Margolis, 1987). Intentionality is not limited to a symbolic, or a reflective, or a transreflective system of psychological meanings. Intentionality also extends to a system of psychological meanings that characterize practical embodied actions operating at the most minimum level of consciousness. These most basic meanings and all others "come from having a body with particular perceptual and motor capabilities that are inseparably linked" (Thelen,

2001, p. 1). Or, again as Johnson (1999) has pointed out, "Human beings are creatures of the flesh. What we can experience and how we make sense of what we experience depend on the kinds of bodies we have and the on the ways we interact with the various environments we inhabit" (p. 81).

As suggested earlier, Stern, Werner, and Piaget—through their insistence on the centrality of sensorimotor actions in the development of mind—have been the traditional champions of a person-centered embodied action synthesis of biology and culture. More recently, person-centered embodiment has come to capture the attention of a wide array of investigators. Varela, Thompson, and Rosch (1991) sketched the general outlines for an embodied theory of cognition. George Lakoff and Mark Johnson (Johnson, 1987, 1999; Lakoff, 1987; Lakoff & Johnson, 1999) presented a systematic conceptual and empirical inquiry into the place of embodiment in language and conceptual functioning. Sebastiano Santostefano (1995) examined the emotional and cognitive dimensions of embodied meanings, and he, like many who have focused on the development of psychopathology from R.D. Laing, (1960) to Donald Winnicott (1965), and Thomas Ogden (1986), made disruptions in the embodied actions of the Person-Agent central to issues in the development of psychopathology (see also Overton & Horowitz, 1991).

At the level of practical actions, Bermudez's (1998) exploration of the development of self-consciousness is central to an understanding of the impact of an embodied person conceptualization. Bermudez's fundamental argument is that late emerging forms of meaning found in symbolic and reflective levels of consciousness develop from—and are constrained by—embodied self-organizing action systems available to the infant. Most important, these early systems entail person-level somatic proprioception and exteroception. As these person-centered processes interpenetrate the physical and sociocultural worlds, proprioception operates as the differentiation mechanism for the emergence of a self-consciousness action system, and exteroception operates as the differentiation mechanism for the emergence of an object-consciousness system. Hence, over the first several months of life a basic practical action associated with "me" and "other" develops, which in turn becomes transformed into the symbolic "me" and "other" of early toddlerhood. Thelen's (2000, 2001) work on the role of movement generally, and specifically body memory in infant cognitive functioning is another closely related area that illustrates the importance of embodiment at the level of practical actions.

Langer's (1994) empirical studies represent important demonstrations of the intercoordination of embodied action systems as these intercoordinations move development from the practical to the symbolic plane of meaning. Earlier work by Held and his colleagues (e.g., Held & Bossom, 1961; Held & Hein, 1958), on the other hand, illustrated the significance of voluntary embodied action at all levels of adaptation. Acredolo's research (e.g., Goodwyn & Acredolo, 1993) on the use of bodily gestures as signs expressing practical meanings in older infants suggested the expressive and instrumental value of embodied practical gesture. Other work has elaborated on the significance of bodily representations at the symbolic and reflective levels of meaning. For example, while the use of fingers for counting is well documented (Gelman & Williams, 1998), Saxe's (1981, 1995) research has shown cross-culturally that other bodily representations enter into counting systems. Further, earlier research by Overton and Jackson (1973) and more recently by Overton and Kovacs (2001) has demonstrated that bodily gestures support emerging symbolic representations at least until the level of reflective meanings.

CONCLUSIONS

In this chapter, I argued and presented evidence to the effect that within the context of a relational metatheory, embodiment—and the research paradigm it entails—bridges and joins together in a unified whole several complementary research standpoints without any need to appeal to split Cartesian concepts involving foundationalism, elements, atomism, reductionism. When the domain of inquiry is any topic that, directly or indirectly, touches on issues of the place of biology, culture, and the person in explanations of human behavior and development, an embodied approach offers an alternative to classical split approaches that is conceptually coherent and empirically productive. This embodied understanding of human behavior and development impacts on the very way science is thought about and the way that science is done. From an embodied perspective, it no longer makes sense to ask questions about genetic influences on or cultural influences on, or the influence of individual characteristics on human behavior and development. "Influence on" is the language of a causal reductionism and a bedrock foundationalism. Within an embodied perspective questions and research strategies focus on functional intra- and interrelations among dynamic self-organizing systems including biological, cultural, and person systems as these arise and develop from the body as a form of lived experience, actively engaged with the world of sociocultural and physical objects.

While an embodied approach offers a positive vision for our psychological science, it also offers caution about the claims of several alternative split approaches including behavior genetics, sociobiology (e.g., Wilson, 1978, 1998), splits forms of evolutionary psychology (e.g., Tooby & Cosmides, 1992), and so-called representational theories of mind (see Mueller & Overton 1998a, 1998b)—including production systems, or symbolic theories (Keil, 1998)—which split mind from world and claim that mind is nothing but calculations made on the inner depiction of an outer reality. Each of these split approaches, as well as others (e.g., social constructivist theories), faces the dismal fate of forever being caught on a pendulum ride that can swing only narrowly between nativism and empiricism. Embodiment, on the other hand, offers the means for moving beyond this narrow compass and addressing issues that will promote a progressive advancement to scientific knowledge of human behavior and development.

REFERENCES

Baldwin, J. M. (1895). *Mental development in the child and the race: Methods and process.* New York: Macmillan.

Bermudez, J. L. (1998). *The paradox of self-consciousness.* Cambridge, MA: MIT Press.

Bloom, L. (2001). The intentionality model and language acquisition. *Monographs of the Society for Research in Child Development, 66*(4, Ser. No. 267).

Boesch, E. E. (1991). *Symbolic action theory and cultural psychology.* Berlin: Springer-Verlag.

Bowlby, J. (1958). The nature of the child's tie to his mother. *International Journal of Psychoanalysis, 39,* 350–373.

Brandstädter, J. (1998). Action perspectives on human development. In W. Damon (Series Ed.) & R. M. Lerner (Vol. Ed.), *Handbook of child psychology: Vol. 1. Theoretical models of human development* (5th ed., pp. 807–863). New York: Wiley.

Brandstädter, J., & Lerner, R. M. (Eds.) (1999). *Action and self-development: Theory and research through the life span.* London: Sage Publications.

Bunge, M. (1962). *Causality: The place of the causal principle in modern science.* New York: World Publishing.

Collins, W. A., Maccoby, E. E., Steinberg, L., Hetherington, E. M., & Bornstein, M. H. (2000). Contemporary research on parenting: The case for nature and nurture. *American Pychologist, 55,* 218–232.

Csordas, T. J. (1999). Embodiment and cultural phenomenology. In G. Weiss & H. F. Haber (Eds.), *Embodiment: The intersection of nature and culture* (pp. 144–162). New York: Routledge.

Damasio, A. (1994). *Descartes' error: Emotion, reason, and the human brain.* New York: Avon Books, Inc.

Damasio, A. (1999). *The feeling of what happens: Body and emotion in the making of consciousness.* New York: Harcourt Brace.

Dennett, D. (1987). *The intentional stance.* Cambridge, MA: MIT Press.

Eckensberger, L. H. (1990). On the necessity of the culture concept in psychology: A view from cross-cultural psychology. In F. J. R. van de Vijver & G. J. M. Hutschemaekers (Eds.), *The investigation of culture. Current issues in cultural psychology* (pp. 153–183). Tilburg, Germany: Tilburg University Press.

Edelman, G. M. (1992). *Bright air, brilliant fire: On the matter of the mind.* New York: Basic Books.

Edelman, G. M., & Tononi, G. (2000). *A universe of consciousness: How matter becomes imagination.* New York: Basic Books.

Erikson, E. H. (1968). *Identity youth and crisis.* New York: Norton.

Gallese, V. (2000a). The acting subject: Towards the neural basis of social cognition. In T. Metzinger (Ed.), *Neural correlates of consciousness* (pp. 325–334). Cambridge, MA: MIT Press.

Gallese, V. (2000b). The "shared manifold hypothesis": From mirror neurons to empathy. *Journal of Consciousness Studies, 8,* 33–50.

Gelman, R., & Williams, E. M. (1998). Enabling constraints for cognitive development and learning: Domain specificity and epigenesis. In D. Kuhn & R. Siegler (Eds.), *Cognition, perception, and language: Vol. 2. Handbook of child psychology* (5th ed., pp. 575–630). New York: Wiley.

Goodwyn, S. W., & Acredolo, L. P. (1993). Symbolic gesture versus word: Is there a modality advantage for onset of symbol use? *Child Development, 64,* 688–701.

Gottlieb, G. (1997). *Synthesizing nature–nurture.* Mahwah, NJ: Lawrence Erlbaum Associates.

Gottlieb, G. (2002). Developmental-behavioral initiation of evolutionary change. *Psychological Review, 109,* 211–218.

Harding, S. (1986). *The science question in feminism.* Ithaca, NY: Cornell University Press.

Harre, R. (1995). The necessity of personhood as embodied being. *Theory & Psychology, 5,* 369–373.

Held, R., & Bossom, J. (1961). Neonatal deprivation and adult rearrangement: Complementary techniques for analyzing plastic sensory-motor coordinations. *Journal of Comparative Physiological Psychology, 54,* 33–37.

Held, R., & Hein, A. (1958). Adaptation of disarranged hand-eye coordination contingent upon re-afferent stimulation. *Perceptual-Motor Skills, 8,* 87–90.

Ingold, T. (2000) Evolving skills. In H. Rose & S. Rose (Eds.), *Alas, poor Darwin: Arguments against evolutionary psychology* (pp. 273–297). New York: Harmony Books.

Johnson, M. (1987). *The body in the mind.* Chicago: The University of Chicago Press.

Johnson, M. (1999). Embodied reason. In G. Weiss & H. F. Haber (Eds.), *Embodiment: The intersection of nature and culture* (pp. 81–102). New York: Routledge

Keil, F. C. (1998). Cognitive science and the origins of thought and knowledge. In R. M. Lerner (Ed.), *Theoretical models of human development: Vol. 1. Handbook of child psychology* (5th ed., pp. 341–413). New York: Wiley.

Lakoff, G. (1987). *Women, fire, and dangerous things: What categories reveal about the mind.* Chicago: University of Chicago Press.

Lakoff, G., & Johnson, M. (1999). *Philosophy in the flesh: The embodied mind and its challenge to western thought.* New York: Basic Books.

Laing, R. D. (1960). *The divided self.* New York: Pantheon Books.

Langer, J. (1994). From acting to understanding: The comparative development of meaning. In W. Overton & D. Palermo (Eds.) *The nature and ontogenesis of meaning* (pp. 191–214). Hillsdale, NJ: Lawrence Erlbaum Associates.

Latour, B. (1993). *We have never been modern.* Cambridge, MA: Harvard University Press

LeDoux, J. (1996). *The emotional brain: The mysterious underpinnings of emotional life.* New York: Touchstone.

Lerner, R. M. (1978). Nature, nurture, and dynamic interactionism. *Human Development, 21,* 1–20.

Lerner, R. M. (2002). *Concepts and theories of human development* (3rd ed.). New York: Random House.

Lewontin, R. C. (1991). *Biology as ideology: The doctrine of DNA.* New York: Harper Perennial.

Lewontin, R. C. (2000). *The triple helix: Gene, organism and environment.* Cambridge, MA: Harvard University Press.

Luhmann, N. (1995). *Social systems.* Stanford, CA: Stanford University Press

McGuire, S., Manke, B., Saudino, K. J., Reiss, D., Hetherington, E. M., & Plomin, R. (1999). Perceived competence and self-worth during adolescence: A longitudinal behavioral genetic study. *Child Development, 70,* 1283–1296.

Magnusson, D. (1998). The logic and implications of a person-oriented approach. In R. B. Cairns, L. R. Bergman, & J. Kagan (Eds.), *Methods and models for studying the individual* (pp. 33–63). London: Sage Publications.

Margolis, J. (1987). *Science without unity: Reconciling the human and natural sciences.* New York: Basil Blackwell.

Merleau-Ponty, M. (1962). *Phenomenology of perception* (Colin Smith, Trans.). London: Routledge.

Merleau-Ponty, M. (1963). *The structure of behavior* (Alden Fisher, Trans.). Boston: Beacon Press.

Miller, J. G. (1996). Theoretical issues in cultural psychology. In J. W. Berry, Y. H. Poortinga, & J. Pandey (Eds.), *Handbook of cross-cultural psychology: Theory and method* (pp. 85–128). Boston: Allyn and Bacon

Mueller, U., & Overton, W. F. (1998a). How to grow a baby. A re-evaluation of image-schema and Piagetian action approaches to representation. *Human Development, 41,* 71–111.

Mueller, U., & Overton, W. F. (1998b). Action theory of mind and representational theory of mind: Is Dialogue Possible? *Human Development, 41,* 127–133.

Ogden. T. H. (1986).*The matrix of the mind: Object relations and the psychoanalytic dialogue.* Northvale, NJ: Jason Aronson.

Overton, W. F. (1973). On the assumptive base of the nature–nurture controversy: Additive versus interactive conceptions. *Human Development, 1972, 16,* 74–89.

Overton, W. F. (1994a). The arrow of time and cycles of time: Concepts of change, cognition, and embodiment. *Psychological Inquiry, 5,* 215–237.

Overton, W. F. (1994b). Contexts of meaning: The computational and the embodied mind. In W. F. Overton & D. S. Palermo (Eds.), *The nature and ontogenesis of meaning* (pp. 1–18). Hillsdale, NJ: Lawrence Erlbaum Associates.

Overton, W. F. (1997a). Relational-developmental theory: A psychology perspective. In D. Gorlitz, H. J. Harloff, J. Valsiner, & G. Mey (Eds.), *Children, cities and psychological theories: Developing relationships* (pp. 315–335). Berlin: de Gruyter.

Overton, W. F. (1997b). Beyond Dichotomy: An Embodied Active Agent for Cultural Psychology. *Culture and Psychology, 3,* 315–334.

Overton, W. F. (1998). Developmental psychology: Philosophy, concepts, and methodology. In R. M. Lerner (Ed.), *Theoretical models of human development: Vol. 1. Handbook of child psychology* (5th ed., pp. 107–188). New York: Wiley.

Overton, W. F. (2002). Understanding, explanation, and reductionism: Finding a cure for cartesian anxiety. In L. Smith & T. Brown (Eds.), *Reductionism* (pp. 29–51). Mahwah, NJ: Lawrence Erlbaum Associates.

Overton, W. F. (2003). Development across the life span: Philosophy, concepts, theory. In R. M. Lerner, M A. Easterbrooks, & J. Mistry (Eds.), *Comprehensive handbook of psychology: Developmental psychology* (Vol. 6, pp. 13–31). New York: Wiley

Overton, W. F., & Horowitz, H. (1991). Developmental psychopathology: Differentiations and integrations. In D. Cicchetti & S. Toth (Eds.), *Rochester symposium on developmental psychopathology* (Vol. 3, pp. 1–42). Rochester, NY: University of Rochester Press.

Overton, W. F., & Jackson, J. (1973). The representation of imagined objects in action sequences: A developmental study. *Child Development, 44,* 309–314.

Overton, W. F., & Kovacs, S. (2001, June). *An embodied action theory of mind approach to the development and transformation of symbolic representation in preschoolers.* Paper presented at the 31st Annual Symposium of the Jean Piaget Society. Berkeley, CA.

Overton, W. F., & Reese, H. W. (1973). Models of development: Methodological implications. In J. R. Nesselroade & H. W. Reese (Eds.), *Life-span developmental psychology: Methodological issues* (pp. 65–86). New York: Academic Press.

Piaget, J. (1952). *The origins of intelligence in children.* New York: Norton.

Pinker, S. (1997). *How the mind works.* New York: Norton

Plomin, R. (1986). *Development, genetics, and psychology.* Hillsdale, NJ: Lawrence Erlbaum Associates.

Plomin, R. (1994). *The limits of family influence: Genes experience and behavior.* New York: Guilford

Plomin, R., & Rutter, M. (1998). Child development, molecular genetics, and what to do with genes once they are found. *Child Development, 69,* 1223–1242.

Russell, J. (1996). *Agency: Its role in mental development.* London: Taylor and Francis.

Sampson, E. E. (1996). Establishing embodiment in psychology. *Theory and Psychology, 6,* 601–624

Santostefano, S. (1995). Embodied meanings, cognition and emotion: Pondering how three are one. In D. Cicchetti & S. L. Toth (Eds.), *Rochester symposium on developmental psychopathology: Vol. 6. Emotion, cognition and representation* (pp. 59–132). Rochester, NY: University of Rochester Press.

Saxe, G. B. (1981). Body parts as numerals. A developmental analysis of numeration among the Oksapmin of New Guinea. *Child Development, 52,* 306–316.

Saxe, G. B. (1995, June). *Culture, changes in social practices, and cognitive development.* Paper presented to the annual meeting of the Jean Piaget Society, Berkeley, CA.

Searle, J. (1992). *The rediscovery of the mind.* Cambridge, MA: MIT Press.

Shanon, B. (1993). *The representational and the presentational: An essay on cognition and the study of mind.* New York: Harvester Wheatsheaf.

Spelke, E. S., & Newport, E. L. (1998). Nativism, empiricism, and the development of knowledge. In W. Damon (Series Ed.) & R. M. Lerner (Vol. Ed.), *Handbook of child psychology: Vol. 1 Theoretical models of human development* (5th ed., 275–340). New York: Wiley.

Stern, W. (1938). *General psychology: From the personalistic standpoint.* New York: Macmillan.

Suomi, S. J. (1999). Attachment in rhesus monkeys. In J. Cassidy & P. R. Shaver (Eds.), *Handbook of attachment: Theory, reserarch, and clinical applications* (pp. 181–197). New York: Guilford Press.

Suomi, S. J. (2000). A behavioral perspective on developmental psychopathology: Excessive aggression and serotonergic dysfunction in monkeys. In A. J. Sameroff, M. Lewis, & S. Miller (Eds.), *Handbook of developmental psychopathology* (2nd ed., pp. 237–256). New York: Plenum.

Sullivan, H. S. (1953). *The interpersonal theory of psychiatry.* New York: Norton.

Taylor, C. (1995). *Philosophical arguments.* Cambridge, MA: Harvard University Press.

Thelen, E. (2000). Grounded in the world: Developmental origins of the embodied mind. *Infancy, 1,* 3–28.

Thelen, E. (2001). The dynamics of embodiment: A field theory of infant perseverative reaching. *Behavioral and Brain Sciences, 24,* 1–86.

Tobach, E., & Greenberg, G. (1984). The significance of T. C. Schneirla's contribution to the concept of integration. In G. Greenberg & E. Tobach (Eds.), *Behavioral evolution and integrative levels* (pp.1–7). Hillsdale, NJ: Lawrence Erlbaum Associates.

Tooby, J., & Cosmides, L. (1992). The psychological foundations of culture. In J. Barkow, L. Cosmides, & J. Tooby (Eds.), *The adapted mind: Evolutionary psychology and the generation of culture.* New York: Oxford University Press.

Valsiner, J. (1998). *The guided mind: A sociogenetic approach to personality.* Cambridge, MA: Harvard University Press.

Varela, F. J., Thompson, E., & Rosch, E. (1991). *The embodied mind: Cognitive science and human experience.* Cambridge, MA: MIT Press.

von Bertalanffy, L. (1968a). *General system theory.* New York: Braziller.

von Bertalanffy, L. (1968b) *Organismic psychology and systems theory.* Barre, MA.: Barre Publishing Co.

von Wright, G. H. (1971). *Explanation and understanding.* Ithaca, NY: Cornell University Press.

Vreeke, G. J. (2000). Nature, nurture and the future of the analysis of variance. *Human Development, 44,* 32–45

Werner, H. (1957). The concept of development from a comparative and organismic point of view. In D. B. Harris (Ed.), *The concept of development: An issue in the study of human behavior* (pp. 125–148). Minneapolis: University of Minnesota Press.

Werner, H. (1958). *Comparative psychology of mental development.* New York: International Universities Press.

Wertsch, J. V. (1991). *Voices of the mind: A sociocultural approach to mediated action.* Cambridge, MA: Harvard University Press.

Wilson, E. O. (1978). *On human nature: The new synthesis.* Cambridge, MA: Harvard University Press.

Wilson, E. O. (1998). *Consilience: The unity of knowledge.* London: Little, Brown.

Winer, B. (1962). *Statistical principles in experimental design.* New York: McGraw-Hill.

Winnicott, D. W. (1965). *The maturational process and the facilitating environment.* New York: International Universities Press.

Winnicott, D. W. (1971). *Playing and reality.* New York: Basic Books.

Zelazo, P. D. (1996). Towards a characterization of minimal consciousness. *New Ideas in Psychology, 14*(1), 63–80.

12

Conclusions: Beyond Nature Versus Nurture to More Complex, Relational, and Dynamic Developmental Systems

Cynthia García Coll
Elaine L. Bearer
Brown University

Richard M. Lerner
Tufts University

Burgeoning biological, developmental, and behavioral evidence suggests that human behavior is the result of complex dynamic interactions between genes and the physical-experiential environment, operating at many dimensions from the molecular to the cultural, social, and historical. Questions that arise from the idea that nature can be separated from nurture during the genesis of behavior—such as "What is the relative contribution of genes versus environment in the development of differences in a particular behavior or developmental process?"—have limitations in how well they can help us understand the way patterns of behavior develop, and, as counter factual, may blind us to fruitful avenues of research, policy, and practice.

The scholarship presented in this book, and the broader literatures from which these ideas draw (see Bearer, 1992; Damasio, 1999; Damasio, Harrington, Kagan, McEwen, Moss, & Shaikh, 2001; Lerner, 1984, 2002; Lewis, 2000; Oyama, 2000;

Thelen & Smith, 1998; Program in Human Biology at Stanford University[1]), lead ineluctably to one key and incontrovertible conclusion: Human development occurs through a process of dynamic relations involving variables from biological through sociocultural and historical levels of organization. Influences from all levels—genes, individual behavior, parental rearing practices, or social policies, for instance—contribute integratively, and *only* integratively, to the structure and function of human behavior and development. No one level of organization, no one set of influences—be it genes or environmental/cultural—can be factually construed as an exclusive, or even prime, impetus to the full development of any organisms. Neither system functions without the other. Functional adaptability and phenotype is not a product of a single system in isolation but of each in concert with others.

The Nobel prize-winning experiments of Hubel and Wiesel (1979) demonstrated definitively and incontrovertibly that brain function relies on both biological and environmental influences. They showed that the very ability to see and respond to the environment was a result of a complex interplay between the biological rules that determine the structure of the visual system in the developing brain and the input of light into the eye. Neurobiologists have further pursued these ideas, with experiments designed to test perception of the physical world and the effect of what is perceived on the structure and chemistry of the brain, beginning with such pioneer studies as those of Hamburg and Elliott (1981). We now know that the brain is not hard wired, nor is it like a computer's hardware—once constructed, always invariant. Instead, the brain responds to its input derived from sensations of the environment and internal memory by changing not only its chemistry but its very structure (Hyman, 2000). This dance of brain and environment continues throughout life, particularly in the realm of emotions which participates in many behaviors. How the genetic program responds to such environmental input specifically is a vigorous area of research in which serious progress will only be made if gene expression is considered within the context of other variables, including the anatomic, chemical, and environmental basis of the historical and autobiographical self (Damasio, 1999). In pursuit of these ideals, cautions from the insightful work of Jane Goodall should not be forgotten, where she warned against an oversimplification of Darwin's theories, which can lead to dangerously inaccurate reductionist conclusions (Flemming & Goodall, 2002).

---

[1] One of us (E.L.B.) was early initiated into these ideas by The Program in Human Biology at Stanford University. This undergraduate curriculum, founded in 1971 by David Hamburg, Nobelist Joshua Lederberg, Paul Ehrlich, Sanford Dornbusch, Norman Kretchmer, and Colin Pittendrigh, included such courses as "Cells, Organisms and Societies," "Behavior as Adaptation," "Man and Nature." The curriculum evolved to become an interdisciplinary interweaving of all aspects of the human condition, from the genetic, molecular, anatomical, to the psychosocial and societal levels. Don Kennedy brought a special energy to the curriculum, and added environmental perspective, and taught "The Human Predicament" up until 2000. Jane Goodall lectured in the late 1970s and lead select students to her research in Gombe. Hamburg went on to become president of the Institute of Medicine in 1975, and president of the Carnegie Corporation from 1982-1997. Lederberg left Stanford to become president of the Rockefeller Foundation and Kennedy served as Director of the FDA, president of Stanford University and is now Editor in Chief of Science Magazine of the American Association of Academic Scientists.

THEMES PERTINENT TO THE USE OF MORE COMPLEX
AND DYNAMIC DEVELOPMENTAL SYSTEMS THEORIES

The conclusions that derive from this book are validated by the commonality of the points made by each of the multidisciplinary set of scholars contributing to this work.[1] We extract below a short list of general principles underlying the new paradigm that a dynamic developmental systems view implies:

1. Adopting a theory that defines a human being as an embodied person functioning as a self-organizing dynamic system of cognitive, emotional, and motivational meanings, thereby moving conceptually away from trying to explain behavior as a product of two distinct processes—nurture or nature.

2. Recognizing the necessity of targeting theory, research, and application to develop experimental methodologies that allow the exploration of development as the product of mutual interactions between genetic expression and its environmental context.

3. Recognizing that gene-environment interactions are ubiquitous, diverse in nature, and detectable even in utero. Developmental systems perspectives—approaches that underscore the dynamism of human development that derives from the ongoing relationship between biology and environments, in cognitive, affective, motivational, and behavioral systems—need to be used to study these interactions from the cellular to the macroinstitutional levels.

4. Understanding that the normal genotype is immensely flexible in its expression and that this expression is regulated as a function of context, experience, and developmental history. Biological systems evolve and function in close connection with their environments. Depending on critical characteristics of these environments, very different structures and functions can develop from similar genetic programs, and very similar structures and functions can develop from different genetic programs.

5. Appreciating that genes require environmental and behavioral inputs to function appropriately during the normal course of individual development. In fact, behavior and environment can each be an agent of natural selection that fosters evolution and, within individual ontogeny, can influence the outcome of genetic programs.

6. Understanding that the genetic program may be influenced by the social and physical environment through a multistep system of complex and flexible biochemical reactions. Behavior is part of the environment that surrounds genetic expression, and behavior can therefore drive genetic change over evolutionary time, thus influencing our gene pool over generations.

7. Appreciating that the developmental system framework has profound implications for a new set of public policy and social program options for people across the life span. As discussed in Lerner (this volume), these implications derive from

the lifelong plasticity of the human development system, promote an optimistic stance in regard to the ability of interventions to enhance the life courses of all individuals, and emphasize the value of sound justice, democracy, and equity to best capitalize on the potential for healthy and positive development in each person. In contrast to policies based on a dualistic concept of nature versus nurture, policies based on an understanding of the dynamic, intimate relationship between the genetic expression and the environment will lead to programs that enhance the lives of each and every individual, such as those proposed in the Spencer and Harpalani chapter (this volume).

CONCLUSIONS

As evidenced by the above points, throughout this volume the contributors—biologists and social and behavioral scientists—advocate a careful scrutiny of notions that split influences in human development and behavior as just the product of genes or of environments. We see this as a plea for a more complex and dynamic developmental systems perspective. We think that this paradigm shift will bring about exciting theoretical and methodological research aimed at understanding human development and at promoting physical, psychological, and social well-being.

However, as also made clear in the contributions to this book, how to achieve such a perspective is far from decided. Indeed, as Overton (1998) explained, the casting of "our fundamental understanding of development into an inclusive relational frame has profound implications for the concepts and theories, as well as the methodology and methods, of developmental inquiry" (p. 114). The need for interdisciplinary efforts, well funded and supported, is critical if we are going to make serious progress in this field. The multidisciplinary agreement about the need to engage on these tasks as evidenced by the scholarship in this book, and the progress that has been made in the use of integrative, developmental systems philsosphy in science and practice, supports the hopefulness of Gottlieb that "the immense gap between molecular biology and developmental psychology will one day be filled with facts as well as valid concepts" (1997, p. 100).

We would add that a developmental systems perspective supports optimism about the potential efficacy of developmentally appropriate public policies including preventive strategies and optimization of interventions. This perspective indicates the importance of reevaluating social policies and programs as to whether they best capitalize on the dynamism of the developmental system approach. Accordingly, scientists and practitioners have considerable work to do to best deploy—to test the limits of—the relational, developmental systems perspective for enhancing theory, methodology, research, and application and, ultimately, for improving human life.

To actualize this hope, however, we must marshal not only the intellectual resources of our scientists and practitioners to embrace a fundamental recasting of our theoretical, methodological, and applied tools into an integrative, relational frame. We need to use developmental systems thinking to alter the training of future scientists and practitioners and, as well, to reeducate government and private funders about the allocation of resources for research and application. We must explain to colleagues, students and the public that to understand how things really work requires knowledge far beyond that which is gained from (mistakenly and simplistically) pursuing a scientific path that seeks to partition variance into genetic and environmental components. We must promote acceptance of the possibility and importance of attaining much more complex, integrated knowledge about all the levels of organization that comprise the biology and ecology of human development and, most critical, about the dynamic system of developmental relations that comprise these highly intertwined systems.

As is made quite evident by various chapters in this book, to obtain and champion such knowledge we must go beyond the limits of any one area of scholarship. Indeed, we will have to go beyond the limits of academe. To fully engage a vision fully reflective of a developmental system approach, the voices and visions of practitioners, policy makers, and the public need to be involved in both supporting and making best use of the approach to scholarship promoted by the conclusions drawn from this book.

In the end, then, each of our disciplinary based perspectives is limited. To effect important and sustained scholarship and social changes through our actions, communities of scholars in concert with communities of citizens will have to coalesce to learn which individual, family, and societal changes are desired and how such changes can be enacted.

In sum, then, a relational, developmental system is a frame for productive science and for applications that may serve to advance the human condition. We believe that it is not too harsh to suggest that the scholarship in this book, along with a growing literature across various disciplines (i.e., Horowitz, 2000; Lerner, 1984, 2002, in preparation; Lewontin, 2000; Oyama, 2000; Siegel, 1999; Thelen & Smith, 1998) sounds the death knell for the nature–nurture dichotomy. The work in this volume contributes to a growing literature that provides scholarly and scientific legitimization of dynamic, relational systematic approaches to key questions about science and policy. For those concerned with using the best of science to inform the policies and programs affecting the quality of human development within and across the nations of our world, dynamic developmental systems approaches to theory and research can serve as a template through which scholars may develop or extend their knowledge about the systemic bases of human development and of the multidisciplinary and scientist-practitioner-community collaborations needed to enhance it.

REFERENCES

Bearer, E. L. (1992). *Cytoskeleton in development.* San Diego, CA: Academic Press, 1992.

Damasio, A. (1999). *The feeling of what happens: Body and emotion in the making of consciousness.* New York: Brace.

Damasio, A. R., Harrington, A., Kagan, J., McEwen, B. S., Moss, H., & Shaikh, R. (Eds). (2001). *Unity of knowledge: A convergence of natural and human science.* New York: New York Academy of Science.

Flemming, C., & Goodall, J. (2002). Dangerous Darwinism. *Public Understanding of Science, 11,* 250–271.

Hamburg, D. A., & Elliott, G. R. (1981). Biobehavioral sciences: An emerging research agenda. *Psychiatric Clinics of North America, 4,* 407–421.

Horowitz, F. D. (2000). Child development and the PITS: Simple questions, complex answers, and developmental theory. *Child Development, 71,* 1–10.

Hubel, D. H., & Wiesel, T. N. (1970). The period of susceptibility to the physiological effects of unilateral eye closure in kittens. *Journal of Physiology, 206,* 419–436.

Hubel, D. H., & Wiesel, T. N. (1979). Brain mechanisms of vision. *Scientific American, 241*(3), 150–162.

Hyman, S. (2000). Mental illness: Genetically complex disorders of neural circuitry and neural communication. *Neuron, 28,* 321–322.

Lerner, R. M. (1984). *On the nature of human plasticity.* New York: Cambridge University Press.

Lerner, R. M. (2002). *Concepts and theories of human development* (3rd ed.). Mahwah, NJ: Lawrence Erlbaum Associates.

Lerner, R. M. (in preparation). *Liberty: America's moral defense of civil society.* Medford, MA: Applied Developmental Science Institute, Tufts University.

Lewontin, R. C. (2000). *The triple helix: Gene, organism, and environment.* Cambridge, MA: Harvard University Press.

Overton, W. F. (1998). Developmental psychology: Philosophy, concepts, and methodology. In W. Damon (Series Ed.) & R. M. Lerner (Ed.), *Handbook of child psychology: Vol. 1. Theoretical models of human development* (5th ed., pp. 107–187). New York: Wiley.

Oyama, S. (2000). *Evolution's eye: A systems view of the biology-culture divide.* Durham: Duke University Press.

Siegel, D. J. (1999). *The developing mind: How relationships and the brain interact to shape who we are.* New York: Guilford Press.

Thelen, E., & Smith, L. B. (1998). Dynamic systems theories. In W. Damon (Ed.), *Handbook of child psychology* (5th ed., Vol. 1, pp. 563–634). New York: Wiley.

Author Index

Subject Index